RETAIL MERCHANDISING AND CONTROL

CONCEPTS AND PROBLEMS IN BASIC RETAIL MATH

The Irwin Series in Marketing
Consulting Editor   Gilbert A. Churchill, Jr.
University of Wisconsin, Madison

RETAIL MERCHANDISING AND CONTROL

CONCEPTS AND PROBLEMS IN BASIC RETAIL MATH

ROBERT J. MINICHIELLO, D.B.A.
Professor of Marketing
Northeastern University

IRWIN

Homewood, IL 60430
Boston, MA 02116

Cover photos:

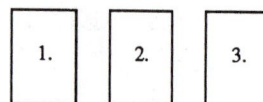

1. R. Iwasaki / AllStock, Inc.
2. L. Bencze / AllStock, Inc.
3. R. Gendreau / AllStock, Inc.

© RICHARD D. IRWIN, INC., 1990

Developmental editor: Eleanore Snow
Project editor: Ethel Shiell
Production manager: Bette K. Ittersagen
Cover designer: Carol Chestnut
Interior designer: Miller and Seper Design
Compositor: Beacon Graphics
Typeface: 10/12 Times Roman
Printer: Malloy Lithographing, Inc.

Library of Congress Cataloging-in-Publication Data

Minichiello, Robert J.
    Retail merchandising and control: concepts and problems/Robert
J. Minichiello.
      p.   cm.
    ISBN 0-256-06767-8
    1. Retail trade—Management. 2. Merchandising. I. Title.
HF5429.M52 1990   89–19858
658.8'7—dc20   CIP

Printed in the United States of America

1 2 3 4 5 6 7 8 9 0 ML 6 5 4 3 2 1 0 9

To:
Pat and Connie, two of the great shoppers

Preface

Retailing's dynamic growth in recent years has intensified the search for management talent and expanded opportunities for prospective employees. Simultaneously, colleges have added programs and courses in retailing to help provide the industry with knowledgeable graduates.

Why Was This Text Written?

Retail Merchandising and Control: Concepts and Problems in Basic Retail Math has been developed and written to help students become knowledgeable about the numerical terminology, concepts, and calculations that are the language of retail management. Many students lack full understanding of basic arithmetical methods. Others lack confidence in their quantitative skills. Yet few will achieve their managerial aspirations unless they are able to calculate, interpret, and use the numbers that retailers regularly apply.

This book seeks to make interesting and understandable the numerical material that many students find dull and difficult. It begins with the relatively easy to understand concept of a simple markup and gradually adds levels of complication and comprehensiveness. By the end of the book, students have been introduced to most of the fundamental concepts and calculations used in retailing, including the relatively recent applications of DPP (direct product profit).

The text engages the reader's interest through short vignettes that place retailing personnel in situations involving the concepts and calculations being introduced. Students thus become familiar with the concepts not as abstract definitions or formulas, but within the contexts in which retailers apply them.

How Does This Text Differ from Other Retail Math Texts?

The author has deviated from the technique used in many books of briefly introducing a concept, then presenting a sample problem with solution, immediately followed by a similar problem to be solved by the student. In the author's experience, many students—particularly those with high quotas of so-called math anxiety—merely copy the method indicated in the sample problem, just changing the numbers. Often they do not understand the problem or its solution.

In this book, a discussion of a concept, its calculation (and sometimes closely related calculations), is followed by a short series of problems that test whether the student has learned the material just presented. The student cannot merely copy a sample solution. If unable to solve a problem, the student should re-study the preceding section of text. The **review problems** test whether the student has mastered all the material discussed in a chapter.

The rote memorization of formulas is deemphasized. Instead, the text immerses students in practical retailing situations to foster their genuine understanding and learning. Calculations are explained in detail, and their value and application are illustrated. Whenever possible, commonsense solutions using simple arithmetic are presented.

At the end of each chapter, an **applications section** using a fictitious retail store, the **Mellow Music Store**, reviews the concepts and calculations presented in the chapter. By the end of the book, students have used a variety of concepts and calculations in dealing with the first year of this store's operation.

Where Does This Text Fit in the Marketing Curriculum?

This book was developed to provide teaching material for courses that might have titles such as Retail Merchandising and Control; Retail Arithmetic; Retail Mathematics; Merchandising Mathematics; Retail Buying; Mathematics of Merchandising; and so forth. It also may be used as a supplement for basic retailing, merchandising, and retailing strategy courses.

Retailing courses taught using the case method of instruction might use the book as a supplement to help students understand and apply basic quantitative analysis to case situations.

With its detailed presentation and discussion of concepts, this book is also useful for self-study purposes.

Acknowledgments

Properly acknowledging all who have contributed in some way to the preparation of this book is not possible. While some primary influences can be recognized, many others from a lifetime of living, working, shopping, studying, and teaching retailing defy deserved credit. My father, Aurelio Minichiello, a 44-year employee of the Great Atlantic and Pacific Tea Company (during the heyday of its reign as the world's largest retailer), was the first person I ever heard use the term *merchandising*. He introduced me to the wonders of that food retailing innovation, the supermarket, when I was a young child. As a teenager working in A&P stores, I could never understand why the produce manager was always talking about his "gross," or why the store manager was so concerned when his "figures were off."

Conceptual understanding began with the late Professor Malcolm McNair's Retail Merchandising and Control course, the source of this book's title. Further understanding resulted from a period as a graduate assistant to the late William Applebaum. My doctoral dissertation, written under the supervision of Mr. Applebaum and Professors Walter Salmon and Robert Buzzell, was the basis for applying many of the concepts and calculations discussed in this book.

The classic volumes of John W. Wingate, Elmer O. Schaller, Robert W. Bell, and F. Leonard Miller also deserve acknowledgment. I taught from these texts for several years, and they undoubtedly influenced my thinking. Likewise worthy of appreciation are the hundreds of students who experienced my efforts to clarify "the numbers of retailing," especially those with whom I used a draft of this book.

Special thanks are due Hyman Dushman, discount department store pioneer, retail executive and consultant, C.P.A., Marketing and Retailing teacher, who read and critiqued most of the manuscript. His comments were very helpful. Professor Linda Jamieson of Northeastern University; Paul Corcoran of the Harvard Shops; James Moody of Hannaford Bros. Company; John Tirrell III, of M&M Supermarkets; Curt Kornblau of the Food Marketing Institute; Thomas Joyce, formerly of Filene's; and Joan Descovich O'Hare, formerly of Jordan Marsh, provided advice and/or material. Phyllis Ashinger, Wayne State University; Calvin D. Bogart, Wayne State University; Elizabeth L. Mariotz, Philadelphia College of Textiles and Science; and John Roman, Rochester Institute of Technology reviewed final-draft manuscript and offered many insightful comments and suggestions.

At Irwin, Senior Developmental Editor Eleanore Snow, Project Editor Ethel Shiell, and other members of the Irwin team were especially helpful throughout the editorial and production processes.

Graduate assistants Michael Cooper, Nancy Gross, Karen Gallagher, and Samuel Solomon were of assistance in various ways. Much appreciation and thanks is due Geraldine Brancato, Virginia Spero, Julia Finn, June Remington, and Gisele Crepeau who prepared the various drafts and suffered with my almost illegible handwriting.

Needless to say, any errors are the responsibility of the author.

Robert J. Minichiello

Contents

11 Break-Even, DPP, and Other Measures of Performance, 183

Appendix A: Terms of Sale and Purchase: Discounts and Dating, 207

Appendix B: Answers to Odd-Numbered Problems, 210

Index, 213

CHAPTER 1

Introduction

Retailing takes place in a wide range of settings. Fruits and vegetables are sold at hot, dusty roadside stands and in elaborate, air-conditioned gourmet food stores. Clothing is sold at rickety tables in drafty flea markets and from fancy racks in the designer boutiques of multi-acred, climate controlled, enclosed shopping malls. The same watch may be purchased from an exquisitely decored, prestige jewelry store, or from Bargain Louie's, a back alley, discount outlet.

Similarly, a retailer may promote a store by advertising on television, or by sponsoring a major parade on Thanksgiving Day, or by putting up a sign in the window, or even by shouting to passersby: "Hey, come on in and look 'em over!"

Variety and Innovation in Retailing

The great diversity in retailing reflects the wide variety of needs, wants, tastes, and styles represented in the market by the customers who patronize the different stores. Some want a high degree of personal service in attractive settings. Others would rather help themselves and pay a lower price. Some seek convenience and wish to minimize the time spent shopping. Others view shopping as a pleasurable experience or as a form of entertainment.

When the retailing system of the United States — the collection of stores serving customers — is examined historically, regular change and innovation is apparent. New store types appear from time to time as innovators seek advantage over competitors by applying new concepts or recognizing opportunities created by changing conditions. The supermarket is a good example. It enabled customers to purchase in one large store a wide variety of foodstuffs previously purchased in several specialty stores. The introduction of "self-service" permitted a reduction in labor costs that enabled the supermarket to lower prices to attract business. Developments in refrigeration allowed supermarkets to store large quantities of perishable foods while maintaining quality. The spread of in-home refrigerators, replacing iceboxes, enabled customers to make fewer shopping trips for perishables and to purchase more per trip because it could be safely stored. Increased ownership and use of the automobile allowed supermarkets to appeal to customers who could drive to the new type of store, park in the newly created parking lot, purchase a wide assortment of food at prices much lower than traditional competitors, drive home, and store the perishables in the refrigerator. Revolutionary at the time, scorned by skeptics, today we take this familiar store type for granted and wonder how anyone could have questioned its viability.

During the last 40 years there have been many new developments in U.S. retailing institutions, such as: branch department stores, shopping centers, enclosed shopping malls, discount department stores, catalog showrooms, self-service building supply centers, so-called superstores of various designs, hypermarkets, and even a few experiments with teleshopping, involving the use of telephone and computer systems to permit automated shopping from the home.

Essence of Retailing

While retailing can be characterized by change and innovation, its essence has not, will not, and cannot change. The essence of retailing is a simple process of exchange. The customer exchanges money (often in the form of a charge card or check) for products and/or services that the retailer offers for sale. The setting may be elaborate or simple, air-conditioned or dusty; the price may be high or low; the promotion may be heavy or nonexistent. The essence of retailing is this transaction between the retailer and the customer.

This fundamental aspect of retailing permeates every kind of retailing, no matter what types of goods are being sold or at what prices. Fundamental to the accomplishment of this process of exchange is the concept of merchandising, which requires that the retailer acquire and have available the goods that the customer will buy.

Merchandising

Merchandising is the retailer's most important activity. It is best understood by referring to the *five rights* of merchandising. These five rights of merchandising are:

The right merchandise.
In the right place.
At the right time.
At the right price.
In the right quantities.

It is apparent from only a brief consideration of the five rights, that without them there is no sale. Thus no matter how beautiful the store, how attractive the decor, how elaborate the fixturing, how creative the promotion — if the merchandise the customer wants is not there when the customer wants it, at a price the customer is willing to pay, and in the amount sought, all the other efforts of the retailer have been in vain.

Furthermore, if the retailer fails often enough, because of faulty merchandising, to bring about the fundamental process of exchange with the customer, the retailer will ultimately go out of business. There have been and continue to be many retail failures including some large, well-known companies.

Merchandising Generates Revenue

The importance of successful merchandising to the continued success of a retailer can be best understood by recognizing that only through the successful completion of the merchandising task, culminating in a sale to the customer, does the retailer generate revenue. This revenue that the retailer generates through selling goods must of course be greater than the amount the retailer paid for the goods. The difference between what the retailer paid suppliers for goods and what the retailer charges customers provides the money to pay the expenses of operating the store: labor, rent, utilities, advertising, equipment, insurance, maintenance, supplies, displays, snow removal, and so forth. When the revenue generated by the retailer exceeds the cost of the goods and all the expenses associated with selling the goods, then the retailer has made a profit. While part of the profit will have to be paid for income taxes, the retailer hopes the balance will be large enough to compensate the owners/stockholders for their investment in the retail enterprise and to provide capital for growth.

Profitable Merchandising Uses Numbers

The long-run success of a retail business, therefore, requires profitable merchandising. Profitable merchandising involves the understanding and application of concepts that have evolved to assist the management of retailing enterprises. These concepts are usually expressed in numerical terms and involve such measures as sales, costs, expenses, profits, markups, markdowns, stockturns, open-to-buys, sale per square foot, and returns on investments. These concepts help the retailer: (1) to plan activities that result in sales, (2) to monitor results against goals so that any desirable changes can be made, and (3) to review and assess performance in preparation for future decisions. They provide the mechanisms used to evaluate on a daily, weekly, monthly, quarterly, seasonal, and annual basis the performance of individual selections of merchandise, merchandise categories, departments, store divisions, total stores, districts and regions of chain stores, entire companies, and the individuals that manage them.

Decisions regarding which individual managers or buyers to promote, to transfer, to reward with a raise, to terminate; which stores to expand, to redesign, to close; which categories of merchandise to expand, to promote, to reduce; which brands of goods to expand, to promote, to reduce; which individual items to expand, promote, reduce — all these decisions are significantly influenced by "what the numbers say." It has been said that "numbers are the language of business;" this is especially so for retail businesses.

Retailing Students Need Numbers Skills

Some students (and retailers) are very comfortable with numerical concepts and relationships. For them the objective of this book is to provide a clear, logically presented exposition of the major merchandising and control concepts, techniques, and systems that are essential for success in retail management.

Other students (and retail trainees and managers) are not comfortable with numerical concepts and relationships. Many who are attracted to retailing because of their desire to own and operate their own store, or because they aspire to become a buyer or merchandise manager for one of the great retail companies, may question the need to study what is sometimes referred to as *retail math*. These individuals may possess such desirable attributes as knowledge of merchandise specifications, familiarity with markets for goods, and strong negotiating skills. Or they may believe that flair and glamour are the keys to success. But unfortunately, experience has shown that without an understanding of and the ability to use fundamental numerical concepts, they constantly struggle to achieve the success that would come more easily with knowledge of the material presented in this book.

For those students who are uncomfortable with numbers, this book has an additional objective: to present the numerical concepts in a simple, understandable way that minimizes the use of threatening quantitative techniques. Most of the ideas presented will only require familiarity with basic arithmetic: addition, subtraction, multiplication, and division; and simple algebra. Successful merchants do not have to be quantitative experts, but they do need to understand some fundamentals of retail merchandising and control. This book will provide these essentials.

Overview

This book will begin with a discussion of some simple, basic, familiar concepts. A knowledge of these concepts will serve as a foundation for developing understanding of more advanced concepts. Numerous examples will be used to assist comprehension.

Chapter 2 introduces and explains the markup concept. Markups represent the difference between what a retailer pays suppliers for goods and what the customer pays the retailer. How retailers calculate markups will be discussed and examples provided.

Chapter 3 explains how retailers determine how much markup is needed for a particular store or merchandise department; how retailers check on the amount of markup being generated; and how they compensate for lower than desired markups.

Most retailers sell a variety of different goods that do not all have the same markup. Chapter 4 discusses how retailers average and balance individual markups to meet overall markup targets.

Sometimes merchandise that a retailer has made available for sale doesn't sell. In an effort to sell the goods, the retailer may reduce the price. Oftentimes, to stimulate customer traffic to a store, a retailer has a "sale." Price reductions and sales result in markdowns. Chapter 5 discusses how retailers calculate and control markdowns.

Chapter 6 presents the refinements that lead to the determination of gross margin—the precise measure of the difference between what the retailer pays for goods and what the customer is charged by the retailer for them. The gross margin is the most accurate indicator of the amount of revenue the retailer has available to cover the expenses of operating a store and to contribute to its profit.

As suggested above, much of the gross margin that the retailer generates in buying and selling goods must be applied to the expenses incurred in operating the store. If the gross margin revenue exceeds the expenses, there is a profit. Chapter 7 introduces the elements of expense and explains the methods of determining retail profits and related measures.

Most retail businesses do not sell the same quantities of the same merchandise every day. Variations in sales are caused by seasonal factors and influenced by holidays, in addition to the efforts of competitors. Furthermore, retailers do not have unlimited amounts of funds available to invest in purchases of merchandise. Consequently, retailers must plan to use available funds wisely in seeking to have the right merchandise available, in the right place, at the right time, at the right price, in the right quantities. Thus retailers must plan regularly what sales are likely to occur and what amounts of merchandise need to be available to support those sales. Chapter 8 introduces concepts and techniques that retailers use to determine stock needs. Chapter 9 then presents the preparation of a seasonal merchandise plan and the determination of the amount of money authorized to be spent for merchandise at any particular time (the so-called buyer's open-to-buy).

In addition to measuring and monitoring such concepts as markups, margins, profits, and expenses, retailers also regularly gather, compare, and interpret other indexes of performance. Those measures based on sales, such as sales per square foot, are discussed in Chapter 10. Chapter 11 presents other methods of evaluating financial performance of a retail enterprise such as break-even points, returns on space and dollar investments, and a newer concept, direct product profit (DPP).

The concepts, terms, techniques, and systems discussed in this book are derived from and applicable to what might be called *mainstream retailing*. This involves stores selling a wide range of tangible goods, such as food, clothing, appliances, electronics, sporting goods, shoes, books, health and beauty aids, jewelry, automotive supplies, housewares, computers, hardware, and so forth. Excluded are restaurants, which may be considered retail establishments, but have specialized systems beyond those discussed here, and retail service establishments, such as dry cleaners, banks, and beauty salons.

CHAPTER 2

Markups

Markup is a fundamental concept in retailing. Whatever your role may be as a retailer—trainee, or clerk, or buyer, or merchandise manager, or store manager, or store owner—you will calculate, analyze, compare, discuss, negotiate, and revise markups. The more you are involved in the actual buying and selling of merchandise, the more your thoughts will focus on markups. In this chapter, we will become familiar with the meaning of markups in retailing and learn the various markup calculations that retailers use.

SOME EXAMPLES OF MARKUPS

A hobby store owner purchases an electric toy train locomotive from the manufacturer for $25. It is sold to the father of a young boy for $50. The *markup* on the toy locomotive is $25.

A buyer for a department store pays $200 for a video cassette recorder that is sold for $349. The *markup* on the video cassette recorder is $149.

The proprietor of a T-shirt shop pays $2.50 each for T-shirts that are sold for $4.99 each. The *markup* on a T-shirt is $2.49.

An automobile dealer obtains a new sedan from the manufacturer for $12,000. The dealer sells the sedan for $14,000. The dealer has a $2,000 *markup* on the sale of the sedan.

A bookstore pays $8 for books that are sold for $10. The *markup* on each book is $2.

The produce buyer of a large supermarket chain purchases bananas for $.25 per pound. They are sold in the stores for $.49 per pound. The *markup* on the bananas is $.24 per pound.

Defining Simple Markup

In the examples given above, the difference between the retail selling price and the retailer's cost has been defined as the *markup*.

So:

$$\text{Retail selling price} - \text{Retailer's cost} = \text{Markup}$$

or:

$$\text{Markup} = \text{Retail selling price} - \text{Retailer's cost}$$

Occasionally you may see or hear a reference to a *markon* or a *margin*. These terms are sometimes used to mean what we have defined above as the markup; that is, the difference between the retailer's selling price and the retailer's cost. *Markup* is the preferred term, and the one we will use.

The term *markup* as we use it refers to a "simple markup"—just the difference between the retail selling price and cost of an individual item or group of items, such as a dozen, case, gross, and so forth. Other terms that include the word *markup*, specifically *initial markup*, *cumulative markup*, and *maintained markup*, have particular meanings in retailing that will be explained in later chapters. Likewise, the term *gross margin* has a precise meaning that will also be discussed in a later chapter.

Markup Calculations in Dollars

Retailers perform a number of calculations that involve simple markups. Let's use our bookstore example cited above to illustrate a few.

We are given:

> Retail price of book $10
>
> Cost of book 8

By *subtracting* the cost from the selling price we obtain the markup of $2 ($10 − $8 = $2).

Suppose we were given:

> Cost of book $8
>
> Markup 2

and asked: What is the selling price? By *adding* the cost and the markup we would obtain the selling price. ($8 + $2 = $10)

Suppose we were given:

> Retail price of book $10
>
> Markup 2

and asked: What is the cost? By subtracting the markup from the selling price we would obtain the cost ($10 − $2 = $8). Now we have learned three relationships:

$$\text{Retail selling price} - \text{Cost} = \text{Markup}$$

$$\text{Cost} + \text{Markup} = \text{Retail selling price}$$

$$\text{Retail selling price} - \text{Markup} = \text{Cost}$$

The Markup Box

A helpful way to visualize the relationship between the retail selling price, the cost and the markup is by use of a box, as illustrated in Figure 2–1.

Figure 2–1 The Markup Box

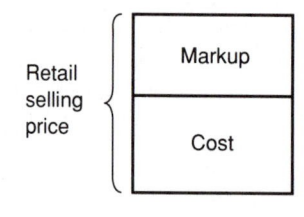

Here the lower part of the box represents the cost; the upper part represents the markup. Put together, the two parts represent the selling price. By drawing a box like Figure 2–1 and filling in what is known, one can quickly determine the unknown quantity. Let's illustrate by using again the bookstore example cited above where the bookstore pays $8 for books that are sold for $10. To determine the markup, given the cost and the selling price we will draw a box as in Figure 2–2. First enter the $10 selling price and the $8 cost. We will quickly see that our question mark (the markup) is $2.

Figure 2–2 Markup Box with Cost $8 and Retail Selling Price $10

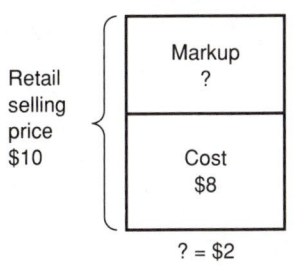

Similarly, in Figure 2–3 we determine the selling price, given the cost and the markup.

Figure 2–3 Markup Box with Cost $8 and Markup $2

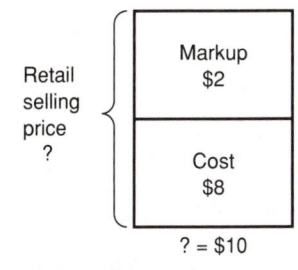

Likewise, in Figure 2–4, we determine the cost, given the selling price and the markup.

Figure 2–4 Markup Box with Selling Price $10 and Markup $2

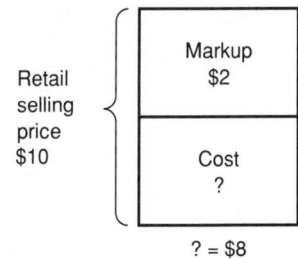

The box solution is easy to understand and is very useful in making other calculations that will be discussed in the following sections.

Markup Percentages

In the examples presented above, we have been considering dollar figures. The retail selling prices, the costs, and the markups used have all been expressed in dollars. Retailers think and talk in dollar terms at times, but often they think and talk in percentage terms. Sometimes retailers are simultaneously thinking and talking in dollar and percentage terms!

A percentage commonly used by retailers is the **markup percentage.** Let's continue with our bookstore example, which had a book selling for $10 with a cost of $8. We have already calculated the markup as $2. But what is the markup percentage?

If you asked, "Percentage of what?" you have asked a very good question and recognized the cause of considerable confusion for beginning retailing students (and even some practitioners!).

A markup can be calculated as a percentage of the retail selling price or as a percentage of the cost. For example, given the book with a $10 retail selling price and an $8 cost, we can calculate the following markup percentages:

$$\text{Markup \% on retail selling price} = \frac{\$2}{\$10} = 20\%$$

$$\text{Markup \% on cost} = \frac{\$2}{\$8} = 25\%$$

So when reference is made to a markup percentage, the student or retailer must be sure to understand the base upon which the percentage is calculated. The calculation requires that the dollar markup be *divided: (a)* by the retail selling price to determine the markup on retail selling price; or *(b)* by the cost to determine the markup on cost.

$$\text{Markup \% on retail selling price} = \frac{\$ \text{ markup}}{\$ \text{ retail selling price}}$$

$$\text{Markup \% on cost} = \frac{\$ \text{ markup}}{\$ \text{ cost}}$$

Markup Percentages Usually Based on Retail Selling Price

All large retail businesses and most smaller ones use and refer to a markup percentage based on retail selling price. This custom has evolved over the years and has become standardized in the reports of merchandising information compiled and distributed by various retail trade associations such as the National Retail Merchants Association (NRMA) and the Food Marketing Institute (FMI).

However, not everyone follows the convention of having the retail selling price as the base for percentage calculations. Some "old-timers" and single-store proprietors still use what they refer to as the "old way of doing it," that is, calculating markups as a percentage of the cost of the item. Also, the practice varies among manufacturers and suppliers. While most large organizations assume a retail selling price base, some smaller suppliers may be represented by salespersons who use the cost base.

Distinguish Markup Percentage on Retail from Markup Percentage on Cost

Retail personnel must understand the difference between markup percentages based on retail and those based on cost. And they must be able to convert from one base to the other. The following example illustrates why this is important.

A salesperson meeting with the buyer for small appliances at a department store extolled the features of a new device developed by his company. The buyer regularly sought a markup of at least 30% on merchandise sold in the department. In wrapping up the presentation, the salesperson exclaimed: "And the best feature from your standpoint, if you sell this at our suggested retail, you'll make a $33\frac{1}{3}\%$ markup!"

The buyer was very interested, then noticed the dollar figures: suggested retail $20, cost $15.

The salesperson was offering a $33\frac{1}{3}\%$ markup on a cost base ($\frac{\$5}{\$15}$). The buyer wanted a 30% markup based on retail. Calculation of the markup based on retail indicated that it was only 25% ($\frac{\$5}{\$20}$) and well below the buyer's minimum. By not clearly understanding markup calculations, the salesperson made an unsuccessful and somewhat embarrassing representation on behalf of the manufacturer. The buyer, however, was familiar with the issue and able to quickly spot the inadequate markup.

The Markup Base Assumption

In this chapter we will specifically label markups as being on retail selling price or on cost. But be aware that many retailing publications, books, and business case studies follow the practice of only labeling markups based on cost. In this text, markups not specified as to base are assumed to be on retail. We will adopt this convention starting with the review problems of this chapter and throughout the following chapters. So beginning with the review problems of Chapter 2, assume that when the base for a markup percentage is not given, the base is retail.

Problems

2–1. A merchant buys a bicycle for $45 and sells it for $79.95. What is the retailer's dollar markup?

2–2. A flower shop sells roses for $25 per dozen that cost $9 per dozen. What dollar markup does the flower shop take on a dozen roses?

2–3. An appliance store sells a brand of color television sets for $399 each. A set costs the store $280. What is the dollar markup? What is the markup as a percentage of retail? What is the markup as a percentage of cost?

2–4. A shoe store purchased a gross (a dozen dozen) of sneakers for $2,880. The sneakers are priced to sell at retail for $29.95 per pair. What is the markup as a percentage of selling price? What is the markup as a percentage of cost?

Using the Markup Box for Percentage Calculations

Figure 2–5 illustrates the use of a variation of the markup box to incorporate percentages, using the example of the book that costs $8 and retails for $10. One rule must be remembered: *The base for a markup percentage must equal 100%*. This means that when considering a markup percentage based upon retail selling price, the retail selling price is 100%. When considering a markup based upon cost, the cost is 100%.

Figure 2–5 Markup Box with Percentages Based on Retail and on Cost

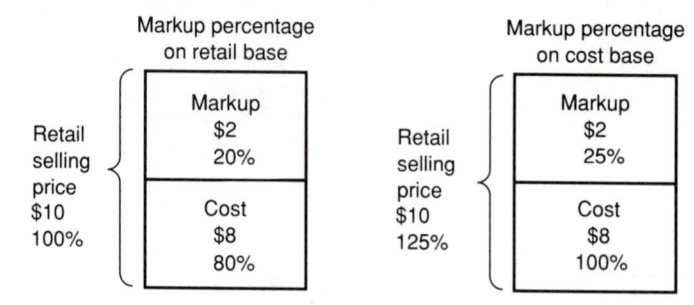

Note that because the cost is 100%, when the markup percentage is based on cost, the total retail percentage, being greater than cost, will be greater than 100%.

As we have seen, problems and calculations that involve markups use three numbers: the retail selling price, the cost, and the markup. If we are given the markup percentage, we can easily figure out the retail selling price and cost percentages. This is because we not only know the markup percentage, but we also know that the base percentage is 100%.

For example, if we are given a markup of 25% based on retail, we know that the retail selling price is 100%, therefore the cost is 75%. This is shown in Figure 2–6.

Figure 2–6 Markup Box with Markup Percentage Based on Retail

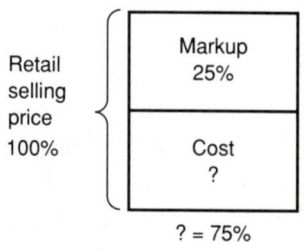

Likewise, if we are given a markup of 25% based on cost, we know that cost is 100%, therefore retail selling price is 125%. This is shown in Figure 2–7.

Figure 2–7 Markup Box with Markup Percentage Based on Cost

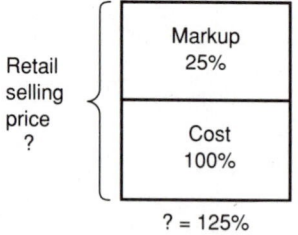

Problems

2–5. A watch has a markup of 45% based on retail. What is the cost as a percentage? What is the retail as a percentage?

2–6. Potatoes have a 50% markup based on cost. What is the cost as a percentage? What is the retail as a percentage?

2–7. A typewriter's cost is 65% of the retail price. What is the markup percentage on retail?

2–8. A yard of sod has a retail percentage of 180% based on cost. What is the percentage markup of the yard of sod based on cost?

The Markup Box Helps to Convert from One Base to the Other

Use of the markup box simplifies the conversion from markup based on cost to markup based on retail selling price, and vice versa. It literally translates from one base to the other. We are given by a manufacturer a markup of $33\frac{1}{3}\%$ based on cost. We want to determine the markup based on selling price. We enter the known numbers into the markup box in Figure 2–8.

Figure 2–8 Markup Box with Markup of $33\frac{1}{3}\%$ Based on Cost

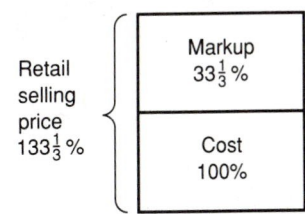

In the markup section we enter $33\frac{1}{3}\%$. Because this markup is based on cost, we enter 100% in the cost section. Adding together the markup and the cost we get a retail selling price percentage of $133\frac{1}{3}\%$. Now to calculate the markup as a percentage of retail, we divide the markup of $33\frac{1}{3}\%$ by the retail of $133\frac{1}{3}\%$. The result is the markup as a percentage of retail:

$$\frac{33\frac{1}{3}\%}{133\frac{1}{3}\%} = 25\%$$

Figure 2–9 illustrates converting a markup based on retail into a markup based on cost. Suppose we have a markup on retail of 25%. We enter that in the markup section. Because the markup is based on retail, the retail is 100%. We enter that in the retail section of Figure 2–9. Subtracting the markup from the cost, gives the cost of 75%. To calculate the markup based on cost, we divide the markup (25%) by the cost (75%):

$$\frac{25\%}{75\%} = 33\frac{1}{3}\%$$

Figure 2–9 Markup Box with Markup of 25% Based on Retail

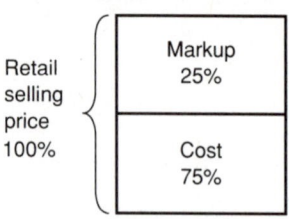

Conversion Formulas Can Be Memorized

Formulas have been developed to convert from one markup base to another. While some students like to memorize formulas, many students (and retailers) are intimidated by them. Furthermore, it is the author's experience that while students may memorize formulas for a test, they quickly forget them. Because it is our purpose to learn concepts in a way that they can be remembered and applied in the world of retailing, this book advocates the logical understanding of the relationship between retail, cost, and markup, and the application of the markup box to clarify momentary confusion. But for those who prefer to memorize formulas, they are provided in the footnote.[1]

Problems

2–9. A necktie has a markup of 45% based on retail. What is the corresponding markup based on cost?

2–10. A lamp has a markup of 55% based on retail. What is the corresponding markup based on cost?

2–11. Watermelons are priced to reflect a 100% markup based on cost. What is the corresponding markup based on selling price?

2–12. Hot dogs were price marked with a 50% markup based on cost. What is the corresponding markup based on selling price?

---

[1]Markup % on cost $= \dfrac{\text{Markup \% on retail selling price}}{100\% - \text{Markup \% on retail selling price}}$

Markup % on retail selling price $= \dfrac{\text{Markup \% on cost}}{100\% + \text{Markup \% on cost}}$

Determining Retail Selling Price in Dollars Given Markup Percentage on Retail

Having now understood the relationships among retail, cost, and markup, and having learned how to calculate markup percentages, we can move ahead and perform a number of calculations regularly done in retailing.

A shoe buyer in a department store pays a manufacturer $50 per pair for shoes. The markup objective based on retail in the shoe department is 45%. What retail selling price should the buyer set for a pair of shoes?

Your first response may be to take the cost ($50) and multiply it by the markup percentage (45%). This would give a markup of $22.50, which when added to the cost of $50, results in a retail selling price of $72.50. BUT THIS IS INCORRECT!

Why is this calculation of $72.50 as the retail selling price wrong? Because the buyer's markup objective of 45% is based on *retail,* not on cost. By multiplying the markup percentage by the cost we were basing the markup on cost. How then do we apply the markup based on retail selling price when we are given only the dollar cost?

Notice that we could convert the markup based on retail selling price to a markup based on cost. Let's try it that way. Figure 2–10 provides assistance. This allows us to find the cost percentage, 55%. Then dividing the markup by the cost, we get the markup percentage based on cost.

Figure 2–10 Markup Box with Markup of 45% Based on Retail

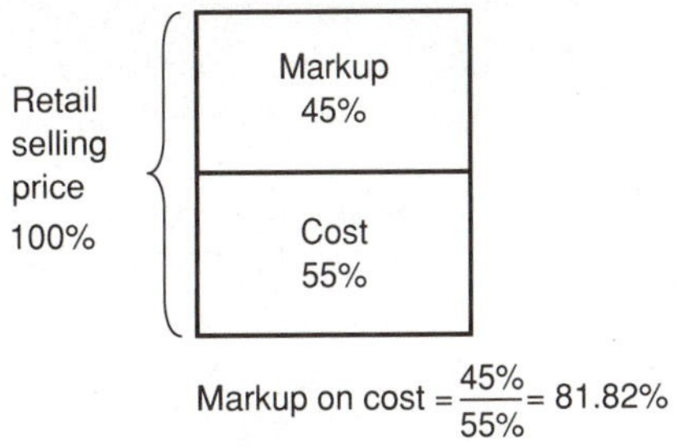

```
                  ┌──────────────┐
Retail           │   Markup     │
selling          │    45%       │
price            ├──────────────┤
100%             │    Cost      │
                 │    55%       │
                 └──────────────┘
         Markup on cost = 45%/55% = 81.82%
```

$$\text{Markup \% on cost} = \frac{45\%}{55\%} = 81.82\%$$

Next we would have to apply the markup percentage based on cost to the cost: $50 × 81.82% = $40.91. Finally we would add this to the cost to get the retail selling price:

$$\$50 + \$40.91 = \$90.91$$

This is a correct but very cumbersome way of determining the retail selling price. It is not how retail professionals would do the calculation. Let's refer for a moment back to Figure 2–10. Notice that we have already determined the cost percentage to be 55%. So we now know that the cost which is $50 is also 55% of the retail selling price. Let's show this in Figure 2–11. What we have done here is to combine both the dollar and percentage numbers in one illustration.

Figure 2–11 Markup Box with Cost in Dollars and as Percentage

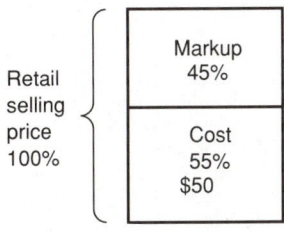

As we can see, the cost, \$50, is 55% of the retail selling price.

or:

$$\$50 = 55\% \text{ retail selling price}$$

so:

$$\frac{\$50}{55\%} = \text{Retail selling price} = \$90.91$$

The retail selling price is \$90.91.[2]

Now let's check to see whether the retail selling price of \$90.91 will provide a 45% markup on retail.

$$\text{Retail selling price} - \text{Cost} = \text{Markup}$$

$$\$90.91 - \$50 = \$40.91 \text{ (the markup)}$$

$$\frac{\$ \text{ markup}}{\$ \text{ retail}} = \frac{\$40.91}{\$90.91} = 45\% \text{ (the markup \% on retail selling price)}$$

So to calculate a retail selling price, given a dollar cost and a markup percentage based on retail, we divide the dollar cost by 100% minus the markup percentage. 100% minus the markup percentage based on retail is often referred to as the *cost complement* or the complement of the cost.

Let's try another example.

A supermarket buyer is paying \$2.40 per pound for a brand of coffee. The buyer usually has a 14% markup on coffee based on retail. What should the retail selling price be? Figure 2–12 organizes the data and helps us understand the problem.

Figure 2–12 Markup Box with Cost of \$2.40 and Markup of 14% Based on Retail

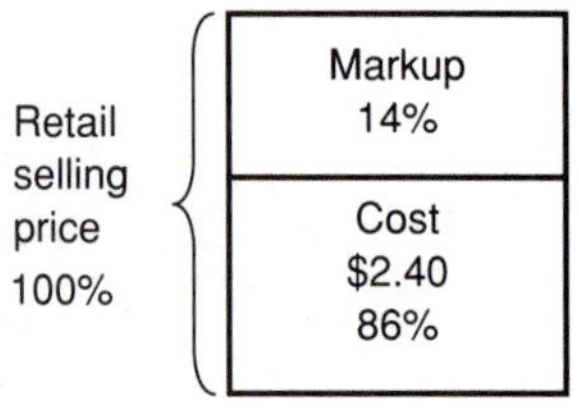

We can now quickly see that \$2.40 is 86% of the retail selling price. So, the retail selling price is:

$$\frac{\$2.40}{86\%} = \$2.79$$

Determining Cost in Dollars Given Markup Percentage on Retail

A department store buyer is considering sources for a line of private-label blouses. The buyer would like to retail the blouses for \$25. The markup objective for this department is 45% based on retail. What is the highest price the buyer can pay for the blouses and still meet the markup objective? Figure 2–13 helps to sort out the data.

---

[2]In this calculation the 55% is retained in percentage form and not converted into a decimal because it is likely that students will be utilizing a calculator that can divide by a percentage. To perform the calculation with pencil and paper it would be beneficial to make the conversion to a decimal (i.e., $55\% = .55; \frac{\$50}{.55} = \$90.91$).

Remember that to convert from a percentage to a decimal you move the decimal point 2 places to the left: $25\% = .25$. To convert from a decimal to a percentage you move the decimal point two places to the right: $.45 = 45\%$.

*Figure 2–13 Markup Box with Retail Selling Price of $25 and Markup of 45%
Based on Retail*

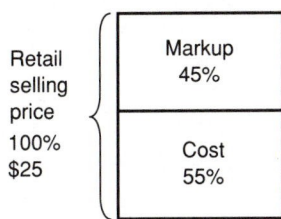

We can see that because the markup is 45%, the cost is 55%. Therefore, on a blouse selling at retail for $25, the cost cannot be more than 55% of the selling price. Thus, the cost would be: $25 × 55% = $13.75.

Let's check to make sure this answer gives a 45% markup on retail. Markup is $25 − $13.75 = $11.25.

$$\text{Markup percentage} = \frac{\$11.25}{\$25} = 45\%$$

It checks!!!

We can also solve the above problem by determining the markup and subtracting that from the retail. That is, the markup is $25 × 45% = $11.25. Then $25 − $11.25 = $13.75, the cost. This approach is just as correct, but once you get in the habit of using the cost complement, you will find it a bit quicker. Often with easy numbers, you will be able to do the calculation in your head.

Problems

2–13. A bookstore manager normally takes a 45% markup based on retail on new books. She purchases from a wholesaler a best seller that cost $14. What retail price should the manager mark on the book?

2–14. A gift shop owner takes a 60% markup based on retail on novelty giftware. An ashtray that has a cost from a jobber of $2 would be priced at what retail?

2–15. A buyer for men's clothing in a department store is seeking sport coats to retail for $125. The markup objective based on retail is 48%. What is the most the buyer can pay a supplier for the jackets?

2–16. A pushcart vendor is negotiating with a jobber for some banners and pennants. He wants to sell them for $3 each and make a 25% markup on retail. What is the maximum amount per item the vendor should pay?

Determining Selling Price in Dollars Given Markup Percentage on Cost

The problems discussed in the preceding section involved markup percentages based on retail. Similar calculations can be made with markup percentages based on cost. Although most students will confront cost based calculations less often, they should be confident of their ability to do any type of markup calculation. Therefore we will review a few calculations with a markup percentage based on cost.

A produce manager for a supermarket usually prices lettuce with a 50% markup based on cost. If lettuce costs $.50 per head, what would the retail selling price be? Figure 2–14 organizes the data and directs us to the solution.

Figure 2–14 Markup Box with Cost of $.50 and Markup of 50% Based on Cost

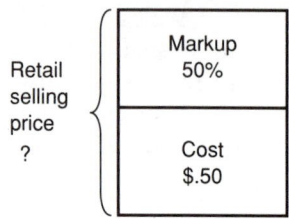

As Figure 2–14 suggests, we can determine the markup by multiplying the dollar cost ($.50) by the markup percentage on cost (50%). This gives a markup of $.25 which when added to the cost results in a selling price of $.75.

$$\$.50 \times 50\% = \$.25 \text{ (markup)}$$
$$\$.50 \text{ (cost)} + \$.25 \text{ (markup)} = \$.75 \text{ (retail selling price)}$$

Notice also that we can calculate the result a second way as illustrated by Figure 2–15. Here we have illustrated the retail as 150% of cost. Thus, by multiplying $.50 (the cost) by 150% (the retail selling price), the result is the same as that calculated above:

$$\$.50 \text{ (cost)} \times 150\% = \$.75[3]$$

Figure 2–15 Variation of Markup Box with Cost of $.50 and Markup of 50% Based on Cost

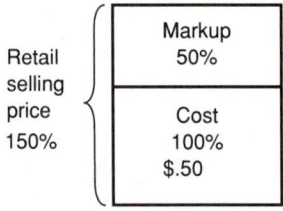

Determining Cost in Dollars Given Markup Percentage on Cost

The owner of an antique store prices merchandise with a 100% markup based on cost. What is the most that could be paid for an old icebox that the owner thought could be sold for $450? Figure 2–16 organizes the solution for us.

---

[3]As suggested in the preceding footnote, the percentage figure (150%) can be used in most calculators. To calculate with pencil and paper, it would be advisable to convert to decimals: 150% = 1.5; $.50 × 1.5 = $.75. This conversion to decimals applies to many other problems in this book.

Figure 2–16 Markup Box with Retail Selling Price $450 and Markup of 100%
Based on Cost

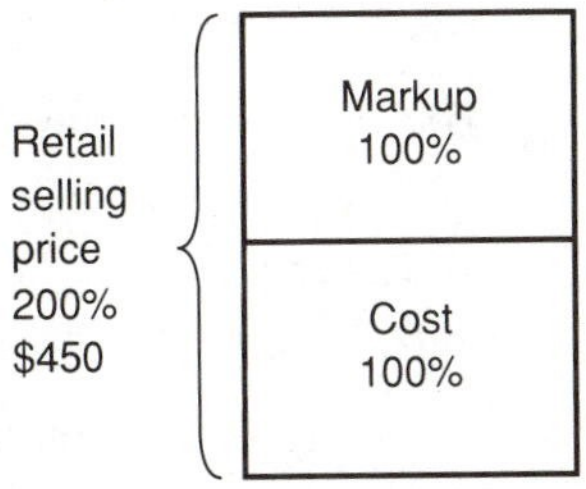

The retail is $450 and the retail in percentages is 200%. Thus $450 is 200% of cost and we can solve for the cost:

$$\$450 = 200\% \text{ cost}$$

$$\frac{\$450}{200\%} = \text{Cost}$$

$$\$225 = \text{Cost}$$

Problems

2–17. The owner of a nursery takes a 125% markup based on cost on shrubs. What price should be charged for evergreens that cost $10 each?

2–18. A florist marks up flowers 150% of cost. What price should be charged for a dozen roses that cost $10 per dozen?

2–19. A secondhand clothing store owner regularly sells coats at a markup of 75% of cost. The owner is offered a coat that upon inspection appears to be resalable for $49. What is the maximum amount that should be offered for the coat?

2–20. A cobbler (shoe repairer) decides to add a few styles of new shoes to his shop. The shoes will be sold for $25 per pair and the cobbler is seeking a markup of 50% based on cost. What is the most the cobbler should pay for the shoes?

Other Calculations Using Markups

There are other calculations you may use as a retailer in pricing merchandise, in analyzing particular options, or in negotiating with suppliers.

A salesperson for a supplier tells you that a certain item carries a markup of $2 when sold at the manufacturer's suggested retail price.

You ask: What's the markup percent?

The salesperson responds: Twenty-five percent.

You inquire further: On cost or retail?

Salesperson: Retail.

Given these facts, what is the suggested retail and cost? Figure 2–17 organizes the facts.

Figure 2–17 Markup Box with Markup of $2 and Markup of 25% Based on Retail

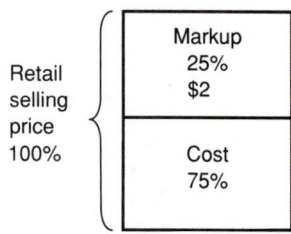

As Figure 2–17 indicates, the markup of $2 is 25% of retail.

Therefore:

$$\$2 = 25\% \text{ retail}$$

$$\frac{\$2}{25\%} = \text{Retail}$$

$$\$8 = \text{Retail}$$

$$\$8 \text{ (retail)} - \$2 \text{ (markup)} = \$6 \text{ (cost)}$$

Suppose the salesperson had said that the markup was 25% based on cost. Figure 2–18 translates that situation for us.

Figure 2–18 Markup Box with Markup of $2 and Markup of 25% Based on Cost

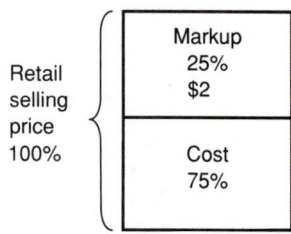

Now the $2 is 25% of the cost.

So:

$$\$2 = 25\% \text{ cost}$$

$$\frac{\$2}{25\%} = \text{Cost}$$

$$\$8 = \text{Cost}$$

$$\$8 \text{ (cost)} + \$2 \text{ (markup)} = \$10 \text{ (retail)}$$

Mellow Music Store Applications

The Mellow Music Store is a small keyboard retailer to be opened soon on Mainstreet, U.S.A. It will sell pianos, organs, synthesizers, and other keyboard instruments, along with accessories and some music. John and Julie Martin, graduates of a well-known music school, will operate the new store. Both had acquired several years of experience working part-time in music stores and in music departments of department stores. After discussions with other music store proprietors and with representatives of musical instrument manufacturers, they decided that their markup objective will be 50% based on retail. They have purchased a piano that costs $1,000. They calculate using Figure 2–19 that the piano will have a retail price tag of $2,000.

Figure 2–19 Markup Box with Cost of $1,000 and Markup of 50% Based on Retail

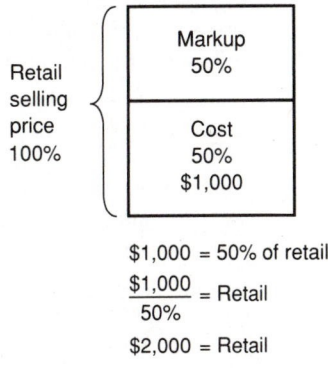

$$\$1,000 = 50\% \text{ of retail}$$

$$\frac{\$1,000}{50\%} = \text{Retail}$$

$$\$2,000 = \text{Retail}$$

A salesman representing a music publisher presented some songbooks that were prepriced at $4.95. The songbooks cost $2.50. John figured the markup to be 49.5%.

$$\text{Retail selling price} - \text{Cost} = \text{Markup}$$

$$\$4.95 - \$2.50 = \$2.45$$

$$\text{Markup } \% = \frac{\$ \text{ markup}}{\$ \text{ selling price}} = \frac{\$2.45}{\$4.95} = 49.5\%$$

He told Julie that he was disappointed that the salesperson would not reduce the price of the songbooks below $2.50. He said that the songbooks should be prepriced at $5 so that the store could make a 50% markup:

$$\text{Retail selling price} = \frac{\$ \text{ cost}}{\text{Cost complement } \%} = \frac{\$2.50}{50\%} = \$5.00$$

A young musician wandered into the store as John and Julie were decorating for their Grand Opening. He carried a used amplifier. Approaching Julie he said, "I'd like to sell you my amplifier. You can resell it for $300, I'm sure. Give me $200 for it and you'll make a nice 50% markup."

Julie turned to John and said, "He wants $200 for this amplifier. I agree with him that we can sell it for $300. But to get the 50% markup that *we* want, we can only pay him $150 for it." Here the seller was basing his markup on cost:

$$\text{Cost} = \$200$$

$$\text{Markup on cost} = 50\% \times \$200 = \$100$$

$$\text{Retail} = \text{Cost} + \text{Markup}$$

$$\text{Retail} = \$200 + \$100 = \$300$$

The store owners want a markup based on retail. With a markup based on retail of 50%, the cost is 50%. Thus, as Figure 2–20 indicates, the cost would have to be $150.

Figure 2–20 Markup Box with Retail of $300 and Markup of 50% Based on Retail

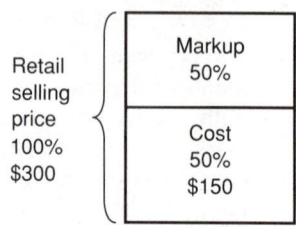

Remember that from now on we will specify the base for a markup percentage only when it is on cost. If the base for a markup percentage is not specified, we will assume it to be on retail.

Review Problems

2–1R.   A manufacturer's representative offers the buyer for a discount department store a special cost of $240 on the current model of refrigerators that will be slightly modified in the new model year. The representative suggests that the buyer sell the refrigerators for $319. What markup percentage is being suggested based on retail? What markup percentage is being suggested based on cost?

2–2R.   A sleepwear buyer in a department store purchases pajamas at a cost of $100 per dozen. If the buyer's markup objective is 44% what retail price should the buyer establish for one pair of pajamas?

2–3R.   The proprietor of a video store regularly applies a 60% markup based on cost to merchandise carried in stock. What should the retail selling price be for video cassette tapes purchased for $3.40?

2–4R.   A radio with a markup of 24% has a markup of $6. What is the retail price of the radio?

2–5R.   A markup of $33\frac{1}{3}$% based on cost would correspond to what markup based on retail?

2–6R.   A markup of 48% based on retail would correspond to what markup based on cost?

2–7R.   The buyer for a supermarket chain wishes to sell private-label soda at a retail price of 2/$1 for liter-sized bottles. If a markup of 25% is desired, what is the maximum price the buyer may pay per bottle?

2–8R.   The owner of a vegetable stand wants to sell fresh tomatoes for $.59 per pound and earn a markup of 50% based on cost. What is the highest price he could pay growers for tomatoes?

2–9R.   A buyer for a supermarket chain is negotiating for ice cream to sell under the chain's private label. Different suppliers have offered varying quotations. The buyer is anxious to achieve a 40% markup. What retail prices would result if the ice cream were purchased from the following suppliers:

Vendor	*Cost per Half-Gallon*
Quality Ice Cream	$1.00
Patriot Ice Cream	1.10
Buttercream Dairy	.95
Guernsey Creamery	1.20

2–10R.   The owner of a small convenience store bases markups on cost. In seeking a supplier for private label potato chips, the following quotations were received:

Vendor	Cost per Pound
Spud Farms	$0.85
Snacks, Inc.	1.10

What retail prices would result if the owner sought a markup of 50% on cost for private-label chips?

CHAPTER 3

Initial Markup and Cumulative Markup

In Chapter 2, while discussing markups and various markup calculations, we occasionally referred to desired markups:

The markup objective in the shoe department is 45%.
A bookstore manager normally takes a 45% markup on new books.
The sleepwear buyer's markup objective is 44%.

How are these markup objectives established? Retailers have a definite process for determining them. But before we learn that process, let's first discuss the need for a markup objective.

Markup Provides Revenue

As we have seen, the buying and selling of merchandise creates revenue for a retailer; and markup is the difference between what a retailer buys something for and what it is sold for. The total of all the markups realized from all the goods that are bought and sold provides the revenue used to cover expenses and to generate a profit.

Retailers should (and most do) have profit goals. Retailers should (and most do) have excellent information about their expenses. Therefore, with a profit goal and knowledge of expected expenses, a retailer can determine how much revenue in markup form is needed.

Markup Objectives Are Necessary

Consider the alternative: having no objective. If the markups are too high, the merchandise is priced too high; many customers will not buy, if competitors have the same goods at a lower price. Not enough revenue will be generated to cover expenses, and the retailer will incur a loss. If the markups are too low and the prices are too low, lots of people will buy. But because the markup is not great enough to cover expenses, the more the store sells the more money it loses! So there is a need for balance; prices must be competitive and yet must generate enough revenue to cover expenses and provide profits. The markup must be planned; the retailer should know how much markup to apply in pricing merchandise.

The Initial Markup

The markup that the retailer plans and applies when goods are originally priced is the **initial markup.** It is sometimes also called the *original markup,* or the *initial markon*. Many goods are sold at the initial markup. As customers, however, we know that retailers often reduce the price before certain goods are sold. They take what is known as a *markdown*. But to aid our understanding of the establishment of the initial markup, let's first consider a situation where there are no reductions in the original price, a store with no markdowns.

The Initial Markup at Adams Hardware

The Adams Hardware store is operated by Ted Adams. It has had the same location on Main Street for 105 years. It was previously operated by Ted Adams's father; before that, his grandfather; and before that, his great-grandfather. The store sells staple hardware merchandise—nuts and bolts, nails and screws, tools, paints, and other supplies. It is open 6 days a week, 49 weeks a year. Ted closes the store for three weeks during the summer for his annual vacation. The store is open from 7:00 A.M. to 6:00 P.M., except between 1:30 P.M. and 2:00 P.M. when Mr. Adams closes for lunch. Sales average $2,000 per week, week-in, week-out, except that they double the week before Christmas.

"Been that way as long as I can remember," muses Mr. Adams. "We're convenient for people and have anything they might want. If I don't have it, I can get it quickly for them from the wholesaler. Never had a sale; never mark anything down. If you wait long enough, there'll be someone who needs it."

The merchandise that Mr. Adams sold the most recent year cost him $50,000. The total cost of operating the store, including Mr. Adams's salary, was $40,000. Mr. Adams's store had a profit of $10,000. A summary statement of his store's operation would indicate:

Sales		
48 weeks at $2,000	$96,000	
1 week at $4,000	4,000	$100,000
Cost of merchandise sold		50,000
Revenue generated (gross margin)		50,000
Expenses		40,000
Profit		$ 10,000

In planning for the next year, Mr. Adams said, "I think everything is gonna' be the same. I was thinking of giving myself a raise, but decided not to. I like to stick to my budget anyway. If the cost of oil goes up again, I'll just turn the thermostat down and put on a sweater. Customers won't notice; they have coats on when they come in."

It's easy to see what markup Mr. Adams needs. He has to cover expenses of $40,000 and a profit of $10,000, in the course of selling $100,000 worth of merchandise. So he needs to generate $50,000 in markup. Relating this to his sales (remember now we are assuming markup on retail) results in a markup of 50%.

$$\frac{\text{Markup needed}}{\text{Sales}} = \frac{\$50,000}{\$100,000} = 50\%$$

Another way of visualizing Mr. Adams's situation is presented in Figure 3–1.

Figure 3–1 Adams Hardware Initial Markup and Sales Components with No Reductions

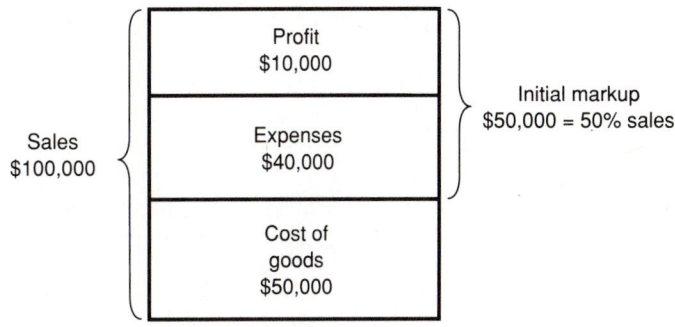

Here we see that added to the cost of the goods ($50,000) are the expenses ($40,000) and the profit ($10,000). The three categories combined comprise the sales. The markup, that is, the difference between the cost of goods and what they were sold for, is $50,000, or 50% of sales.

Thus, with Mr. Adams never selling an item at less that the regular price, if he took a 50% initial markup on all the merchandise that is in the store and that he added to the store's inventory, he would generate $50,000 in revenue (gross margin) to cover his expenses and profit—as long as he sold $100,000 worth of goods.

Adams Hardware Not a Typical Retailer

Unfortunately, most retail operations are not as simple, predictable, and stable as Adams Hardware. Sales vary, expenses change, and there are markdowns. These factors and others that are parts of the dynamic world of retailing, place even greater emphasis on planning. For with a plan you: *(a)* have some idea where you are going; and *(b)* have something against which to measure how well you are doing. **Measuring current accomplishment against what was planned is the major control device of the retailer.** Retail merchandising and control, as the title of this book suggests, are closely intertwined.

The first major difference from Mr. Adams's operation that we must consider is the normal expectation in retailing that everything will not sell at the original retail price and at the same markup. Many items will be sold at a reduced price. There are four categories of what retailers call *reductions:*

Markdowns.
Employee discounts.
Discounts to special classes of customers.
Shortages.

Markdowns

Retailers classify two major types of price reductions as markdowns. One considers merchandise that for some reason—perhaps color, style, fabric, a defect of some sort—is not selling in desired quantities. It will be lowered in price in an effort to induce sale. Sometimes there will be more than one reduction. For example, an overcoat has been in stock for three months at a retail price of $200. Day after day it hangs on the rack, while other coats are being sold. The buyer reduces the price to $175. The coat still does not sell. The buyer takes a second markdown to $149. At this price someone buys the coat.

Likewise at the end of the fall-winter season, in anticipation of bringing in spring merchandise, and not wishing to carry overcoats in inventory until the next fall season, the same buyer may reduce the price of all remaining overcoats. In both of these examples the reduction in price is motivated by a desire to sell merchandise that might be considered to have some negative association: merchandise undesired by customers at the regular price or going out of season.

A second major type of markdown is when a retailer reduces the price of merchandise that sells well at the regular price and that is in season. But the merchant wishes to use the attraction of a price reduction on these desired goods to bring customers into the store. As customers we recognize this as a **sale.** It is usually promoted by advertising and in-store signs. Often the event will also be used by the merchant to sell merchandise that has been marked down for reasons of style, color, and so forth, as described above. This is especially characteristic in the sale of fashion related merchandise such as clothing. In the food retailing area, some managements will take markdowns on perishable food such as overripe bananas or day-old bread, but most of the markdowns will consist of regularly selling merchandise reduced in price to attract customers to the store.

Employee Discounts

A second category of reductions is **employee discounts.** Many stores follow the practice of giving store employees the privilege of purchasing merchandise from the store at a special reduced price, for example, 20% off the regular price.

Special Customer Discounts

A third category of reductions is **discounts to particular groups of customers.** For example, many stores will give a senior citizen's discount of 10% to qualifying customers. Some stores will give a discount to members of the clergy. Some hardware stores will give a special discount to professional painters or other tradesmen. Some music stores may give a special discount to professional musicians.

Shortages

The fourth category of reductions is **shortages.** These represent several different actions such as damaged goods and shoplifting. If the jar of mayonnaise that is dropped and broken in the supermarket aisle must be thrown away, it brings no revenue to the store. It represents, however, the loss in regular price which the store would have realized had the jar been sold.[1]

Likewise, there is the item that is taken from the store by a shoplifter. The store's revenue has been reduced by the amount that would have been generated if the item had been sold at its regular price.

An additional category of shortages comprises recordkeeping and other clerical errors that have escaped detection and correction and that result in bookkeeping discrepancies which must be reconciled.

If Adams Hardware had Reductions

Let's return to Ted Adams and the Adams Hardware store and make the operation more realistic by adding some reductions.

In planning for next year, Ted Adams anticipates that he will occasionally reduce the price of an item that becomes shopworn; he expects to have a couple of *sales;* and he will allow the part-time help he employs to take a 15% price reduction on merchandise they buy from the store. His best estimate is that such reductions will total $2,500 next year. He still has the profit and sales goals of $10,000 and $100,000, respectively, and he estimates total operating expenses of $40,000. Figure 3–2 illustrates Mr. Adams's plan for next year with the addition of reductions.

Figure 3–2 Adams Hardware Initial Markup and Sales Components with Reductions

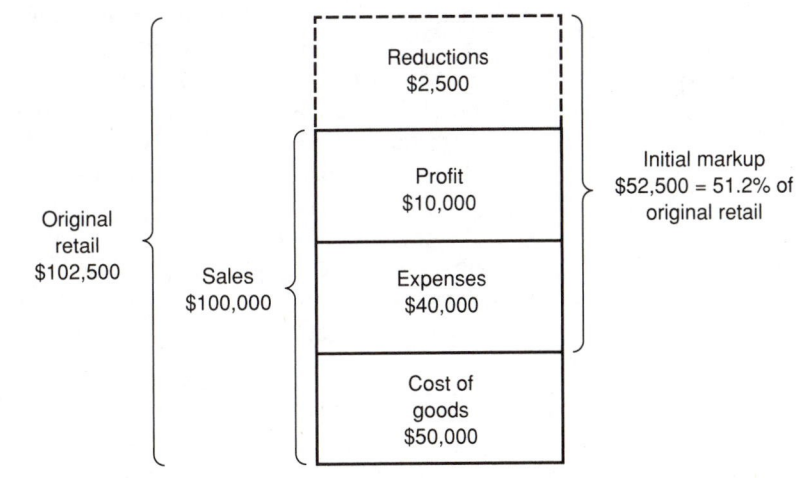

Notice that now the initial markup has to include an allowance for the reductions in the original prices of merchandise that is not sold at the original retail price. So when Mr. Adams sets his initial markup, he has to plan it to be higher than 50% of original retail so that after the reductions in price, he still has 50% of sales to cover expenses and profit.

---

[1]Some vendors will accept such damaged merchandise as a return for credit.

Remember that the initial markup is based on the original retail value. The goods that were planned to be sold for $100,000 had an original retail value of $102,500. Because the original retail prices were reduced by a total of $2,500, the sales value of the merchandise when sold (the amount rung up on the cash registers) was $100,000. Therefore, allowing for reductions, Mr. Adams needs an initial markup of:

$$\text{Initial markup needed} = \frac{\text{Expenses} + \text{Profit} + \text{Reductions}}{\text{Original retail value of goods sold}}$$

$$\text{Initial markup} = \frac{\$40,000 + \$10,000 + \$2,500}{\$100,000 + \$2,500}$$

$$\text{Initial markup} = \frac{\$52,500}{\$102,500}$$

$$\text{Initial markup} = 51.2\%$$

Many retailers incur two additional corrections that must also be considered when determining initial markup. These are cash discounts from suppliers and so-called alteration costs.

Allowing in Initial Markup for Cash Discounts

Up to this point, we have not accurately defined *cost* when considering the cost of merchandise as part of markup calculations. The cost of merchandise for this purpose is the *billed cost,* including any transportation expenses incurred by the retailer in getting the merchandise from the supplier to the retailer. Thus, if Mr. Adams purchased 2 dozen hammers at a price of $54 per dozen, with the shipping charges paid by the manufacturer, his total cost for the hammers would be $108; and his cost per hammer would be $4.50. If, on the other hand, Mr. Adams had to pay a $6 shipping cost, his total cost for 2 dozen would be $114; and his cost per hammer would be $4.75.[2]

For some categories of merchandise, especially soft goods, many vendors offer a cash discount. Initially established to motivate prompt payment, cash discounts are sometimes allowed by suppliers even though payment may not be made on a prompt basis. While the effect of the cash discount is to reduce the cost of the merchandise if the discount is taken, most retailers do not correct for the discount in pricing goods. Possible reasons for this are temporary cash flow problems or clerical oversights resulting in a particular discount not being taken. That is, the bill for the merchandise is not paid by the expiration date for taking the cash discount.

However, in setting the initial markup needed to achieve profit objectives and cover expenses, the expected cash discounts are included. Because the cash discounts reduce the actual cost of the goods, their net effect is to add to revenue. Thus the cash discounts are subtracted in determining the amount of initial markup needed. So for retailers anticipating the generation of cash discounts:

$$\text{Initial markup} = \frac{\text{Expenses} + \text{Profits} + \text{Reductions} - \text{Cash discounts}}{\text{Sales} + \text{Reductions}}$$

Cash Discounts Are Worth Taking

Retailers should manage their accounts payable so as to take available cash discounts unless their financial position is so tight that it precludes doing so. Even though the amounts of cash discounts offered may seem small, for example, 2%, 4%, or 6%, these discount rates are for very short periods of time and on an annual basis reflect a very favorable rate of interest.

---

[2]Whether the retailer or the supplier pays the cost of transporting merchandise to the store varies among suppliers and is sometimes negotiable.

Thus, a 4% cash discount that may be offered for paying a bill 20 days early (that is, 20 days before the full amount is due) represents a 75% rate of interest on an annualized basis.[3] By not taking the cash discount, the retailer is in effect paying a high rate of interest for the short-term use of the funds involved.

Allowing in Initial Markup for Alteration Costs

For some lines of goods, retailers make certain refinements or modifications to the merchandise after it is received in the stores. For example, many stores provide clothing alterations. Some do not charge for this service, others may have fees for some alterations that sometimes do not cover the full cost. Some musical instrument departments find it necessary to tune pianos after receiving them from manufacturers, and while they are on the selling floor prior to sale. Some, upon purchase, provide a *free* tuning to the purchaser. Such adjustments become a part of the cost of the particular category of merchandise. While these associated expenses could be included as part of total operating expense, it is the practice in most large stores to separately account for these alteration expenses and to include them in the calculation of the initial markup. Thus, for retailers experiencing both cash discounts from suppliers and these so-called alteration expenses, the initial markup is calculated as follows:

$$\text{Initial markup} = \frac{\begin{array}{c}\text{Expenses} + \text{Profits} + \text{Reductions} \\ + \text{ Alteration costs} - \text{Cash discounts}\end{array}}{\text{Sales} + \text{Reductions}}$$

Problems

3–1. The proprietor of a greeting card and stationery store was planning sales for next year of $60,000. Total operating expenses were estimated to be $25,000. No cash discounts, reductions, or alteration costs were anticipated. What initial markup percentage would provide the proprietor with an $8,000 profit?

---

[3]On a bill of $1,000 with a 4% cash discount, the retailer would save $1,000 × 4% = $40 by taking the discount and paying early. So the net amount paid would be $960. To not take the cash discount, the retailer would be paying $40 to use $960 for 20 days. On an annual basis, using a 360 day business year, there are 18 20-day periods. So the annual interest would actually be $40 × 18 = $720. This is an interest rate of $720/$960 = 75%.

Another way of looking at the situation is to say that the retailer is loaning the supplier $960 for 20 days. The retailer is paid $40 interest for the loan. The annual rate of interest earned by the retailer is:

$$\frac{\$40}{\$960} \times \frac{360}{20} = 75\%$$

Appendix A discusses terms of sale and purchase in more detail.

3–2. The manager of a sporting goods store estimated sales for the next season would be $200,000. Reductions of $20,000 were expected along with total expenses of $60,000. What initial markup would generate a $15,000 profit for the store?

3–3. The buyer for women's blouses was planning spring season sales of $120,000. Markdowns were expected to be $10,000. Employee discounts were expected to be $500. Shortages were expected to be $250. Cash discounts of $2,000 were forecast. Operating expenses were estimated to total $30,000. The buyer's profit objective was $12,000. What initial markup should the buyer plan?

3–4. A men's clothing buyer was planning for sales of $185,000. The following figures were estimated: total reductions $12,000; operating expenses $50,000; cash discounts $18,000; and alteration costs $3,000. What initial markup should the buyer plan in order to achieve a profit objective of $15,000?

Calculating Initial Markup with Percentage Figures

The above discussion of establishing the initial markup was based upon dollar figures. The same results can be achieved by using percentage figures based upon sales as 100%. The following figures are for a furniture retailer:

	In Dollars	*As a Percent of Sales*
Sales	$500,000	100.0%
Operating expenses	190,000	38.0
Reductions	50,000	10.0
Cash discounts	1,000	.2
Alteration costs	4,000	.8
Profits	25,000	5.0

Using dollar figures:

$$\text{Initial markup} = \frac{\begin{array}{c}\text{Expenses} + \text{Profit} + \text{Reductions} + \\ \text{Alteration costs} - \text{Cash discounts}\end{array}}{\text{Sales} + \text{Reductions}}$$

$$\text{Initial markup} = \frac{\$190,000 + \$25,000 + \$50,000 + \$4,000 - \$1,000}{\$500,000 + \$50,000}$$

$$\text{Initial markup} = \frac{\$268,000}{\$550,000}$$

$$\text{Initial markup} = 48.7\%$$

Using percentage figures:

$$\text{Initial markup} = \frac{\begin{array}{c}\text{Expenses \%} + \text{Profit \%} + \text{Reduction \%} \\ + \text{Alteration costs \%} - \text{Cash discounts \%}\end{array}}{100\% + \text{Reduction \%}}$$

$$\text{Initial markup} = \frac{38\% + 5\% + 10\% + .8\% - .2\%}{100\% + 10\%}$$

$$\text{Initial markup} = \frac{53.6\%}{110\%}$$

$$\text{Initial markup} = 48.7\%$$

Calculating Initial Markup with Both Percentage and Dollar Figures

Given a mix of dollar and percentage figures, the calculations can be done on either basis. You are provided with the following figures:

Expenses	35%
Reductions	9%
Cash discounts	2%
Alteration costs	2%
Profits	10%, $60,000

What should the initial markup be?

Because we are using a retail base, we know that sales are 100%. Profits which are 10% of sales are $60,000.

Therefore,

$$10\% \text{ sales} = \$60,000$$

$$\text{Sales} = \frac{\$60,000}{10\%}$$

$$\text{Sales} = \$600,000$$

Now we can list the relevant figures in dollars and percentages:

	In Dollars	*In Percentages*
Sales	$600,000	100%
Expenses	210,000	35
Reductions	54,000	9
Cash discounts	12,000	2
Alteration costs	12,000	2
Profits	60,000	10

and calculate the initial markup on either a dollar or percentage basis.

$$\text{Initial markup} = \frac{\text{Expenses + Profit + Reductions} + \text{Alteration costs} - \text{Cash discounts}}{\text{Sales + Reductions}}$$

$$\text{Initial markup} = \frac{\$210,000 + \$60,000 + \$54,000 + \$12,000 - \$12,000}{\$600,000 + \$54,000}$$

$$\text{Initial markup} = \frac{\$324,000}{\$654,000}$$

$$\text{Initial markup} = 49.5\%$$

$$\text{Initial markup} = \frac{\text{Expenses \% + Profit \% + Reductions \%} + \text{Alteration costs \%} - \text{Cash discounts \%}}{100\% + \text{Reductions \%}}$$

$$\text{Initial markup} = \frac{35\% + 10\% + 9\% + 2\% - 2\%}{100\% + 9\%}$$

$$\text{Initial markup} = \frac{54\%}{109\%}$$

$$\text{Initial markup} = 49.5\%$$

Problems

3–5. A video shop manager estimated the following figures in planning for next year: expenses 31%; markdowns 7%; employee discounts 3%; shortages 1.5%; and profits 6%. No alteration costs or cash discounts were expected. What initial markup percentage should be planned?

3–6. The owner of a men's apparel shop wished to establish the initial markup percentage needed if operating figures were as follows: profit 7%; reductions 18%; cash discounts 4%; alteration costs 4%; and expenses 29%.

3–7. Determine the initial markup percentage on a dollar basis and on a percentage basis from the following figures:

Sales	$200,000
Profit	15,000
Employee discounts	6,000
Expenses	63,000
Markdowns	22,000

Senior citizen discounts	4,000
Cash discounts	7,000
Alteration costs	5,000
Shortages	2,000

3–8.   Determine the initial markup percentage on a dollar basis and on a percentage basis from the following figures:

Profit	$18,000, 6%
Cash discounts	3
Reductions	16
Expenses	32
Alteration costs	4

When Reductions and Expenses Vary

Retailers will often explore different combinations of expenses, profits, and reductions, in establishing objectives and plans. The impact of being more *promotional*, having higher markdowns, can be estimated. Similarly, the effect of raising expenses to increase service can be explored.

For example, a department had the following results for last season:

Reductions	14%
Expenses	28%
Cash discounts	4%
Profits	5%

Management is wondering what effect a combination of higher reductions (up to 18%) and higher expenses (up to 30%) would have on the initial markup, if profits and cash discounts are maintained at existing levels and there are no alteration costs.

Let's first calculate last season's initial markup:

$$\text{Initial markup} = \frac{\text{Expenses \% + Profit \% + Reductions \% − Cash discounts \%}}{100\% + \text{Reductions \%}}$$

$$\text{Initial markup} = \frac{28\% + 5\% + 14\% - 4\%}{100\% + 14\%}$$

$$\text{Initial markup} = \frac{43\%}{114\%}$$

$$\text{Initial markup} = 37.7\%$$

With the changes in reductions and expenses, we'll calculate the initial markup that would be needed:

$$\text{Initial markup} = \frac{\text{Expenses \% + Profit \% + Reduction \% − Cash discounts \%}}{100\% + \text{Reductions \%}}$$

$$\text{Initial markup} = \frac{30\% + 5\% + 18\% - 4\%}{100\% + 18\%}$$

$$\text{Initial markup} = \frac{49\%}{118\%}$$

$$\text{Initial markup} = 41.5\%$$

Now management must judge the wisdom of implementing the changes. The higher initial markup would result in some increases in average original retail prices. For example, we recall from Chapter 2 that an item that costs $10 with an initial markup of 37.7% would have a retail of:

$$\frac{\$ \text{ cost}}{\text{Cost complement \%}} = \frac{\$10}{62.3\%} = \$16.05$$

The same item with an initial markup of 41.5% would have a retail of:

$$\frac{\$ \text{ cost}}{\text{Cost complement \%}} = \frac{\$10}{58.5\%} = \$17.09$$

Would the greater markdowns and higher service offset the higher prices? Notice that if sales stayed the same, and the other results were as estimated, the dollar profits earned would be the same. For example, let's assume that sales were $100,000. Then both the first and second sets of figures give the same profit, 5% of $100,000, or $5,000.

But if sales were to increase under the revised conditions to let us say $120,000, what would the profits be?

$$\text{Profits} = \$120,000 \times 5\% = \$6,000$$

So if sales increased, profits would increase. But if sales decreased, so would profits. Now management must judge the likelihood of an increase in sales. Would taking the risk of the plan not working, that is, sales falling, be justified by the possible increase in profits? These are the judgments that managements are paid to make!

Impact of Higher Profits on Initial Markup

In the above example, profits were held constant in percentages. Another kind of analysis retailers like to do is to determine what increase in initial markup would be needed to increase the profit percentage.

For example, a department had experienced the following results:

Operating expenses	34%	Cash discounts	5%
Profits	1%	Alteration costs	3%
Reductions	15%		

The new buyer was of the opinion that his predecessor had operated at an initial markup that was too low. The new buyer thought that the department could raise prices somewhat and remain competitive. With somewhat higher prices, it was further estimated that markdowns would increase by 2% bringing total reductions to 17%. If the new buyer sought to achieve a profit target of 5%, what should the initial markup be?

The previous buyer's initial markup was:

$$\text{Initial markup} = \frac{\text{Expenses \% + Profit \% + Reductions \% + Alteration costs \%} - \text{Cash discounts \%}}{100\% + \text{Reductions \%}}$$

$$\text{Initial markup} = \frac{34\% + 1\% + 15\% + 3\% - 5\%}{100\% + 15\%}$$

$$\text{Initial markup} = \frac{48\%}{115\%}$$

$$\text{Initial markup} = 41.7\%$$

The new buyer's estimates would result in the following initial markup:

$$\text{Initial markup} = \frac{\text{Expenses \% + Profit \% + Reductions \% + Alteration costs \%} - \text{Cash discounts \%}}{100\% + \text{Reductions \%}}$$

$$\text{Initial markup} = \frac{34\% + 5\% + 17\% + 3\% - 5\%}{100\% + 17\%}$$

$$\text{Initial markup} = \frac{54\%}{117\%}$$

$$\text{Initial markup} = 46.2\%$$

Let's examine the impact on retail prices of this increase in initial markup. Under the former buyer's initial markup, an item that cost $10 would have a retail of:

$$\frac{\$ \text{ cost}}{\text{Cost complement \%}} = \frac{\$10}{58.3\%} = \$17.15$$

With the new buyer's proposed initial markup, the item costing $10 would carry a retail of:

$$\frac{\$ \text{ cost}}{\text{Cost complement \%}} = \frac{\$10}{53.8\%} = \$18.59$$

Would price increases of this magnitude allow the department to continue to be competitive with other stores? The buyer (and the merchandise manager) would have to make that judgment.

Let's suppose that they decide that it would be too risky to increase prices that much. Can't you just hear the merchandise manager saying, "I really admire your desire to get our profits up there where they should be. But let's proceed a little more cautiously until you get to really understand your customers and the competition. Let's just shoot next year for a profit of 2%. After all, that's a doubling over your predecessor!"

What impact would doubling profits have on the initial markup if the buyer estimates that reductions, expenses, cash discounts, and alteration costs would stand at previous levels?

$$\text{Initial markup} = \frac{\begin{array}{c}\text{Expenses \% + Profit \% + Reductions \%}\\ \text{+ Alteration costs \% − Cash discounts \%}\end{array}}{100\% + \text{Reductions \%}}$$

$$\text{Initial markup} = \frac{34\% + 2\% + 15\% + 3\% - 5\%}{100\% + 15\%}$$

$$\text{Initial markup} = \frac{49\%}{115\%}$$

$$\text{Initial markup} = 42.6\%$$

Thus the item that cost $10 would now carry a retail price of:

$$\frac{\$ \text{ cost}}{\text{Cost complement \%}} = \frac{\$10}{57.4\%} = \$17.42$$

Once again a management judgment would have to be made about whether this change should be implemented.

Estimating Profit

Another type of analysis that retail executives do is to estimate the profit resulting from a set of related figures. For example, what profit would a department operating with an initial markup of 48% realize if it also achieved the folowing results:

Operating expenses	30%
Reductions	16%
Alteration costs	5%
Cash discounts	3%

To solve this problem it is necessary to use some simple algebra. (Initially we will set up the relationships with percentages but then convert to decimals to make the algebraic steps easier.)

$$\text{Initial markup \%} = \frac{\begin{array}{c}\text{Expenses \% + Profit \% + Reductions \%}\\ \text{+ Alteration costs \% − Cash discounts \%}\end{array}}{100\% + \text{Reductions \%}}$$

$$48\% = \frac{30\% + 16\% + 5\% - 3\% + x}{100\% + 16\%} \qquad \text{(Defining profit as } x \text{, the unknown.)}$$

$$.48 = \frac{.30 + .16 + .05 - .03 + x}{1.00 + .16} \qquad \text{(Converting percentages to decimals.)}$$

$$.48 = \frac{.48 + x}{1.16} \qquad \text{(Adding and subtracting.)}$$

$$.48(1.16) = .48 + x \qquad \text{(Multiplying by 1.16.)}$$

$$.5568 = .48 + x$$

$$.0768 = x \qquad \text{(Subtracting .48.)}$$

$$7.68\% = x \qquad \text{(Converting decimal back to percentage.)}$$

Now let's check to see if our answer is correct. What initial markup would be needed to meet the following results?

Operating expenses	30%	Cash discounts	3
Reductions	16	Profits	7.68
Alteration costs	5		

$$\text{Initial markup} = \frac{\begin{array}{c}\text{Expenses \% + Profit \% + Reductions \%}\\ \text{+ Alteration costs \% − Cash discounts \%}\end{array}}{100\% + \text{Reductions \%}}$$

$$\text{Initial markup} = \frac{30\% + 16\% + 5\% - 3\% + 7.68\%}{100\% + 16\%}$$

$$\text{Initial markup} = \frac{55.68\%}{116\%} = 48\%$$

It checks!!!

Estimating Sales Volume

Understanding the factors that influence the initial markup and how they interrelate is also very helpful when trying to analyze the following type of situation:

Marie O'Neill, the owner of a women's ready-to-wear shop, was experiencing strong competition from a discount department store chain. As the owner explained:

> *Take the same item that I pay $6 for and retail regularly at $9.99; they price it at $8.99. Some of my loyal customers are starting to grumble a little. I'd like to know what sales volume I need to maintain my profits if I match their markup. Right now my figures are: expenses $40,000 (I don't think they'll change at all.); reductions $16,000 (I think they'll drop to $12,500 because I won't take as many markdowns with lower prices.); cash discounts around $5,000 (They might go up, say $1,000, with higher volume.); and I don't do any alterations. My profits are now $15,000, and I want to keep them at that level. My sales are right around $150,000.*

The shop owner is asking us to determine, based on her estimates, the sales volume she must achieve at a lower initial markup in order to make a profit of $15,000.

Let's first determine the change in the shop's initial markup, assuming the example cited accurately represents the initial markups of the two stores.

Present initial markup of Marie's women's shop:

$$\text{Markup \%} = \frac{\text{Dollar markup}}{\text{Retail price}} = \frac{\$3.99}{\$9.99} = 39.9\%$$

Markup of competing discount department store:

$$\text{Markup \%} = \frac{\$2.99}{\$8.99} = 33.3\%$$

If Marie O'Neill prices with an initial markup of 33.3% and her estimates are accurate, what sales volume will generate a $15,000 profit? Once again we use simple algebra:

$$\text{Initial markup \%} = \frac{\begin{array}{c}\text{Expenses + Profit + Reductions}\\ \text{+ Alteration costs − Cash discounts}\end{array}}{\text{Sales + Reductions}}$$

$$33.3\% = \frac{\$40,000 + \$15,000 + \$12,500 - \$6,000}{\text{Sales} + \$12,500}$$

$$33.3\% = \frac{\$61,500}{x + \$12,500} \qquad \text{(Defining sales as } x\text{, the unknown.)}$$

$$.333\,(x + \$12,500) = \$61,500 \qquad \text{(Multiply by } x + \$12,500.\text{)}$$

$$.333x + \$4,162.50 = \$61,500$$

$$.333x = \$57,337.50 \qquad \text{(Subtracting } \$4,162.50.\text{)}$$

$$x = \$172,185$$

Thus with a lower initial markup, Marie would have to experience a sales increase from $150,000 to $172,185 assuming her estimates to be accurate. This is an increase of 14.8%:

$$\frac{\$172,185 - \$150,000}{\$150,000} = \frac{\$22,185}{\$150,000} = 14.8\%$$

Marie must now judge the advisability of changing her initial markup.

Problems

3–9. The buyer for men's clothing was examining results for last year which were as follows: reductions 19%; cash discounts 6%; alteration costs 5%; expenses 34%; and profits 5%. The buyer wondered what initial markup would be needed if reductions dropped to 16%, expenses increased to 36%, and the profit objective was to maintain last year's level. Cash discounts and alteration costs were expected to be the same as last year's figures.

3–10. A buyer for women's sleepwear wished to increase profits which last year were only 2.5%. Last year's expenses were 30%, reductions were 9%, cash discounts were 3%, and there were no alteration costs. What initial markup would be needed to double the profit percentage, if the other factors were all kept at last year's levels?

3–11. The owner of a small variety store was confronted with strong discount store competition. A strategy of lowering prices in an effort to maintain sales volume was being considered. The owner had been operating with an initial markup of 44%. Other operating figures were: expenses 30%; reductions 15%; and profit 5.5%. There were no cash discounts or alteration costs. If the initial markup is lowered to 37.5%, expenses are maintained at 30%, and reductions reduced to 12%, what operating profit would result?

3–12. Raising the initial markup from 42% to 45% would have what impact on average original retail prices?

3–13. Lowering the initial markup from 32% to 25% would have what impact on average original retail prices?

3–14. In the face of strong competition from an off-price retailer, the management of a women's apparel shop was considering a reduction in the initial markup from 44% to 37.5%. Under the new initial markup policy the following operating results were estimated: expenses $37,000; reductions $15,000; cash discounts $5,500; and alteration costs $500. What sales volume would have to be achieved to produce a profit of $10,000?

When the Initial Markup Is Not Followed

While planning the initial markup is an important part of retail merchandise management, retailers do not always price all goods at the original price determined by using the initial markup that is established as a goal. For example, a store may be carrying merchandise that is prepriced by the manufacturer; that is, a retail price is printed on the package or wrapper, or the manufacturer affixes to the item a tag that indicates the retail price. Sometimes the price is designated as the "manufacturer's suggested retail price," but often there is no designation other than the number indicating the price. The retailer selling the merchandise is not required to sell it at the suggested price. Clearly, if the price reflects the retailer's desired initial markup, there is a strong likelihood that the item will be sold at that price. But what if the manufacturer's preticketed price does not reflect the retailer's initial markup?

Let's look at some examples:

A buyer has established 40% as the initial markup. An item that has a cost of $6.00 comes from the manufacturer preticketed with a retail price of $9.99. Competitors regularly sell the item for $9.99. Applying a 40% initial markup would result in an original retail price of $10.00 ($\frac{\$6.00}{60\%} = \$10$). The buyer would in all likelihood sell the item for $9.99. At that price the initial markup is 39.9%.($\frac{\$3.99}{\$9.99}$)

The same buyer purchases another item for $6.00 with a preticketed original retail price of $10.99. Competitors regularly sell the item for $10.99. At that price the retailer would generate an initial markup of 45.4%($\frac{\$4.99}{\$10.99}$). Given the opportunity to make some extra margin, and in the absence of competitive pressure, the buyer would probably sell the item for $10.99.

The buyer has another item purchased for $6.00 that has a preticketed original retail price of $8.99. At that price the initial markup is only 33.3%($\frac{\$2.99}{\$8.99}$). Competitors have been selling the item at that price. The buyer has the practical choices of: (a) selling the item at the going competitive price and not achieving the desired initial markup; (b) removing the price-ticket and repricing the item at the price which provides the higher desired initial markup; or (c) dropping the item from the assortment.

Even when merchandise is not preticketed by the manufacturer there are times when the buyer is forced to deviate from the initial markup objective. A common example would be when a product becomes suddenly popular, and competitors, attempting to attract customers, establish and widely promote a price lower than that needed to generate the desired markup. Usually the buyer is forced to price the item lower than the initial markup objective would require.

On the other hand, there are occasions when a buyer may purchase at a very attractive price an item not stocked by competition. Assessment of the item may suggest that at what seems to be a reasonable price, the buyer can earn a markup substantially greater than the initial markup. It is very likely that in such a situation the buyer will price the item to earn the higher than initial markup, generating additional revenue either to offset items with lower than desired markups, or to provide some additional profit.

Price Lines and Initial Markups

Other deviations from the initial markup target occur when a store or department is using price lines. **Price lining** is a common practice used by retailers whereby merchandise is assembled into categories of comparable quality or appeal and given the same price. Many stores utilize at least three price categories, which can be broadly labeled *good*, *better*, and *best*. They might be defined as follows:

Good — The minimum level of quality expected by the store's customers.

Better — A moderate level of quality expected by the store's customers.

Best — The top level of quality expected by the store's customers.

These obviously are relative terms and have specific meaning only for a particular store. The best quality men's sport jacket sold by a particular discount department store might, on an objective basis, be below the quality of the good quality sport jacket in a high fashion men's clothing boutique.

Stores that utilize price lining will usually attach a specific price to a particular price line. Let's illustrate: A men's clothing store has an extensive assortment of men's ties. The customer can select among many colors, fabrics, weaves, designs, and labels. But there are only three price lines: $9.99, $14.99, and $19.99.

The buyer has four suppliers of ties and in acquiring merchandise for the fall season made the following purchases of ties to be sold in the $9.99 price line:

Supplier A:	4 dozen at $66 per dozen
Supplier B:	2 dozen at $70 per dozen
Supplier C:	6 dozen at $60 per dozen
Supplier D:	2 dozen at $62 per dozen

The buyer's initial markup is 45%.

Let's first determine what original retail prices would result by applying the initial markup of 45% to each of the purchases.

$$\text{Ties from supplier A:} \quad \frac{\$66}{12} = \frac{\$5.50 \text{ each}}{55\%} = \$10.00 \text{ retail price}$$

$$\text{Ties from supplier B:} \quad \frac{\$70}{12} = \frac{\$5.83 \text{ each}}{55\%} = \$10.61 \text{ retail price}$$

$$\text{Ties from supplier C:} \quad \frac{\$60}{12} = \frac{\$5.00 \text{ each}}{55\%} = \$9.09 \text{ retail price}$$

$$\text{Ties from supplier D:} \quad \frac{\$62}{12} = \frac{\$5.17 \text{ each}}{55\%} = \$9.39 \text{ retail price}$$

Thus, the original retail prices would range from $9.09 to $10.61 each. The buyer, however, has decided to sell them all at the same price, $9.99. On some, the store will make a little more than the target initial markup; and on others, a little less. The confusion that might result from customers trying to determine the justification for the slight differences in prices is avoided. The customers have a broad assortment from which to choose at a reasonable price. The actual markups that would be earned by selling all the ties at $9.99 are as follows:

Supplier A:	Retail	$9.99
	Cost	5.50
	Markup	$4.49, 44.9%
Supplier B:	Retail	$9.99
	Cost	5.83
	Markup	$4.16, 41.6%
Supplier C:	Retail	$9.99
	Cost	5.00
	Markup	$4.99, 49.9%
Supplier D:	Retail	$9.99
	Cost	5.17
	Markup	$4.82, 48.2%

In the unlikely event that all the ties were sold at the $9.99 original retail — that is, with no markdowns, no employee discounts, and no shortages — what markup would the department earn on the sale of these ties?

	Total Retail	*Total Cost*	*Total Markup*
Supplier A ties	48 × $9.99 = $ 479.52	4 × $66 = $264	$215.52
Supplier B ties	24 × 9.99 = 239.76	2 × 70 = 140	99.76
Supplier C ties	72 × 9.99 = 719.28	6 × 60 = 360	359.28
Supplier D ties	24 × 9.99 = 239.76	2 × 62 = 124	115.76
	$1,678.32	$888	$790.32

The overall markup earned would be $\frac{\$790.32}{\$1,678.32} = 47.1\%$

The Cumulative Markup

As the above examples indicate, there are reasons why, in the course of every day retailing activity, merchandise is originally priced at somewhat more or somewhat less than the price that would result if the initial markup were applied exactly. This does not diminish the importance of the initial markup. It is a vital planning objective. But because there are deviations from the established initial markup, retailers calculate a measure called the **cumulative markup** (also called the *cumulative markon*) which reports what the total (aggregate) initial markups applied up to a certain date actually are.

To illustrate further, let's continue with the example presented above, the necktie department in a men's clothing store. We were considering purchases of ties to be retailed for $9.99 and had already accounted for:

Purchases of $9.99 Ties

Total cost	$ 888.
Total retail	$1,678.32

In addition the buyer had made purchases of ties to be sold for $14.99 and $19.99. The total amounts involved were:

Purchases of $14.99 Ties

Total cost	$ 992.
Total retail	$1,978.68

Purchases of $19.99 Ties

Total cost	$ 740.
Total retail	$1,439.28

At the start of the season the buyer's inventory of ties had the following values:

Total cost	$3,200
Total retail	$5,962

Now we can calculate the cumulative markup for ties, that is, the aggregate initial markup for all merchandise put into stock to date:

	Retail	Cost
Inventory	$ 5,962.00	$3,200
Purchases		
$19.99 ties	1,439.28	740
$14.99 ties	1,978.68	992
$ 9.99 ties	1,678.32	888
Total	$11,058.28	$5,820

The aggregate markup for the merchandise available for sale to date, based on the initial markups, was:

Total retail	$11,058.28
Total cost	5,820.00
Total markup	$ 5,238.28

The cumulative markup percentage to date was:

$$\frac{\text{Total markup}}{\text{Total retail}} = \frac{\$5,238.28}{\$11,058.28} = 47.37\%$$

With a cumulative markup to date of 47.37%, the buyer is somewhat ahead of the initial markup objective for ties which was 45%.

Problems

3–15. The buyer for the shoe department has an initial markup objective of 42%. At the start of the season the inventory consisted of shoes with a retail value that totalled $16,200. The cost of these shoes was $9,680. During the first three months of the season, the buyer had received into stock the following purchases: from Ace Shoes shipments with a total cost of $4,440 that were priced to sell for a total of $7,800 at retail; from Brown Shoe Company shipments with a total cost of $1,864 that were priced to sell for a total of $3,000 at retail; and from Cook Footwear shipments with a total cost of $3,588 that were priced to sell for a total of $6,175 at retail. What was the buyer's cumulative markup at the start of the fourth month of the season?

3–16. A proprietor of a new video shop has been acquiring inventory and placing it on display in anticipation of opening day. He has been keeping a journal in which he has recorded each individual item purchased, the cost and retail. Two days before opening, the proprietor totalled the costs and retails for the various categories of products to be sold:

	Total Cost	*Total Retail*
Videocassette recorders	$18,400	$28,000
Videocassettes		
Films/movies	2,200	3,200
Exercise/self-improvement	1,800	2,800
Music	650	1,200
Other	1,400	2,100
Videocassettes — blank	1,250	1,800
Books/booklets	425	750
Supplies	650	1,000

What is the proprietor's cumulative markup to date?

Mellow Music Store Applications

As they continued preparations for the opening of the Mellow Music Store, John and Julie Martin discussed their progress with Julie's father, Mr. James Flynn, an experienced retail executive and also an investor in the new store. He had inquired about the markup that they were using to price merchandise. John and Julie told about their discussions with other music store operators and with representatives of musical instrument manufacturers. "We both think 50% is a reasonable markup to shoot for," said John.

Mr. Flynn inquired whether they had reconciled the 50% markup with their estimated operating expenses and expected markdowns. "Didn't you calculate the initial markup you'll need to cover everything? How do you know 50% will be enough?" he asked.

With Mr. Flynn's guidance, John and Julie prepared the following estimates:

Sales (average $3,000/week $\times$ 52 weeks)	$156,000
Total expenses (including John's and Julie's salaries)	50,000
Total reductions ($250 per week $\times$ 52 weeks)	13,000
Alteration costs (including piano tuning and instrument adjustments)	3,000
Profit	15,000

They then calculated the initial markup needed:

$$\text{Initial markup \%} = \frac{\text{Expenses} + \text{Profit} + \text{Reductions} + \text{Alteration costs}}{\text{Sales} + \text{Reductions}}$$

$$\text{Initial markup \%} = \frac{\$50,000 + \$15,000 + \$13,000 + \$3,000}{\$156,000 + \$13,000}$$

$$\text{Initial markup \%} = \frac{\$81,000}{\$169,000}$$

$$\text{Initial markup \%} = 47.9\%$$

"Well," Mr. Flynn said, "it looks like you eyeballed it pretty well. Maybe you two have the merchant's sense. Or maybe you were just lucky. Why don't you stay with the 50%, that will provide a little cushion. You'll know pretty quickly, however, if your prices are not competitive."

With Mr. Flynn's suggestion, John decided to check on the markup that had been applied to all the goods already in stock. He summarized the results as follows:

	Cost	*Retail*
Pianos — consoles	$ 6,750	$ 13,500
Spinets	2,500	4,998
Organs, full size	11,000	21,985
Keyboards	7,200	14,340
Synthesizers	19,800	39,750
Amplifiers	8,644	18,285
Music and music instruction books	3,200	6,350
Miscellaneous	2,950	6,145
Totals	$62,044	$125,353

John then calculated the resulting markup:

$$\$125,353 - \$62,044 = \frac{\$63,309}{\$125,353} = 50.5\%$$

"We call that your cumulative markup," said Mr. Flynn, "and it looks good compared to your planned initial figure. But just remember that you haven't sold anything yet!"

Review Problems

3–1R. The buyer of women's shoes was developing plans for the upcoming season. Discussions with the merchandise manager led to the following objectives; sales $128,000; markdowns $15,000; employee discounts $3,000; expenses $39,400; profit $10,000; and shortages $1,200. What initial markup should the buyer set?

3–2R. The manager of a children's clothing store established the following planned figures for next year: sales $175,000; reductions $20,000; cash discounts $8,500; expenses $50,000; alteration costs $2,000; and profit $18,000. What should the initial markup be?

3–3R. A sweater shop owner was establishing objectives for the spring season. What initial markup should be planned given the following estimates: markdowns 12.5%; employee discounts 4%; senior citizen discounts 5%; theft 2%; expenses 28%; profit 8.5%; and cash discounts 4%?

3–4R. Determine the initial markup for a department that has the following projections for the upcoming season: markdowns $15,000; employee and other customer discounts 5%; expenses 30%; cash discounts 3%; shortages 2%; shortages $2,200; and profit 6%.

3–5R. The owner of a sporting goods store wished to increase annual profits from $5,000 to $15,000. He anticipated that his operating expenses would increase from 28% to 30%, principally to support increased advertising. He expected reductions to stay at last year's level. They were 15.5% of sales. There were no cash discounts or alteration costs. Last year's profits were 2.5% of sales. What was last year's initial markup? What initial markup would be needed this year to achieve the owner's objectives at the same sales volume?

3–6R. What profit percentage would be achieved by a department that experienced the following operating results: expenses 31.3%; markdowns 12.3%; shortages 2.5%; employee discounts 3.5%; other customer discounts 2.3%; cash discounts 3.3%; alteration costs 4.5%; and initial markup 48.2%?

3–7R. A retailer facing strong new discount competition decides to sacrifice short-term profits in order to maintain market position. The retailer expects expenses to continue to be 25% of sales. Reductions are forecast to drop from 12% to 10%. Last year's profits were 5%. There are no cash discounts or alteration expenses. What was the retailer's initial markup last year? What initial markup would result in a break even (no profit/no loss) for the upcoming year? What average percentage decrease in retail prices would result from the lowering of the initial markup to the break-even level?

3–8R. If a buyer operating with an initial markup of 47.5% raised this markup to 50%, what would be the impact on average retail prices?

3–9R. What is the cumulative markup to date for the department whose figures are listed below:

	Cost	Retail
Beginning inventory	$36,834	$78,373
Purchases supplier 101	12,000	23,950
Purchases supplier 202	6,770	12,500
Purchases supplier 303	15,445	28,333

3–10R. A manager setting up a new outlet for a chain store is keeping a record of the cost and retail of merchandise being stocked in the store. The results for the first day are presented below. What cumulative markup has been achieved to date?

	Cost	Retail
Category A		
3 dozen	$ 2.55 each	$ 5.00 each
6 dozen	3.50 each	6.95 each
2 dozen	4.90 each	9.95 each
Category B		
1 dozen	$10.00 per dozen	$ 1.99 each
5 dozen	15.00 per dozen	2.99 each
3 dozen	18.00 per dozen	3.99 each
Category C		
3 cases/24 per case	$ 2.75 each	$ 5.95 each
2 cases/12 per case	95.00/case	14.99 each

CHAPTER 4

Averaging and Balancing Markups

In Chapter 3 we learned that initial markup is an important planning and control tool for retailers. It enables the buyer or manager to price merchandise so that if forecasts of sales, expenses, and reductions are accurately made, a profit objective can be achieved. The task of planning initial markup also enables the retailer to analyze the impact on pricing of the elements of expenses, reductions, and profit. As a control device, the initial markup provides an objective against which actual pricing decisions can be compared. The calculation of cumulative markup in Chapter 3 illustrated this use.

Initial Markup Not Always Followed

We also noted that because of competition, rounding of prices, preticketing by manufacturers, and the use of price-lining, retailers often deviate from the prices that would result if absolute adherence to initial markup percentages were followed. In practice, the overall markup reflects the markups of particular subcategories of goods or even individual items. So real world retailing is actually an averaging or balancing of markups of the different departments, categories, or items.

A buyer who regularly compares the cumulative markup with the initial markup objective is able to determine whether special efforts have to be taken to bring markups in line with objectives. For example, a buyer establishes 48% as the initial markup objective for the coming spring season. Seasonal plans are set far in advance of the actual start of a season. At the start of the season the buyer has in-stock merchandise with a retail value of $59,200 that has a cost value of $33,300. The markup on this merchandise was:

$$\frac{\$59,200 - \$33,300}{\$59,200} = 43.75\%$$

Clearly, the buyer is going to have to achieve a markup higher than 48% on the new merchandise brought into the department to achieve a 48% markup overall. Assume that merchandise in stock at the start of the season represents half the total stock, and that the other half will come from new purchases. So total stock will be $118,400, at retail value, with $59,200 represented by the stock with a 43.75% markup. What markup must be earned on the new purchases in order to average 48% overall?

If total stock is $118,400 at retail value and the markup is 48%, the cost would be 52%, or $61,568. As $59,200 is merchandise with a markup of 43.75%, the cost of that merchandise is 56.25% or $33,300. The markup needed on the new purchases can now be calculated:

	Retail Value	Cost Value	Markup
Total stock	$118,400	$61,568	48.00%
Stock from inventory	59,200	33,300	43.75%
Stock from new purchases	59,200	28,268	52.25%

As the table above indicates, subtracting the cost value of the stock on hand ($33,300) from the total cost value of merchandise needed to fully stock the department ($61,568) results in the cost value of merchandise to be acquired ($28,268). This merchandise is to be retailed for $59,200. Thus the markup can be determined:

$$\frac{\$59,200 - \$28,268}{\$59,200} = 52.25\%$$

The buyer would need a 52.25% markup on new purchases in order to average out at a markup of 48% overall.

Markups Are Weighted Averages

What we are considering here is a *weighted* average. The total markup equals the sum of the individual markups each multiplied by the proportion of the total at that markup.

In the example above, 50% of stock multiplied by 43.75% plus 50% of stock multiplied by 52.25% = 48% overall.

$$50\% \times 43.75\% = 21.875\%$$

$$50\% \times 52.25\% = 26.125\%$$

$$21.875\% + 26.125\% = 48\%$$

Another example can be seen in a supermarket where the percentages of total sales and the markups vary among the different departments. The following data are illustrative:

Department	Percent of Total Sales	Markup Percent
Dry grocery	46%	20%
Meat	25	27
Produce	7	33
Dairy	9	23
Frozen foods	6	28
Bakery	3	40
Health/beauty aids	2	23
General merchandise	2	30

What is the overall markup for the store?

The overall markup is a weighted average that may be calculated as follows:

	Weighted Share
Dry grocery	46% × 20% = 9.20%
Meat	25% × 27% = 6.75
Produce	7% × 33% = 2.31
Dairy	9% × 23% = 2.07
Frozen foods	6% × 28% = 1.68
Bakery	3% × 40% = 1.20
Health/beauty aids	2% × 23% = .46
General merchandise	2% × 30% = .60
Total store markup	24.27%

In all facets of retailing, markups realized are weighted markups. The overall markup in the men's shirt classification reflects the markups on the different brands carried.

	Percent of Stock	*Markup Percent*	*Weighted Share*
Brand A	24%	47.0%	11.28%
Brand B	32	44.0	14.08
Brand C	18	48.5	8.73
Brand D	26	42.5	11.05
Overall markup on stock			45.14%

Similarly, the markup on a particular brand of shirts reflects the markup on the individual styles:

Brand A Style	*Percent Stock of Brand A*	*Markup Percent*	*Weighted Share*
100	10%	50.0%	5.00%
101	9	48.0	4.32
102	16	48.0	7.68
103	12	46.0	5.52
104	8	46.0	3.68
105	15	47.0	7.05
106	16	47.0	7.52
107	14	44.5	6.23
Markup on brand			47.00%

Buyers Constantly Balance Markups

One might wonder why there are these variations in the markups of different styles of a men's shirt. A good reason is the application of price lining. The shirts might have slight differences in cut and detail reflected in the prices of the manufacturer. The buyer can judge these differences as not readily apparent to the average customer and not justifying a price distinction. Also, the buyer might have notions of what consitutes "good retail prices." For example, goods with prices that ended in $.14, $.76, $.32, $.87, and so forth, after initial markups were applied, might all be marked with a price ending in $.95 or $.99. This is a common practice.

So, retailing practice can be considered to be markup balancing. Most retailers sell a mix of goods with varying markups. They have as a guidepost the initial markup calculated to be necessary to achieve objectives. Buyers cannot humanly juggle the interaction of the various individual markups and the proportions of sales to determine where they stand on every pricing decision. That can only be done by the computers in many stores that periodically, via the controller's office, give the buyer a reading on the cumulative markup to date.

But on a day-to-day basis, the alert buyer is averaging, or weighing, or balancing, or juggling the markups, striving to achieve overall goals. The remainder of this chapter will present some types of problems confronted by buyers.

Calculating Markup Needed on Purchases

Let's first review in detail a problem like the one presented above. A department store buyer determines that the total amount of merchandise needed to meet sales objectives during the next season is $180,000. The initial markup objective was 45%. Merchandise on hand at the start of the season had a retail value of $40,000; the cumulative markup on these goods was 46.8%. What initial markup does the buyer have to achieve on merchandise to be purchased?

Because the total merchandise needed is $180,000 and the initial markup sought is 45%, the cost of the goods would be $180,000 × 55%, or $99,000. We can determine the balance needed and the corresponding markup as follows:

	Retail Value	Cost Value	Markup	Markup Percentage
Merchandise needed	$180,000	$99,000	$81,000	45.0%
Merchandise on hand	40,000	21,280	18,720	46.8
Merchandise to be purchased	$140,000	$77,720	$62,280	44.5%

As the table indicates, knowing that the merchandise on hand has a markup of 46.8%, we can calculate the cost of that merchandise: $100\% - 46.8\% = 53.2\% \times \$40,000 = \$21,280$.

Then, by subtracting the cost and retail values of the merchandise on hand from the merchandise needed, we can determine how much has to be purchased. Finally, we calculate the markup on the merchandise to be purchased: $\$140,000 - \$77,720 = \$62,280$; and the percentage: $\frac{\$62,280}{\$140,000} = 44.5\%$.

Now let's check our answer by calculating a weighted average.

The merchandise on hand is $\frac{\$40,000}{\$180,000} = 22.22\%$ of the total needed; so the purchases are $100\% - 22.22\% = 77.78\%$ of the total. Weighting these proportions by the markups, we get the weighted average:

$$(22.22\% \times 46.8\%) + (77.78\% \times 44.5\%) = 10.4\% + 34.6\% = 45\%$$

Recall that 45% was the initial markup objective.

Recalculating Markup on Remaining Purchases

One third of the way through the season, the department store buyer in the above situation had purchased $33,900 worth of merchandise that had been priced to total $60,000 at retail. What markup did the buyer have to achieve on the balance of purchases?

	Retail Value	Cost Value	Markup Percentage
Merchandise needed	$180,000	$99,000	45.0%
Merchandise on hand: Inventory	40,000	21,280	46.8
Purchases to Date	60,000	33,900	43.5
Total on hand	$100,000	$55,180	44.8%
Merchandise to be purchased	$ 80,000	$43,820	45.2%

By subtracting the total merchandise on hand from the total needed, we determine the amount to be acquired. Note that earlier we had determined the initial markup on purchases to be 44.5%. But on purchases to date the buyer had only taken a markup of 43.5%. Therefore for the balance of purchases, the buyer has to achieve a markup of 45.2% in order to achieve the overall objective of 45%.

Let's consider another example of the same type of problem. A department store buyer determines in preparation for an upcoming buying trip that a markup of 46.5% is needed on purchases. After seeing several vendors and making purchases, the buyer decides to recalculate the markup needed on the balance of purchases to be made. The buyer proceeds as follows:

	Retail Value	Cost Value	Markup Percentage
Planned purchases	$62,500	$33,438	46.5%
Purchases to date:			
Vendor A	17,360	9,600	44.7
Vendor B	8,575	4,460	48.0
Vendor C	5,418	2,844	47.5
Vendor D	14,960	8,378	44.0
	$46,313	$25,282	45.4%
To be purchased	$16,187	$ 8,156	49.6%

As the above table indicates, the buyer had purchased from four vendors $46,313 of the $62,500 needed, valued at the retail prices the buyer planned to sell the items. The buyer had paid a total of $25,282 for these goods. Notice that the markups on each vendor's merchandise varied. The buyer had judged that each selection of merchandise should be represented in the store's assortment. But the result to date was that on the purchases from the four vendors, the buyer would be achieving a markup of 45.4% — less than the target of 46.5%. Now the buyer has to purchase merchandise that can be retailed for $16,187, at a cost of $8,156 (incorporating a markup of 49.6%) to meet the goal set for the trip.

So the buyer has to be alert for purchases that have sufficient potential appeal that the buyer can obtain a higher markup on them than has been obtainable on the merchandise purchased so far. The value of having an initial markup target (calculated to cover expected expenses and desired profits) and of determining regularly the cumulative markup (to measure adherence to the initial markup target) should be apparent to the thoughtful reader.

Problems

4–1. A bake shop owner has been keeping statistics on the sales of different items. The owner believes that by taking a low markup percentage on bread, customers will be attracted who might be tempted to purchase "on impulse" other pastry priced with a high markup percentage. If the percentages of total sales and markups are as presented below, what is the overall (weighted) markup percentage for the bakery?

	Percentage of Sales	*Markup Percentage*
Bread	22%	15%
Doughnuts	15	20
Rolls	10	20
Pies	6	30
Squares/Tarts	6	30
Loaf cakes	4	35
Layer cakes	6	35
Cream pastries	5	50
Filled and fancy pastries	10	60
Decorated cakes	16	60

4–2. A discount department store is organized into several departments. The percentages of total sales forecasted for the next season and the planned initial markups are listed below. What is the initial markup percentage for the entire store?

	Percentage of Sales	Markup
Hardware	5%	32%
Sporting goods	3	28
Health and beauty aids	12	22
Pharmacy	8	35
Books and stationery	3	30
Men's clothing	18	32
Women's clothing	16	28
Children's clothing	20	26
Records and tapes	15	20

4–3. The buyer for men's clothing projected the total merchandise needed for the upcoming season was $280,000 at retail value. The initial markup objective was 49.5%. At the start of the season, the inventory consisted of $168,000 worth of merchandise at retail prices. These goods had a total cost of $88,000. What markup percentage did the buyer have to obtain on purchases to achieve the initial markup objective?

4–4. In preparation for a buying trip, a buyer noted that the cumulative markup was 38.5%. The initial markup had been planned to be 40%. The inventory at the beginning of the season had been valued at retail at $74,500. Purchases to date had totaled $50,000 at retail. The buyer had determined that merchandise with a retail value of $35,500 was to be acquired on the trip to complete purchasing for the season. What is the maximum amount the buyer could pay (at cost) for the goods to be purchased so as to bring the cumulative markup to 40%?

4–5. In the midst of a buying trip, a buyer was analyzing purchases to date. The buyer's objective had been to spend $18,500 (at cost) for merchandise to be retailed for $32,000. What markup percentage must the buyer obtain on the balance of purchases to meet objectives, after making the following purchases:

	Cost	*To Be Retailed for*
Vendor A	$2,800	$4,500
Vendor B	2,450	4,080
Vendor C	3,180	9,660
Vendor D	5,320	8,430

Balancing Sales to Average a Markup

Often in stores or departments, buyers or managers want to balance item purchases and sales so as to remain in line with markup objectives. For example, Ed Peters the owner of a hardware store, determines that he needs a 40% markup on barbecue grills. Given the limited space in the store, he decides to stock two grills. One grill appears to be popular with customers. It costs $66. Because many stores are selling it for $99, Mr. Peters believes that he has to be competitive with these stores, so he prices the grill at a retail of $99. The second grill, made by a respected manufacturer, costs $75 and has features not present on the $99 grill.

According to Mr. Peters, "To get my 40% markup on the grill costing $75, I have to sell it for $125, but I think I can get more than $125 for it. Not many other stores carry this particular brand, though it is very popular in other parts of the country. They don't have much distribution here. I think that customers who see the $99 grill and want something better, can be traded up to this one. Besides I'm not making my 40% on the $99 grill. I have to make up for that. I'm going to sell the better one for $139. It is a good value at that price. I wonder how many of each I have to sell to average out at 40%?"

The answer to Mr. Peters's question can be readily determined. The grill that costs $66 would have to be priced at $110 to earn a 40% markup ($\frac{\$66}{60\%}$). So on each grill Mr. Peters sells for $99, he loses $11 from what he needs to achieve his 40% goal. However the grill that he is selling for $139 would need to be sold for only $125 to generate a 40% markup ($\frac{\$75}{60\%}$). So on each grill that he sells for $139, Mr. Peters makes $14 more than he would need to achieve his 40% goal. Let's organize these data:

	Grill Costs $66	*Grill Costs $75*
Actual retail	$ 99	$139
Retail needed to make 40% markup	110	125
Difference	−$ 11	+$ 14

Therefore we might consider that on each $99 grill Mr. Peters sells he "loses" $11, but on every $139 sale he "makes an extra" $14. If Mr. Peters sold one $139 grill for every $99 grill he would be ahead of his markup objective. Let's look at that more carefully:

	Sales	*Cost*	*Dollar Markup*	*Percentage Markup*
1 grill	$139	$ 75	$64	46.0%
1 grill	99	66	33	33.0
	$238	$141	$97	40.8%

Thus if he sold a $139 grill for each $99 grill sold, he would be somewhat above his objective. Actually he can sell slightly more $99 grills than $139 grills to balance out as he wishes. We can determine the precise amount as follows:

1. Add together the differences shown above IGNORING THE SIGNS: $11 + 14 = 25$.
2. Determine the percentage of the total each difference is:

$$\frac{11}{25} = 44\%$$

$$\frac{14}{25} = 56\%$$

3. Remember that *you need to sell more of the item with the smaller difference.*

According to our results, Mr. Peters would need to have 56% of the units sold at $99, and 44% of the units sold at $139. Let's check this answer.

If Mr. Peters sold 100 grills, in order to achieve a 40% markup he would have to sell 56 at $99 and 44 at $139.

	Sales	*Cost*	*Markup*
$ 99 grills	56 × $99 = $ 5,544	56 × $66 = $3,696	$1,848
$139 grills	44 × 139 = $ 6,116	44 × 75 = 3,300	2,816
Totals	$11,660	$6,996	$4,664

$$\text{Overall markup: } \frac{\$4,664}{\$11,660} = 40\%$$

The key to understanding the above situation is to recognize the balancing involved. You are short of your goal by $11 on each $99 grill, but over your goal by $14 on each $139 grill. Just as you need more pieces of smaller weights on a balance scale to offset a lesser number of larger weights, so a given number of additions to markup of $14 can offset a larger number of subtractions of $11.

Balancing within Price Lines

Let's consider another similar example.

A small manufacturer of ski boots offers a sporting goods buyer in a department store a "deal" on a lot of ski boots. There are 150 pairs of ski boots in the lot. The owner tells the buyer, "We're changing our styles for next season and want to clear these styles out. We've been selling them to stores for $45 to $65. You can have the whole lot for $6,000."

The buyer is attracted because the boots are in excellent condition; the brand name is known to the store's customers; they are in popular sizes; and there are several weeks remaining in the selling season for ski boots. He adds, "I've really been looking for something that I can make some extra markup on. I'd like to make 45% on the lot. They'll fit right into my $69 and $89 price lines. But what percentage would I have to sell at $69 and at $89 to make 45% on the lot?"

Our approach is similar to the grill problem. The boots cost $40 each. $\left(\frac{\$6,000}{150} = \$40\right)$. To obtain a 45% markup, the buyer would need an average retail price of $72.73.

$$\frac{\$40}{55\%} = \$72.73$$

So on the boots selling for $69, the buyer "loses" $3.73. On the boots selling for $89, the buyer "makes an extra" $16.27. Let's organize these data:

	Boots Sell for $69	*Boots Sell for $89*
Actual retail	$69.00	$89.00
Retail needed to make 45% markup	72.73	72.73
Difference	−$ 3.73	+$16.27

Here we can quickly see that one boot sold for $89 can offset several boots sold for $69. But we can determine the precise proportion following the procedure explained above:

1. Add together the differences IGNORING THE SIGNS: $3.73 + $16.27 = $20
2. Determine the percentage of the total each difference is:

$$\frac{\$3.73}{\$20} = 18.65\%$$

$$\frac{\$16.27}{\$20} = 81.35\%$$

3. Remember that *you need to sell more of the item with the smaller difference.*

Thus, we would need to sell 81.35% at $69 and 18.65% at $89 to achieve a 45% markup overall. Let's check our answer:

$$150 \text{ pairs} \times 81.35\% = 122 \text{ pairs}$$

$$150 \text{ pairs} \times 18.65\% = 28 \text{ pairs}$$

	Sales	*Cost*	*Markup*
$69 boots	122 × $69 = $ 8,418	$ 6,000 for lot	
$89 boots	25 × 89 2,492		
Total	$10,910	$ 6,000	$4,910

$$\text{Overall markup } \frac{\$4,910}{\$10,910} = 45\%$$

Figures Don't Substitute for Buyer's Judgment

Now you might say, "I'll bet the buyer has the opportunity to sell many more at $89 if the quality of the boots is as good as it appears. Why not, say, sell half at $89 and half at $69?"

Of course the answer to this question depends on the buyer's judgment of the goods and the situation in the department at that particular time. Possibly, the buyer has had to take higher markdowns than originally projected and is looking for some purchases that would provide much needed extra markup. If so, the buyer might decide to follow your suggestion. On the other hand, the buyer might consider featuring the boots as an extraordinary value at $69, hoping to attract customers who might purchase skis and other related merchandise at higher markups. Our arithmetical analysis cannot answer these judgmental questions. The figures just assist the buyer in knowing what proportion would have to be sold at what price to achieve desired goals. Numbers provide guidelines for actual decisions.

Balancing Different Costs

There is another similar type of problem that is often confronted. A produce buyer for a supermarket has two suppliers of "farm fresh vegetables." The markup objective is 35%. One farm supplier has fresh sweet corn at a cost per bushel that averages $1.04 per dozen. The second farm, much smaller in size, has corn of slightly better quality that averages $1.17 per dozen. The buyer would like to sell only the second farmer's corn, but the farm has limited daily output and the retail needed to achieve a 35% markup is not competitive. The buyer decides to buy corn from both farms, mix it together on the produce tables, and sell it for $1.69 per dozen. In what proportion would the buyer have to sell the corn to average a markup of 35%?

Following the approach described above, we can quickly determine the answer:

	Corn Costs *$1.04*	*Corn Costs* *$1.17*
Actual retail	$1.69	$1.69
Retail needed for 35% markup	1.60	1.80
Difference	+$0.09	−$0.11

$$\textit{Proportions}: \quad \$.09 + \$.11 = \$.20$$

$$\frac{\$.09}{\$.20} = 45\%$$

$$\frac{\$.11}{\$.20} = 55\%$$

The buyer would have to sell the corn in the proportion of 55% of the $1.04 corn to 45% of the $1.17 corn. Let's check our answer: for each 100 dozen sold, if 45 dozen were corn costing $1.17, and 55 dozen were corn costing $1.04, the result would be as follows:

Sales	100 dozen at $1.69	$169.00
Cost	45 dozen × $1.17 = $52.65 55 dozen × 1.04 = 57.20	109.85
Markup		$ 59.15 = 35%

A More Complicated Situation

We can complicate these situations somewhat by adding a third price line, and still retain our ability to resolve the problem with simple arithmetic.

The buyer for women's slacks in the budget basement of a department store is offered a closeout stock of various styles, fabrics, and colors that the manufacturer wishes to sell as a lot to one retailer. The stock contains 400 pairs, and the cost of the lot is $4,800. The buyer inspects the lot very carefully and determines that 100 pairs are the same slacks presently being sold in the $30 price line. The remaining pairs are of varying quality; because the buyer did not wish to establish additional price points, these garments would have to be sold at the $14 and $21 price points. How many of the remaining 300 pairs of slacks would have to be sold in the regular $14 and $21 price lines for the buyer to realize an overall markup objective of 40%?

The total cost of the slacks is $4,800. To achieve a markup of 40%, the buyer would need a total retail of $8,000 ($\frac{\$4,800}{60\%} = \$8,000$). 100 pairs could be sold for $30 each and these would total $3,000 at retail (100 × $30). Thus the remaining 300 pairs would have to achieve a total retail of $5,000 ($8,000 − $3,000). Each remaining pair would have to average a retail of $16.67 ($\frac{\$5,000}{300 \text{ pair}}$).

At this point the problem is just like the ones discussed earlier:

	Slacks Selling *for $14*	*Slacks Selling* *for $21*
Actual retail	$14.00	$21.00
Retail needed	16.67	16.67
Difference	−$ 2.67	+$ 4.33

Proportions: $2.67 + $4.33 = $7

$$\frac{\$2.67}{\$7.00} = 38\%$$

$$\frac{\$4.33}{\$7.00} = 62\%$$

The buyer would have to sell 62% of 300 pairs, or 186 pairs at $14, and 38% of 300 pairs, or 114 pairs at $21.

Now let's see if everything checks out. If sales were:

100 at $30	$3,000
186 at 14	2,604
114 at 21	2,394
Total	$7,998

The markup would be $7,998 − $4,800 = $3,198. The markup percentage would be $\frac{\$3,198}{\$7,998} = 40\%$.

(Note that the very slight difference between the $7,998 calculated above and the $8,000 figure earlier results from rounding of decimal numbers. Also remember that we cannot sell a fraction of a pair of slacks!)

Buyer Must Still Judge Opportunity

Don't forget that the calculations developed above provide guidance to the buyer. Now the buyer must judge whether it is very likely that 114 pairs could be sold at $21. If the buyer judges that only 75 pairs could be sold at $21, and that the balance could only bring $14, the buyer should turn down the opportunity, or make another effort to negotiate with the manufacturer for a lower price. On the other hand, if the buyer judged that many more than 114 pairs could be sold for $21, the opportunity to buy the entire lot for $4,800 would appear to be very attractive.

Problems

4–6.   A sporting goods buyer in a department store is offered a gross (a dozen dozen) of baseball gloves at a cost of $20 each. The initial markup in this sporting goods department is 40%. What proportion of the gloves would have to be sold in the regular $29 and $39 price lines for the buyer to achieve the markup goal?

4–7. An audiovideo shop buys blank cassette tapes from two suppliers. One charges $45 per case of 24, the other charges $42 per case of 24. The manager of the shop considers the two brands of equal quality and has observed customers asking for each by brand. He decides to sell both brands for $2.99 each. In what proportion would the two brands have to sell for the buyer to make a 40% markup on blank cassette tapes?

4–8. A men's accessories department stocks belts in $12 and $18 price lines. Belts retailing for $12 cost $78 per dozen. Belts retailing for $18 cost $98 per dozen. In what proportion would the belts have to be sold for the buyer to achieve the markup objective of 48%.

4–9. A supermarket manager buys 300 watermelons of various sizes for $2 each. He decides to sell the smaller ones for $2.49 each and the larger ones for $3.99 each. How many would the manager have to sell at each price to meet a 33% markup objective for the lot of watermelons?

4–10. A manufacturer of women's jeans quotes a department store buyer $3,360 for a lot of jeans of various styles. There are 420 pairs of jeans in the lot. The buyer judges that one third of the lot is comprised of the jeans currently being sold in the $9.99 price line. The balance of the lot would be retailed in the $12.99 and $14.99 price lines. If the buyer was able to sell one third of the lot at $9.99, how many pairs would have to be sold at $12.99 and at $14.99 for the buyer to achieve the markup objective of 38% on the entire lot?

Balancing Total Dollar Markups and Sales Volume

There is one other type of problem that involves a balancing of markups that we will consider at this point. Sometimes a retail manager or buyer will confront the following situation.

Debbie Walsh, the buyer for giftware in a department store has been pricing merchandise with a 50% initial markup. She has been selling an attractive decorator plate that costs $6 for $12. "I noticed," she says, "that customers often walk into the department, look around, pick up and examine those plates, then leave without buying anything. I've been wondering whether I would sell a lot more of them at $10. I think many of my customers are looking for something nice to give as a gift that won't cost them more than $10. Of course at $10, I am reducing my markup to 40%. But if I sell more, there must be a point at which I would make more markup dollars. I wonder what that point is?"

What Debbie is inquiring about is the trade-off between selling *(a)* a lesser volume at a greater markup; and *(b)* a greater volume at a lesser markup. This can be determined very easily both in terms of dollar sales and unit sales. Let's first take the situation of dollar sales.

We will assume that Debbie has been selling 100 plates per season. Thus her total sales would be $100 \times \$12 = \$1,200$. On sales of $1,200, the markup generated would be $\$1,200 \times 50\% = \$600$.

If we divide the *old markup* percentage (50%) by the *new markup* percentage (40%) we get: $\frac{50\%}{40\%} = 1.25$. We will call this the *volume factor*. It says that the new dollar sales have to be 1.25 times the old dollar sales for the dollar markups to be equal. Note that this is the same as saying that the dollar volume has to increase by 25% ($1.25 = 1 + 25\%$). The old dollar sales ($1,200) multiplied by the volume factor (1.25) results in:

$$\text{New sales} = \$1,200 \times 1.25 = \$1,500$$

The markup generated would be:

$$\$1,500 \times 40\% = \$600$$

Thus as indicated above, the dollar markup is the same. What is the difference in unit sales?

$$\text{Old sales} = \$1,200 \div \$12 \text{ each} = 100 \text{ plates}$$

$$\text{New sales} = \$1,500 \div \$10 \text{ each} = 150 \text{ plates}$$

We can also find the new sales in units using the same approach employed to determine the new dollar sales. But instead of dividing the old markup percentage by the new markup percentage, we divide the old markup dollars by the new markup dollars.

$$\frac{\text{Old markup in dollars}}{\text{New markup in dollars}} = \frac{\$12 - \$6}{\$10 - \$6} = \frac{\$6}{\$4} = 1.5 \text{ unit volume factor}$$

Here the volume factor is 1.5. It says that the new unit sales have to be 1.5 times the old unit sales for the total dollar markups to be equal. This is the same as saying that the unit volume has to increase by 50% ($1.5 = 1 + 50\%$).

The old sales (100) multiplied by the volume factor (1.5) results in: $100 \times 1.5 = 150$.

This agrees with the result determined above. Can we also calculate from these unit figures the relevant dollar figures?

"Old sales" in dollars = 100 plates $\times$ \$12 each = \$1,200

"New sales" in dollars = 150 plates $\times$ \$10 each = \$1,500

What we have illustrated above is the trade-off between sales volume and markup percentage that generates the same amount of markup dollars.

$$\text{The dollar sales volume factor} = \frac{\text{Old markup \%}}{\text{New markup \%}}$$

$$\text{The unit sales volume factor} = \frac{\text{Old markup \$}}{\text{New markup \$}}$$

The question that lingers is whether Debbie Walsh should lower the markup she is taking on the plates. The figures once again do not provide a clear-cut answer. They do provide the basis for analyzing the situation more carefully. The uncertainty is the response of customers. Will the result of lowering the markup percentage be to increase sales beyond the points indicated in the figures above; that is, increases greater than 25% in dollar volume, or 50% in unit volume? If so, then Debbie should make the reduction in markup percentage, as long as the departmental costs do not increase. If it is likely that expenses would increase because of the greater volume, the problem becomes further complicated. Clearly, it would appear to be unwise to lower the markup percentage if Debbie strongly doubted that sales would increase by 25% in dollars (or 50% in units). The overall result would then be a reduction in the total dollar markup generated by the plates.

Why Reduce the Markup Percentage?

You may continue to wonder why a buyer would be thinking about lowering the initial markup percentage on merchandise after all the planning expended in establishing the initial markup to begin with. If the initial markup objective is 50%, why consider 40%? Recognize that the initial markup objective was established with a particular sales volume in mind. What we are contemplating is a lowering of markup that would have the effect of increasing sales.

This increasing volume effect can be illustrated with some hypothetical figures. In these figures we will ignore markdowns and other reductions, alteration costs, and cash discounts. (We shall be dealing with a situation where everything is sold at the original retail price—like Ted Adams's Hardware in Chapter 3.)

	Old Situation		*New Situation*
Sales	$100,000	Sales	$125,000
Markup (50%)	50,000	Markup (40%)	50,000
Expenses	40,000	Expenses	40,000
Profit	$ 10,000	Profit	$ 10,000

These numbers present a 25% increase in sales. This is what we determined Debbie Walsh would need to retain the total dollar markup, if the markup percentage was reduced from 50% to 40%. If the expenses do not increase (a big assumption) the profit would be the same.

Now let's examine a similar situation where the sales increase associated with the reduction in margin is actually 33%. The results would be:

Sales	$133,000
Markup (40%)	53,200
Expenses	40,000
Profit	$ 13,200

Here there is an increase in profits which could justify the reduction in markup. This volume effect is the underlying reasoning behind the changes in a retailer's pricing strategy that you sometimes experience as a customer. A store that may have been struggling, will suddenly announce that it has "gone discount" and reduced its prices. Management is hoping the resulting increase in total sales volume will generate enough markup dollars to more than offset the reduction in prices.

But, it is unrealistic to think that expenses will not increase. In Debbie Walsh's giftware department, it is possible that an increase in sales of one item could be handled without increased departmental expenses. On a storewide basis, one can expect at a minimum that advertising will increase, additional employees will be needed to handle the increased sales volume, and expenses such as bags and supplies will also increase. The overall hope of managements making such a change is that the new combination of markup and expense will generate a higher dollar profit than is being earned under the old combination.

Problems

4–11. An appliance buyer has been selling for $399 a washing machine that costs $315. The manufacturer notifies the buyer that the cost of the washing machine will increase to $325. The buyer is reluctant to raise his price believing that $399 is a "good price." The buyer further speculates that a major competitor will raise prices "probably to $419." If the retail price of the washing machine is not increased, what percentage increase in unit sales would the buyer have to realize to make the same dollar markup as was generated before the cost increase?

4–12. The owner of a typewriter shop has been selling packages of ribbons costing $3 for $5.99. A reduction of the retail price to $4.99 is being considered. What percentage increase in dollar volume would be needed at the lower price to produce the same total amount of dollar markup being produced at the higher price? What increase in unit volume would be required?

Mellow Music Store Applications

Julie Martin decided to examine more closely the markups for music and music books. She had noticed that everything came from the suppliers with the retail price already preprinted on the front of the music or music book. Julie divided the various items into five categories and added together the various costs and retail prices. The results were:

	Total Retail	Total Cost	Markup Percentage
Sheet music	$2,832	$1,442	49.1%
Songbooks	1,292	658	49.1
Instruction books	1,185	592	50.0
Exercise books	764	382	50.0
Blank music sheets and notebooks	277	126	54.5
Totals	$6,350	$3,200	49.6%

She observed to John Martin, that whereas the cumulative markup to date on all music and music books was 49.6%, this was really a weighted average of the markups on the different items in stock. These markups varied somewhat, but all were consistent with the initial markup objective of 50%.

John Martin was concerned that there was a noticeable difference in the initial markup of the two amplifiers from one company that he decided to stock. The costs and manufacturer's suggested retails of these amplifiers were:

	Retail	Cost	Markup Percentage
Model 220	$499	$290	41.9%
Model 550	729	340	53.4

"I think I am going to have to sell a lot more of the 550s to average a 50% markup on that line. Let's see," John pondered.

Actual retail	$499	$729
Retail needed to make 50% markup	580	680
Difference	−$ 81	+$ 49

"Sales between those two amplifiers are going to have to be divided 62% of the 550s to 38% of the 220s. That's almost 2 to 1. I wonder if we can achieve that?"

$$\$81 + \$49 = \$130; \frac{81}{130} = 62\%; \frac{49}{130} = 38\%$$

Julie was also examining some imported music boxes. They had cost $10 each, and the salesman for the supplier had recommended a $25 retail price. "I'll bet," Julie said to John, "we would sell many more at $19." John then scribbled on the back of an envelope and said, "We'll have to sell two thirds more at $19 than we would have to sell at $25 to make the same total dollar markup. Do you think there'd be that much difference in sales?"

$$\frac{\text{Old markup \$}}{\text{New markup \$}} = \frac{\$15}{\$9} = 1.67 \text{ unit volume factor}$$

Unit sales would have to increase by a factor of 1.67. This is the same as a 67% increase in sales, or an increase of two thirds.

Review Problems

4–1R. An executive of a supermarket chain planning the opening of a new store makes the following projections:

	Percentage of Total Sales	Initial Markup Percentage
Grocery	42%	21%
Meat	28	28
Produce	8	35
Dairy	8	22
Frozen Foods	7	30
Bakery	4	45
Nonfoods	3	25

What is the initial markup percentage for the entire store?

4–2R. The buyer for junior dresses in a department store had an initial markup objective of 49.5%. At the start of the new season, the merchandise on hand had cost $43,600 and had a retail value of $92,375. What markup percentage did the buyer have to take on the purchases planned for the season, totaling $85,000 at cost, to achieve the initial markup objective?

4–3R. A department store buyer at a merchandise show had planned to acquire goods with a cost value of $28,000 to which would be applied an initial markup of 42.5%. After the buyer had purchased $16,000 at cost value, a tally indicated that these goods were priced to total $30,200 at retail. What markup percentage did the buyer have to obtain on the balance of purchases at the show to meet the initial markup objective?

4–4R. The buyer for outerwear in a men's shop planned to purchase from three vendors $4,200 worth of merchandise at cost. This merchandise was to carry a total retail of $7,000. After meeting with two of the vendors, the buyer had made purchases as follows:

	Cost	Retail
Alpha clothing	$2,170	$3,500
Beta coats	1,860	3,150

What markup percentage must the buyer take on purchases from the third vendor to meet the markup objective?

4–5R. A produce buyer for a supermarket purchases a pickup truckload of cucumbers from a farmer for $100. In unloading the cucumbers from the truck, a clerk counted a total of 1,232. The buyer decides to sell the smaller ones for 10¢ each and the larger ones for 15¢ each. How many would the buyer have to sell at each price in order to make his accustomed 33% markup on cucumbers?

4–6R. The owner of a coffee shop purchases fresh doughnuts each morning from a bakery that charges $1.65 per dozen for plain doughnuts and $2 per dozen for filled doughnuts. The coffee shop owner purchases 20 dozen doughnuts each day and usually sells out by closing time. In what proportion should the owner purchase plain and filled doughnuts to average a 50% markup on doughnut sales if the doughnuts are sold for 30¢ each?

4–7R. The buyer for the art supplies department in a department store purchases a lot of 18 dozen reproductions for $972. Five dozen are the same as those presently in stock at a retail of $10. The buyer planned to sell these at the regular price. Of the balance, those judged by the buyer to be more attractive would be sold at $12, those judged to be less attractive would be sold as a "special" at $6. In what proportion would the buyer have to sell the $12 and $6 reproductions to earn a markup of 50% on the lot?

4–8R. A buyer for a basement shoe department purchased a lot of shoes from a jobber for $5,000. The lot consisted of 200 pairs of mixed styles and quality. After carefully inspecting the shoes, the buyer concluded that 50 pairs were worth only $25 per pair at retail. The buyer planned to sell the other pairs in the $39 and $59 price lines. How many must the buyer sell at $39 and $59 in order to earn a markup of 40% on the lot?

4–9R. The owner of a variety store is contemplating an increase in the markup from 36% to 40%. What percentage reduction in sales could the store incur and still generate the same total dollar markup currently achieved?

4–10R. A proprietor of an auto parts outlet would like to stimulate volume by cutting prices. A reduction in markup percentage from 50% to 40% is being analyzed. What would be the average reduction in prices? What percentage increase in dollar sales would be needed to generate the same total dollar markup that is currently being achieved?

CHAPTER 5

Markdowns

As customers, we know that every item of merchandise does not sell at the original retail price; we are very familiar with markdowns. Sometimes we purposefully shop with the hope of finding some bargains—attractive merchandise with the original price lined out, re-marked at a lower price. Markdowns are a vital component of retail merchandising. One store, Filene's Basement, located in Boston, is known for its famous "automatic markdown" plan.[1]

Retailers Plan for Markdowns

Markdowns were introduced in Chapter 3 as part of the *reductions* that retailers include when establishing the initial markup. Because of their significant impact on the revenues generated to cover expenses and provide profits, retailers carefully plan for and control markdowns. Our discussion of markdowns in this chapter combines together the two major types: (1) merchandise that because of some characteristic (color, style, fabric, size, defect, lack of customer appeal, or seasonality) a buyer or manager wishes to dispose of; and (2) first quality merchandise in demand, that is reduced in price to induce customer traffic. The key element in both cases is that the merchandise is sold at a price less that the original retail price.

Two other categories of reductions mentioned in Chapter 3, employee discounts and discounts to special classes of customers, also involve sales of merchandise at less than the original retail price. Some retailers may not make the distinction and instead will include these price reductions as part of markdowns. Other retailers do make the distinction, considering the employee discounts a kind of quasi-fringe benefit, and the special customer discounts a form of promotion.

Taking a Markdown

Bill Edwards, the buyer for women's coats in a department store noticed that a particular style of winter coat that he had purchased in anticipation of good volume was not selling. He had purchased 12 dozen of these coats in various colors, with a range of sizes. Midway through the fall selling season 25 coats had been sold.

"This is a nice coat," he said, "I really don't know why it's not selling. But I've overheard more than one customer tell salespeople who have been suggesting it, 'I don't know just why, but I really don't care for it.'"

He continued, "I've noticed, too, that my competitor has the same coat and hasn't sold many. I don't think it's going to be a big Christmas item. I'd better mark them down and see if I can get some movement."

Bill Edwards then directed the assistant buyer to take a count of the number of coats on the selling floor and in the stock room, and to change the price from $99 to $69. "And have the sign shop make a couple of signs "Sale—Coats—$69" to place on the racks," he added.

---

[1]Price tags of goods are dated when placed on the selling floor. After 12 selling days goods are reduced in price by 25%; after 18 days by 50%; after 24 days by 75%; and after 30 selling days, unsold merchandise is given to charity.

The assistant buyer counted the coats. There were 118 coats and she reported the figure to Edwards. "Don't tell me someone walked out with a coat on," he exclaimed. "Please count them again."

There were 118 coats hanging from the racks on the selling floor and in the stockroom.

Let's overlook briefly the missing coat and focus on the reduction in the retail price from $99 to $69 — a reduction of $30. The unit dollar markdown was $30. The markdown on this particular lot of coats was 118 × $30, for a total of $3,540. The cost of the coats had been $50 each. The planned initial markup for the department in which the coats were being sold was 50%. In pricing these coats, Bill Edwards had applied the 50% initial markup resulting in a price of $100 ($\frac{\$50}{50\%} = \$100$). He then lowered the price to $99 which he thought was a psychologically better retail.

How Markdowns Reduce the Markup

Consider the impact of this markdown on the markup. For the coats that were marked down, the markup has been reduced from 49.5% ($\frac{\$49}{\$99}$) to 27.5% ($\frac{\$19}{\$69}$). The result may be even more striking for the entire lot of coats. For if all the coats had been sold at the original retail price, the amount of markup dollars generated would have been:

$$\begin{aligned} \text{Sales } 144 \times \$99 &= \$14,256 \\ \text{Cost } 144 \times \$50 &= \underline{7,200} \\ \text{Markup} &\quad \$\ 7,056, \quad 49.5\% \text{ sales} \end{aligned}$$

If the remaining coats are all sold at the $69 price, the amount of markup dollars generated will be:

$$\begin{aligned} \text{Sales}\ \ 25 \times \$99 &= \$\ 2,475 \\ 118 \times\ \ 69 &= \underline{8,142} \\ &\quad \$10,617 \\ \text{Cost } 144 \times \$50 &= \underline{7,200} \\ \text{Markup} &\quad \$\ \ 3,417, \quad 32.2\% \text{ sales} \end{aligned}$$

Here we also see the effect of the possible shoplifting or other loss of one coat. The missing coat provides no sales revenue, but the department has incurred the $50 cost of buying the coat. The total impact is a loss of $3,639 ($7,056 − $3,417) in potential markup revenue. This is a loss of $\frac{\$3,639}{\$7,056} = 51.6\%$ of the potential markup.

Taking a Second Markdown

Often despite the markdown taken, all remaining goods do not sell in what the buyer might consider a reasonable time period. Some buyers may then take an additional, or second markdown. Let's revise the situation described above somewhat and say that in the month following the $30 markdown, 100 of the 118 coats were sold at $69. The remaining coats were further marked down by Bill Edwards to $57. They sold out quickly at this price. What were the total markdowns? To determine the total markdowns we add together the first and second markdown as follows:

First Markdown

Number of coats: 118
Amount of markdown: $99 − $69 = $30
Total dollar markdown: 118 × $30 = $3,540

Second Markdown

Number of coats: 18
Amount of markdown: $69 − $57 = $12
Total dollar markdown: 18 × $12 = $216

Combined total dollar markdown: $3,540 + $216 = $3,756.

The total markdown taken on this lot of coats was $3,756.

Calculating the Maintained Markup

Now let's recalculate the markup that was actually generated by this lot of coats. (For the moment we will consider the "lost" coat as a sale at $0.)

Sales	25 × $99	$ 2,475
	100 × $69	6,900
	18 × $57	1,026
	1 × $0	0
Total		$10,401
Cost	144 × $50	$ 7,200
Markup		$ 3,201, 30.8% sales

So the actual markup earned selling the coats was 30.8%. This markup retailers call the **maintained markup**.

The maintained markup measures the amount of markup that was actually generated in *selling* the goods, distinguished from the initial markup, the markup planned when *originally pricing* the goods. If all the coats had been priced by applying the initial markup and sold at the original retail price, the initial markup and the maintained markup would have been the same. However, because there are usually some reductions, in the case of the winter coats, the two markdowns, plus the shortage of one coat, the maintained markup is normally lower than the initial markup.

Of the two markup measures, it is important to remember that the initial markup is a *planned* figure. It reflects the expenses and profit that we anticipate, allowing for the markdowns and other reductions. The maintained markup is an *actual* figure. It tells how many dollars more than the billed cost of the merchandise we actually generated in selling the goods. In Chapter 6 we will examine more closely the maintained markup, and its mathematical relationship to the initial markup.

Markdown Cancellations

The situation involving Bill Edwards and the women's coats exemplifies the use of markdowns to expedite the sale of slow-moving merchandise. In such a case, the markdown is permanent and may later be increased. But when markdowns are used for promotional purposes, they are often temporary and may later be cancelled.

Linda James, the buyer for the furniture department of a department store decided to have a sale of upholstered chairs to bring some additional customer traffic into her department. She thought that "25% off" the regular retail price would be an attractive inducement and planned newspaper advertising along with "sale" signs in the department. The initial markup in the furniture department was 54%. Linda thought that people attracted to the chair sale might buy a sofa, occasional table, or a rug at regular prices. Linda priced upholstered chairs in three price lines: $399, $559, and $699. Only the styles and fabrics in stock were on sale. Customers desiring a "special order" chair would have to pay the regular retail price. In preparation for the sale, Linda counted the available stock and determined the markdowns as follows:

Regular Price	Sale Price	Unit Markdown	Quantity	Markdown Amount
$399	$299	$100	42	$ 4,200
559	419	140	35	4,900
699	524	175	28	4,900
Total markdown taken				$14,000

During the two-week sale period, sales were as follows:

Price	Quantity Sold
$299	33
419	21
524	12

At the conclusion of the sale, the chairs were repriced at the presale retails: $399, $559, and $699. Linda James now calculated the **markdown cancellations** as follows:

Sale Price	Regular Price	Unit Markdown Cancellation	Quantity	Cancellation Amount
$299	$399	$100	9 (42–33)	$ 900
419	559	140	14 (35–21)	1,960
524	699	175	16 (28–12)	2,800
	Total markdown cancellations			$5,660

Now we can calculate the actual net markdowns incurred:

Net markdowns = Markdowns taken − Markdown cancellations

Net markdowns = $14,000 − $5,660 = $8,340

Repricing below Original Retail

Sometimes after a sale a buyer may reprice the merchandise at a price above the markdown price but below the original retail. When this happens the markdown cancellation is the difference between the markdown price and the new retail. For example, the owner of an appliance store has a sale on kitchen ranges. Ranges normally retailing for $599 are sale priced at $499; those retailing at $519 are sale priced at $459; and those at $449 are sale priced at $399.

The quantities of ranges on hand were:

Regular Price	Amount on Hand
$599	16 ranges
519	24 ranges
449	26 ranges

During the sale, customers purchased ranges as follows:

Sale Price	Number Sold
$499	6 ranges
459	10 ranges
399	15 ranges

Following the sale, the ranges were repriced:

From $499 to $579
From 459 to 499
From 399 to 429

What were the net markdowns?
The total markdowns taken were:

$599 − $499 = $100 × 16 = $1,600
519 − 459 = 60 × 24 = 1,440
449 − 399 = 50 × 26 = 1,300
Total $4,340

The markdown cancellations were:

$$\$579 - \$499 = \$80 \times 10 = \$ \ \ 800$$
$$499 - \ \ 459 = \ \ 40 \times 14 = \ \ \ \ 560$$
$$429 - \ \ 399 = \ \ 30 \times 11 = \underline{\ \ \ \ 330}$$

Total $1,690

The net markdowns were:

$$\$4,340 - \$1,690 = \$2,650$$

Repricing Above Original Retail

Occasionally when repricing merchandise after a sale, a buyer may decide to establish the new retail price above the former original retail. For example, a retailer sells a radio costing $60 for $89. For a sale, the radio is marked down to $75. At the conclusion of the sale, the remaining radios are priced at a new retail of $95. Here the unit markdown would be $14 ($89 − $75). The markdown cancellation would only be $14. That is the actual cancellation of the unit markdown. The difference between the former regular retail and the new regular retail, that is $6 ($95 − $89) would be considered an *additional markup*. In effect it raises the markup on the radio from 32.6% ($\frac{\$89 - \$60}{\$89}$) to 36.8% ($\frac{\$95 - \$60}{\$95}$).

Markup Cancellations

Likewise, a reduction in a retail price that is not a markdown per se, but rather a price change, for example, to correct an erroneous price would be considered a *markup cancellation* or *a revision of retail downward*. A buyer notices scarves with a retail price ticket of $19.99. A check of the unit cost reveals it to be $8.50. The initial markup is 50%. The buyer has the scarves reticketed at $16.99. The three dollar reduction from $19.99 to $16.99 is not recorded as a markdown, but rather as a markup cancellation (or as a revision of retail downward).

Problems

5–1. Anticipating the start of the spring season, a department store buyer for women's coats decided to markdown the remaining women's winter coats in stock. The original retail prices, new lower prices, and quantities on hand are indicated below. What were the total markdowns taken?

Original Retail	New Price	Quantity
$199	$129	133
149	99	84
119	69	77

5–2. In preparation for a sale, the manager of sporting goods marked down the baseball gloves as follows:

Original Retail	New Sale Retail	Quantity
$89	$75	24
75	59	30
59	45	44
45	33	32

During the sale, customers purchased the following amounts at sale prices: 14 at $75; 15 at $59; 18 at $45; and 16 at $33. Following the sale, the remaining stock was repriced at the original retails. What were the markdown cancellations? What were the net markdowns?

5–3.　A department store had a small appliance "warehouse sale." Data are presented below for toasters and can openers. From these data determine the markdown cancellations and the net markdowns.

Toasters

Original Retail	Sale Price	On Hand Start of Sale	Units Sold	New Retail After Sale
$49	$39	3 dozen	15	$49
35	27	3 dozen	18	39
29	21	4 dozen	21	29
19	15	5 dozen	14	17

Can Openers

Original Retail	Sale Price	On Hand Start of Sale	Units Sold	New Retail After Sale
$33	$25	2 dozen	10	$35
27	23	3 dozen	15	29
19	14	3 dozen	22	19
13	9	5 dozen	35	12

5–4.　A shoe retailer decided to analyze the results of a purchase of shoes from a new supplier. The total purchase has been 216 pairs at a cost of $10,800. The retailer had set an original retail of $99 at which 148 pairs were sold. A first markdown to $79 resulted in the sale of 42 pairs. A second markdown to $59 sold 24 pairs. The remaining two pairs has been sold to employees at cost. What were the retailer's total reductions? What maintained markup did the retailer generate on the purchase from the new supplier? What percentage of the potential total markup dollars did the retailer lose because of the reductions?

5–5.   A retailer operating with an initial markup of 48% achieved a maintained markup of 43%. What percentage of the potential dollar markup did the retailer lose because of reductions?

Calculating the Markdown Percentage

In analyzing markdowns, retailers usually employ percentage relationships for control purposes. Like the percentage markup calculations in Chapter 2 that can cause confusion if one is not aware of cost and retail base differences, markdown percentage calculations also involve two different bases and the opportunity for confusion. Let's consider again the winter coats Bill Edwards marked down from $99 to $69. We determined that the markdown was $30. But what is the markdown percentage?

We could divide the $30 by either $99 or by $69 and obtain a percentage. You are probably saying that the $30 should be divided by $99 because that is the original price from which the markdown is being taken. While $30 divided by $99, equaling 30.3% is the reduction in price, it is *not* what retailers call the markdown percentage. The result of dividing $30 by $99, or 30.3%, is referred to as the *off retail* percentage, or the *markdown off* percentage. It indicates the percentage reduction in the retail price. It can be used to tell customers in signs or advertising the amount of percentage reduction in price.

The retailer, however, calls the *markdown* percentage, the dollar markdown divided by the new, or revised price. Thus, for one of Bill Edwards's winter coats, the markdown percentage would be:

$$\text{Markdown percentage} = \frac{\text{Dollar markdown}}{\text{Revised retail price}}$$

$$\text{Markdown percentage} = \frac{\$30}{\$69} = 43.5\%$$

While the above refers to just one unit, the same convention applies to multiple markdowns. Thus, if a department marked down goods with a total original retail value of \$3,500 to \$2,500, the following percentage calculations could be made:

$$\text{Dollar markdown} = \$3,500 - \$2,500 = \$1,000$$

$$\text{Off-retail \%} = \frac{\text{Dollar markdown}}{\text{Original retail}} = \frac{\$1,000}{\$3,500} = 28.6\%$$

$$\text{Markdown \%} = \frac{\text{Dollar markdown}}{\text{Revised retail}} = \frac{\$1,000}{\$2,500} = 40\%$$

The Cumulative Markdown Percentage

Retailers also calculate a markdown percentage that relates markdowns not only to the particular goods marked down, but also to the total sales during a period of time. For example if the department cited above had had total sales of \$9,500 during the period in which the reductions from \$3,500 to \$2,500 took place, a markdown percentage of $\frac{\$1,000}{\$9,500}$, or 10.5% for the department would be reported. While this percentage is usually simply referred to as the *markdown percentage,* we will use the term *cumulative markdown percentage* when referring to it. So the cumulative markdown percentage relates markdowns taken to total sales at regular and markdown prices during a period.

The Markdown Goods Percentage

Retailers also pay careful attention to the mix, or balance of the sales, between goods that have been marked down and those being sold at original retail prices. A percentage called the *markdown goods percentage* relates the total dollar sales at marked down prices to the total sales at all prices during a period. For example, for the department cited above with total sales of \$9,500, let's assume that all the goods that were marked down from \$3,500 to \$2,500 sold out at that price. The markdown goods percentage would be:

$$\text{Markdown goods \%} = \frac{\text{Sales of goods at marked down prices}}{\text{Total sales}}$$

$$\text{Markdown goods \%} = \frac{\$2,500}{\$9,500}$$

$$\text{Markdown goods \%} = 26.3\%$$

Relating Markdowns to Sales

Retailers' practice of relating dollar markdowns to dollar sales is consistent with the overall practice of using sales as the base for most analytical ratios. Sales are the measure of retail performance that reflect retailers' skill in converting merchandise into customer purchases, thereby generating the revenue to cover expenses and produce profits. Sales also are a much more valid measure of the worth of merchandise than are prices at which the goods are not selling. Artificially inflated original retail prices used as a base for markdown calculations would result in smaller percentage numbers, but would be self-deluding. A more useful figure would be realistically based on what merchandise can be sold for. If the markdown percentage is high relative to objectives, other stores, or industry figures, it suggests the need to examine carefully initial markup planning, or perhaps, buyer's skills in monitoring market trends and negotiating purchases.

Summary Example of Markdown Calculations

Let's consider an integrated example showing the various markdown related percentage calculations. Gerri Revere, a buyer for giftware in a department store was reviewing results for the most recent season. Total sales had been \$62,000. Sales of goods that had been marked down totaled \$12,500. These goods had an original retail that totaled \$22,000. In anticipation of the semiannual clearance sale, Gerri had reduced these goods to \$14,725. A second markdown of \$1,725 had been taken on these goods, and finally, a third markdown of \$500 which resulted in the final sale of all the marked down merchandise.

Total markdowns taken were:

First markdown	$22,000 - $14,725 = $7,275
Second markdown	1,725
Third markdown	500
Total	$9,500

$$\text{Off-retail \%} = \frac{\text{Markdowns taken}}{\text{Original retail of goods marked down}} = \frac{\$9,500}{\$22,000} = 43.2\%$$

$$\text{Markdown \%} = \frac{\text{Markdowns taken}}{\text{Revised retail of goods marked down}} = \frac{\$9,500}{\$12,500} = 76\%$$

$$\text{Cumulative markdown \%} = \frac{\text{Markdowns taken}}{\text{Total sales}} = \frac{\$9,500}{\$62,000} = 15.3\%$$

$$\text{Markdown goods \%} = \frac{\text{Sales of goods at markdown prices}}{\text{Total sales}} = \frac{\$12,500}{\$62,000} = 20.2\%$$

The relationships among these concepts can be visualized in Figure 5–1.

Figure 5–1 The Markdown Box

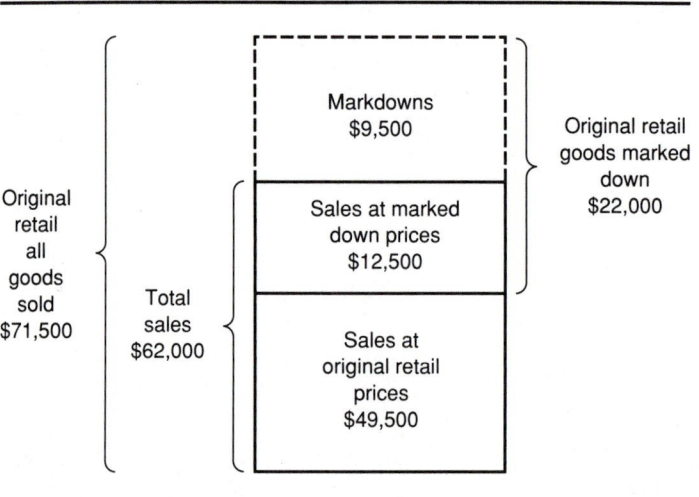

Figuring the Off-Retail Percentage

Understanding these relationships permits a merchant to perform calculations such as the following in situations where all marked down goods are sold during a period, or when the value of marked down goods in stock at the beginning of a period closely approximates the values of marked down goods on hand at the end of a period. (We will use figures from the example above of Gerri Revere's department to illustrate and also to check our answers.)

A buyer wishes to limit the markdown goods percentage to 20.2% and to have a cumulative markdown percentage of 15.3%. What would be the off-retail percentage? Figure 5–2 organizes the data assuming a total sales base of $1,000.

Because the cumulative markdown percentage is 15.3%, dollar markdowns would be $153 on a sales base of $1,000. Likewise, as the markdown goods percentage is 20.2%, sales of goods at marked down prices would be $202. Thus the goods selling for $202 that were marked down $153 had an original retail of $355.

We can then calculate the off-retail percentage:

$$\text{Off-retail \%} = \frac{\text{Markdowns taken}}{\text{Original retail}} = \frac{\$153}{\$355} = 43.1\%$$

Figure 5–2 Applying the Markdown Box Given the Markdown Goods Percentage and the Cumulative Markdown Percentage

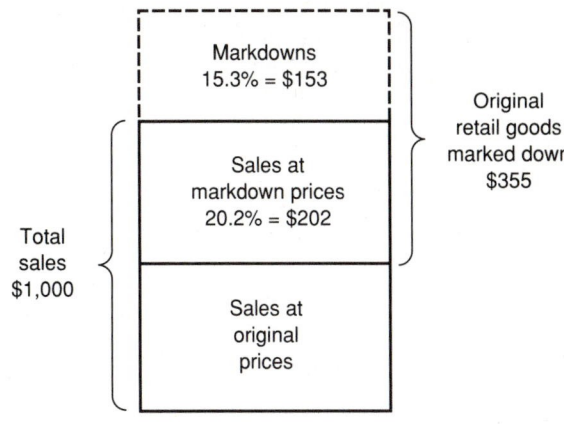

(Note: the difference between this percentage and that calculated for Gerri Revere's department (43.2%) is simple rounding discrepancy.)

Now we can also calculate the markdown percentage for the goods that were reduced in price:

$$\text{Markdown } \% = \frac{\text{Markdowns taken}}{\text{Revised retail}} = \frac{\$153}{\$202} = 75.8\%$$

(Also rounding discrepancy.)

Figuring the Cumulative Markdown Percentage

Let's take a situation where we have the markdown goods percentage and the off-retail percentage and want to determine the cumulative markdown percentage.

If the markdown goods percentage is 20%, and the off-retail percentage is 40%, what is the cumulative markdown percentage?

Figure 5–3 organizes the data using again a sales base of $1,000.

Figure 5–3 Applying the Markdown Box Given the Markdown Goods Percentage and the Off-Retail Percentage

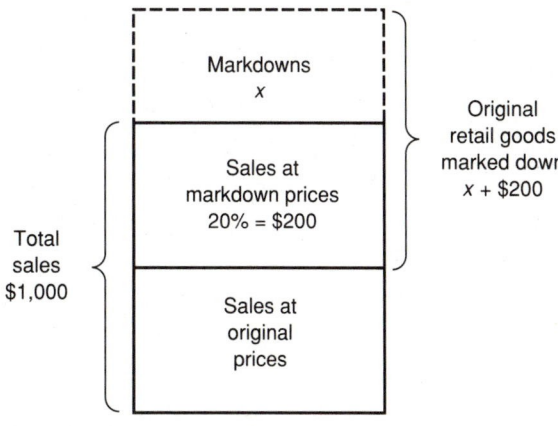

Because the markdown goods percentage is 20%, then on total sales of $1,000, $200 would be sold at reduced prices. The markdowns we do not know, so we will call them X. The original retail of the goods marked down is, therefore, $X + \$200$; that is; the amount of the markdowns plus what the goods were sold for. Now to get the markdown amount, we relate the markdowns to the original retail of the goods marked down. That equals the off-retail percentage, 40%.

$$\text{Off retail }\% = \frac{\text{Markdowns taken}}{\text{Original retail}}$$

$$40\% = \frac{X}{X + \$200}$$

$$.4(X + \$200) = X$$

$$.4X + \$80 = X$$

$$\$80 = .6X$$

$$\$133.33 = X$$

So the markdowns are $133.33. Thus the cumulative markdown percentage is:

$$\text{Cumulative markdown }\% = \frac{\text{Markdowns taken}}{\text{Total sales}} = \frac{\$133.33}{\$1,000} = 13.3\%$$

The same result can also be obtained by reasoning as follows: the goods that were sold for $200 were marked down 40% of their original retail value. Therefore, they were sold for 60% of their original retail value. Thus $200 is 60% of the original retail value, or:

$$\$200 = 60\% \text{ Original retail value}$$

$$\frac{\$200}{60\%} = \text{Original retail value}$$

$$\$333.33 = \text{Original retail value}$$

From the original retail value of $333.33 we would subtract the sales value, $200, to get the markdowns, $133.33.

Again relating the markdowns to the total sales ($\frac{\$133.33}{\$1,000}$) results in the cumulative markdown percentage, 13.3%. We can also calculate the markdown percentage for the goods that were reduced in price:

$$\text{Markdown }\% = \frac{\text{Markdowns taken}}{\text{Revised retail}} = \frac{\$133.33}{\$200} = 66.7\%$$

Figuring the Markdown Goods Percentage

Similarly, given a cumulative markdown percentage of 10% and an off-retail percentage of 25%, we can calculate the markdown goods percentage. Figure 5–4 organizes the relevant data.

Figure 5–4 Applying the Markdown Box Given the Cumulative Markdown Percentage and the Off-Retail Percentage

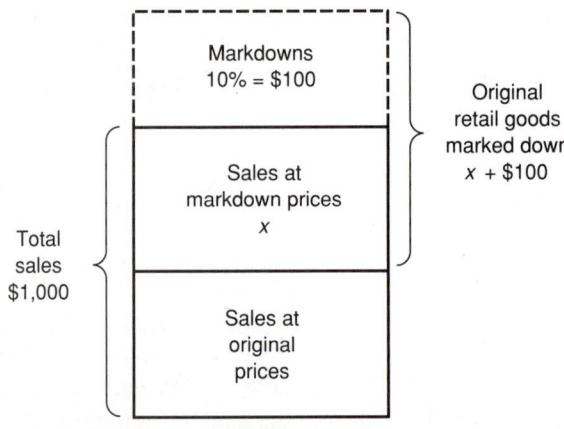

As the cumulative markdown percentage is 10%, the dollar markdowns are $100 on a total sales base of $1,000. We do not know the sales of goods at marked down prices so we will call them X. The original retail of the goods marked down is therefore $X + \$100$. As we did in the example above, we now relate the markdowns to the original retail of the goods marked down which equals the off-retail percentage, 25%.

$$\text{Off retail } \% = \frac{\text{Markdowns taken}}{\text{Original retail}}$$

$$25\% = \frac{\$100}{X + \$100}$$

$$.25(X + \$100) = \$100$$

$$.25X + \$25 = \$100$$

$$.25X = \$75$$

$$X = \$300$$

So the marked down goods were sold for $300. Thus the marked down goods percentage is:

$$\text{Markdown goods } \% = \frac{\text{Sales of goods at markdown prices}}{\text{Total sales}} = \frac{\$300}{\$1,000} = 30\%$$

The same result can also be obtained by reasoning as follows: the markdowns of $100 also represented 25% of the original retail of the goods that were marked down.
Therefore:

$$\$100 = 25\% \text{ Original retail value}$$

$$\frac{\$100}{25\%} = \text{Original retail value}$$

$$\$400 = \text{Original retail value}$$

Subtracting the markdowns ($100) from the original retail value ($400) results in $300 as the sales value of the goods marked down. Relating $300 to total sales of $1,000 results in the marked down goods percentage, $30\% (\frac{\$300}{\$1,000})$.
Now we can also calculate the markdown percentage:

$$\text{Markdown } \% = \frac{\$100}{\$300} = 33.3\%$$

Problems

5–6. A shoe department in a department store had total sales of $66,000. Included in these sales were $12,000 representing sales of goods at marked down prices. The marked down goods had a combined original retail value of $18,000. Calculate the off-retail percentage and the markdown percentage.

5–7. The millinery department had total sales during the last period of $48,000. The only markdowns taken were during the seasonal clearance sale. Fifty hats with an original retail of $29 were reduced in price to $19. Forty sold at the revised price. The balance were further reduced to $11 and sold out. Calculate the off-retail percentage, the markdown percentage, the cumulative markdown percentage, and the markdown goods percentage.

5–8. After Valentine's Day, the buyer for the candy department marked down the $15 heart-shaped assortments to $9, taking total markdowns of $144. $10 hearts were each marked down to $6, with these markdowns totaling $72. Six of the $15 hearts did not sell at $9 and were reduced to $5 and cleared out. Four of the $14 hearts took a second markdown to $3 and sold out. Total sales during February were $9,650. Calculate the off-retail percentage, the markdown percentage, the cumulative markdown percentage, and the markdown goods percentage.

5–9. If the cumulative markdown percentage is 12% and the off-retail percentage is 35%, what is the markdown goods percentage?

5–10. If the markdown goods percentage is 22% and the off-retail percentage is 40%, what is the cumulative markdown percentage?

5–11. If the markdown goods percentage is 18% and the cumulative markdown percentage is 15%, what is the off-retail percentage? What is the markdown percentage?

5–12. Eighty percent of a retailer's sales were at original prices, the balance at marked down prices. The retailer had a cumulative markdown percentage of 14%. What was the retailer's markdown percentage? Off-retail percentage?

Setting the Off-Retail Percentage for a Sale

Understanding markdown relationships enables retailers to make other useful analyses. For example, a buyer is planning to markdown everything in the department for a major promotional sale. The total original retail value of the goods that the buyer hopes to sell is $20,000. The buyer's markdown objective is 12%. The buyer asks, "What average percentage reduction from the original retail value of these goods can I take?"

What the buyer is asking us to calculate is the off-retail percentage for this lot of merchandise. The sales value realized plus the markdowns taken would have to equal the original retail, $20,000, as represented by Figure 5–5.

Figure 5–5 Applying the Markdown Box Given the Original Retail and the Markdown Percentage

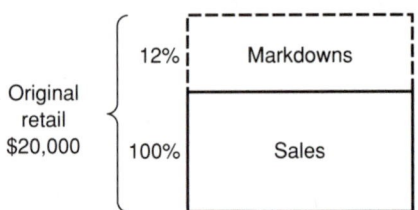

Therefore:

$$\text{Sales} + 12\% \text{ Sales} = \$20,000$$

$$1.12 \text{ Sales} = \$20,000$$

$$\text{Sales} = \frac{\$20,000}{1.12}$$

$$\text{Sales} = \$17,857$$

$$\text{Markdown} = \$20,000 - \$17,857 = \$2,143$$

As the above figures indicate, the buyer could markdown the goods a total of $2,143 and stay within the objective. The off-retail percentage would be $\frac{\$2,143}{\$20,000}$ = 10.7%. Thus the average reduction in price would be 10.7%. Would that result in a 12% markdown percentage? Let's check:

$$\text{Markdown}^2 \% = \frac{\text{Markdown taken}}{\text{Revised retail}} = \frac{\$2,143}{\$17,857} = 12\%$$

It checks!!!

---

[2]Here we are calling the markdown percentage a simple markdown percentage because it is related only to the merchandise sold at marked down prices.

Changing the Off-Retail Percentage

Suppose the buyer then said, "I don't think a 10.7% across the board cut will have enough impact. I want to be able to say *25% off*. What amount of these goods can I mark down 25% and stay within my markdown objective?"

Now the buyer is saying that the off-retail percentage should be 25% for the goods that are marked down. Therefore: $2,143 would be 25% of the original retail of the goods to be marked down.

$$\frac{\$2,143}{25\%} = \text{The original retail of the goods to be marked down}$$

$$\frac{\$2,143}{25\%} = \$8,572, \text{ the original retail of goods to be marked down}$$

So, $20,000 − $8,572 = $11,428, the value of goods to be sold at original retail prices

$8,572 worth of goods at original retail would be marked down to be sold at $8,572 − $2,143 = $6,429

If the buyer accomplished the sales objectives the results would be:

Sales at original retail	$11,428
Sales at marked down prices	6,429
Total sales	$17,857
Markdowns	$ 2,143
Total original retail	$20,000

The original retail of goods marked down = $8,572 ($6,429 + $2,143)

$$\text{The cumulative[3] markdown \%} = \frac{\text{Markdowns taken}}{\text{Total sales}} = \frac{\$\,2,143}{\$17,857} = 12\%$$

$$\text{The off-retail \%} = \frac{\text{Markdowns taken}}{\text{Original retail of goods marked down}} = \frac{\$2,143}{\$8,572} = 25\%$$

Balancing Sales between Full Retail and Markdowns

Some retailers pay very careful attention to the mix or balance of sales between merchandise sold at original retail and that sold at marked down prices. In planning for this year's Labor Day Sale, Fred Wise, buyer for the sporting goods department in a department store had set the following objectives: (1) to increase last year's total sales volume of $15,000, for the sale, by 20%; (2) to maintain the same dollar volume of sales at marked down prices, achieving the additional sales volume from goods sold at original retail; (3) to repeat last year's off-retail percentage of 30%; and (4) to lower the cumulative markdown percentage for the sale, which last year was 20%.

Fred is trying to figure out what volume of sales at original prices he should be striving for, and what the cumulative markdown percentage for the sale would be, if he achieved his objectives.

He might analyze his problem as follows:

a. To achieve a 20% increase in sales volume would require sales of $15,000 + (20% × $15,000) = $18,000.
b. Last year's cumulative markdown percentage was 20%, so the markdowns taken were 20% of sales: 20% × $15,000 = $3,000.

---
[3]Here we are calling the markdown percentage a cumulative markdown percentage because it is related to sales at both original retail and marked down prices.

c. These markdowns taken represented 30% of the original retail of the goods that were marked down, so the original retail of these goods was:

$$\$3,000 = 30\% \text{ Original retail}$$

$$\frac{\$3,000}{30\%} = \text{Original retail}$$

$$\$10,000 = \text{Original retail}$$

d. Merchandise with an original retail of $10,000 was marked down $3,000; therefore it was sold for $7,000.

Fred Wise wants to achieve the same sales volume at reduced prices as last year. That means of a total sales of $18,000, the plan is to sell $7,000 at marked down prices and therefore, $18,000 − $7,000 = $11,000 at original retail prices.

If Fred achieves his objectives his cumulative markdown percentage would be:

$$\text{Cumulative markdown \%} = \frac{\text{Markdowns taken}}{\text{Total sales}} = \frac{\$3,000}{\$18,000} = 16.7\%$$

In summary, Fred would have: (1) increased his sales by 20% from $15,000 to $18,000; (2) achieved the same sales volume in marked down goods, $7,000; (3) had an off-retail percentage of $\frac{\$3,000}{\$10,000} = 30\%$; and (4) lowered his cumulative markdown percentage from 20% to 16.7%. In addition, the markdown goods percentage would be reduced from 46.7% $\left(\frac{\$7,000}{\$15,000}\right)$ to 38.9% $\left(\frac{\$7,000}{\$18,000}\right)$.

How Improved Sales Balance Increases Markup Dollars

Let's take Fred's situation a step further and see the impact on markup dollars generated. We assume that Fred's cumulative markup in sporting goods was 42% for both years. With a 30% off-retail percentage, the markup on goods reduced would be lowered on average as determined below:

An item with an original retail of $10 would cost, $10 × 58% = $5.80.

Taking a 30% off-retail on the item would result in a revised selling price of $10.00 − (30% × $10) = $7.00.

The markup at the reduced price would be $7.00 − $5.80 = $1.20.

$\frac{\$1.20}{\$7.00} = 17.1\% =$ the average markup on goods after a 30% price reduction.

So last year, Fred's markup generated was

$$
\begin{array}{rl}
\$8,000 \times 42\% & = \$3,360 \\
7,000 \times 17.1 & = \underline{1,197} \\
\text{Total} & = \$4,557
\end{array}
$$

If he achieves his targets, this year's markup generated would be:

$$
\begin{array}{rl}
\$11,000 \times 42\% & = \$4,620 \\
7,000 \times 17.1 & = \underline{1,197} \\
\text{Total} & = \$5,817
\end{array}
$$

The increase in what we have learned is called the maintained markup was $5,817 − $4,557 = $1,260, or $\frac{\$1,260}{\$4,557} = 27.6\%$.

Thus with a 20% increase in sales volume, Fred increased the maintained markup by 27.6% because he increased the proportion of higher markup merchandise in the sales mix. This achievement is a constant striving of analytical retailers.

Calculating a Markdown Price

There is another common retailing situation that we can use our understanding to analyze.

A buyer for the bed and bath department of a department store purchases a closeout lot of down quilts. There are 72 quilts in the lot, and the cost is $80 for each quilt. The buyer wishes to earn a maintained markup of 40% on the entire lot. The quilts are priced at a retail of $149. The most attractive ones sell readily; eventually all but 18 are sold. The buyer decides to markdown the remaining quilts. What price can the buyer charge for these quilts and still achieve the maintained markup objective?

The 72 quilts represent a total cost of $72 \times \$80 = \$5,760$.

To earn a 40% maintained markup the quilts must generate a total of $\frac{\$5,760}{60\%} = \$9,600$ in sales revenue.

After selling 54 quilts at $149, the buyer has generated $54 \times \$149 = \$8,046$.

The remaining quilts must bring $\$9,600 - \$8,046 = \$1,554$.

Therefore, each remaining quilt must generate an average of $\frac{\$1,554}{18} = \$86.33$ in sales revenue.

Now the buyer must exercise judgment in deciding what reduced price to mark on the quilts. The buyer knows that each must average $86.33. If the buyer can sell them at a higher price, extra markup dollars will be generated. If the buyer finds the price has to be less than $86.33 to sell the remaining quilts, the maintained markup goal will not be achieved.

Problems

5–13. The proprietor of a small clothing store is planning an end of season "the entire store's on sale" promotion. The owner would like to announce that all merchandise in the store will be reduced in price by a fixed percentage when processed at the checkout counter. The store has in stock merchandise with a total retail value of $22,800. Based on experience the owner wishes to limit the markdown percentage to 15%. What fixed percentage reduction in price should the owner establish?

5–14. A department store buyer, in planning for the upcoming season, sets a sales objective of $125,000. The cumulative markdown objective is 18%. For sale purposes, the buyer would like to promote off-retails of 30%. If the buyer achieves the objectives, what total dollar markdowns would be taken? What would be the original retail value of the goods marked down?

5–15.   A chain store manager achieved a sales volume of $150,000 for last year's "Presidents' Birthday Sale." This year company management is pushing for a 25% increase in total sales. The manager would like to achieve most of the sales increase in merchandise at original retail prices, in order to boost the maintained markup. Last year the markdown goods percentage was 25%. The manager hopes to limit the increase in sales of marked down goods to 10% over last year and to have an off-retail of 20%. What is the sales target for merchandise sold at original retail? If the manager achieves objectives, what would be the cumulative markdown percentage for the sale?

5–16.   A book buyer purchases 2,000 books for $4,500. The buyer dumps many books on two large tables with a retail price of $4.95 per book. Clerks replenish the tables as books are sold. After three weeks, there are 500 books left and the buyer decides to mark them down to clear them out. To what price can the buyer markdown the remaining books and achieve the maintained markup objective of 48%?

Mellow Music Store Applications

John and Julie Martin decided to have some opening week specials to help attract customers to their new store. They decided to offer 30% off on all prepriced sheet music, songbooks, instruction books, exercise books, blank music sheets, and blank music notebooks. Because this price reduction would only apply during the first two weeks of the store's operation, Julie decided not to put a new price tag on all the merchandise. This would eliminate the task of removing these tags to reestablish the regular retail prices. Instead, she drew several signs and attached them to the racks holding the various sheets and books. She recorded a total markdown of 30% of $6,350, the total retail value of the stock, or $1,905. At the end of the two-week period, total sales of all music books and sheets had been $2,100.

Julie determined that this represented 70% of the original retail value of the merchandise sold. Thus she figured that the merchandise sold at "30% off" had an original retail value of $3,000 ($\frac{\$2,100}{70\%}$). The total markdowns actually incurred were $3,000 − $2,100 or $900. Julie then recorded a markdown cancellation of $1,905 − $900, or $1,005.

Sales during the first four weeks the store was opened totaled $10,400. Sales of marked down merchandise, promotional specials, totaled $4,300. The cumulative markdown percentage was 17.7%. While John was satisfied with these results, he hoped during the next month to increase sales. He wondered about taking some markdowns on keyboards in which customers had shown very little interest.

"Perhaps, if I reduce the price on some of these keyboards, I might attract some customers who if they buy a keyboard also purchase an amplifier, a stand, and some music," John said.

He assembled the following package:

	Retail	Cost	Markup	
Keyboard	$ 999.00	$500.00	$499.00	49.9%
Stand	115.00	50.00	65.00	56.5
Amplifier	499.00	290.00	209.00	41.9
Music	9.90	5.00	4.90	49.5
	$1,622.90	$845.00	$777.90	47.9%

"If I markdown the keyboard to $799 what will my maintained markup be on this package?" he asked. On a scratch pad he figured:

$$\frac{\$777.90 - \$200}{\$1,622.90 - \$200} = \frac{\$577.90}{\$1,422.90} = 40.6\%$$

"Wow, that'll cut my maintained to 40.6%, I don't think that's such a good idea." Then, he added: "But these keyboards aren't selling, we should try to move them before they become dust collectors."

Julie had found the music boxes to be surprisingly good sellers. Of the 12 that had been stocked, 8 had been sold. As she prepared a reorder of music boxes, she examined again those still in stock. Most customers had commented that these were not as attractive or pleasant sounding as others that had been sold.

"Maybe I should mark these down to clear them out and only reorder those that have already sold. Let's see, I've already had sales of $200 (8 × $25) at the original retail prices. How much can I mark these others down and still make the 50% maintained markup I'd like to get on music boxes?" She figured quickly:

$$\text{Total cost: 12 units} \times \$10 = \$120$$

$$\text{For a 50\% markup: } \frac{\$120}{50\%} = \$240 \text{ Total retail needed}$$

$$\text{Retail to date: } \$200$$

$$\text{Balance needed: } \$240 - \$200 = \$40$$

$$\text{Balance per unit: } \frac{\$40}{4} = \$10$$

Julie concluded, "I only need to get $10 each for them; I think I'll mark them down to $15 and give customers 40% off."

Review Problems

5–1R. At the end of the summer, the manager of the home and garden shop in a discount department store marked down all lawnmowers in stock by reducing the original retail price by 25%. Before any were sold, a competing store followed with the same reduction. The manager then decided to take as a second markdown an additional 10% off the markdown prices. What were the manager's total markdowns if the original retails and quantities on hand were as follows:

Original Retail	On Hand
$399	4
299	4
199	6
119	10

5–2R. The auto parts department of a discounter has a "Washington's Birthday" sale. Temporary reductions in price are offered on antifreeze, oil filters, snow scrapers, and windshield wipers. Following the sale, prices are returned to regular levels. What were the net markdowns if the regular prices, marked down prices, quantities on hand, and quantities sold were as follows:

Item	Regular Retail	Sale Price	On Hand Start of Sale	Sold
Antifreeze	$3.99	$2.99	150	96
Oil filters	4.59	3.99	72	46
Snow scrapers	1.19	.79	144	115
Windshield wipers	2.99	1.99	96	58

5–3R. The appliance department of a department store had a sale of microwave ovens. The original retail prices, sale prices, units on hand at the start of the sale, units sold, and new retails established after the sale are presented below. Determine the markdown cancellations and the net markdowns.

Original Retail	Sale Price	On Hand Start of Sale	Units Sold	New Retail After Sale
$349	$269	10	6	$329
299	249	12	5	269
279	239	12	3	249
249	209	15	12	229

5–4R. A retailer, pricing with an initial markup of 38%, determined that the maintained markup for the most recent period was 32%. What percentage of the potential dollar markup was lost because of the reductions?

5–5R. A giftware department had total sales of $18,000 during the most recent period. Of this total, $2,200 represented sales of marked down goods that had an original retail of $3,300. Calculate the markdown goods percentage, the off-retail percentage, the markdown percentage, and the cumulative markdown percentage.

5–6R. A department had the following figures: off-retail percentage, 35%; and markdown goods percentage, 18%. What was the cumulative markdown percentage?

5–7R. If the cumulative markdown percentage is 9% and the markdown goods percentage is 14%, what is the off-retail percentage?

5–8R. A department with a 32% off-retail percentage and a 15% cumulative markdown percentage would have what marked down goods percentage?

5–9R. A buyer planning a sale wished to increase last year's sales volume of $18,000 by 15%. Additional objectives are to use the same off-retail percentage, which was $33\frac{1}{3}\%$, but to limit sales of markdown goods to last year's figures, achieving the additional sales in regularly priced goods. Last year the cumulative markdown percentage for the sale was 25%. What would the markdown goods percentage and the cumulative markdown percentage be for this year if the buyer's objectives are achieved?

5–10R. The buyer for carpeting makes a special purchase of a lot of 9′ × 12′ rugs at a cost of $10,800. There are 144 rugs in the lot. The rugs are retailed for $159. After selling 75 rugs, the buyer reduces the price to $129. At this price an additional 35 rugs are sold. The buyer then decides to further mark down the remaining rugs to clear them out. If the buyer's maintained markup objective for the lot of rugs was 45%, what additional markdown could the buyer take on each remaining rug and still achieve the maintained markup goal?

CHAPTER 6

Gross Margin, Maintained Markup, and Initial Markup Relationships

Chapter 5 introduced the maintained markup, that is the difference between what the retailer sells merchandise for and the retailer's billed cost of that merchandise. The important distinction between the maintained markup and the initial markup was also emphasized. The initial markup is a planned figure used in establishing original retail prices. If, in practice, all merchandise taken into stock is actually priced at the initial markup and then sold at that original price, the initial markup and the maintained markup are the same.

Maintained Markup Less than Initial Markup

But this usually does not happen. Typically, the retailer has markdowns and other reductions. So the maintained markup is usually less than the initial markup. Chapter 3 described how retailers plan for these reductions in establishing the initial markup. The major objective of this planning is for the retailer to generate enough revenue from selling merchandise to cover all expenses and make a profit. The maintained markup, then, is an important measure of this revenue because it is the difference between what the merchandise is sold for and what it costs.

Fine-Tuning for Cash Discounts and Alteration Costs

But remember that the *cost* is billed cost, that is the amount that appears on the vendor's invoice (including any applicable transportation costs). Chapter 3 explained that while planning the initial markup, allowances had to be made for available cash discounts and any alteration costs incurred in selling the merchandise. Because all vendors do not provide cash discounts, because all cash discounts offered may not be taken, because the amounts that are offered vary among vendors, and because alteration costs are not incurred on every item sold, retailers use the billed cost in pricing individual units of merchandise. Thus, some "fine-tuning" must occur to correct for cash discounts and alteration costs so that the retailer can determine just how much revenue has actually been generated. Fine-tuning the maintained markup for the cash discounts and alteration costs produces the **gross margin.** For a retailer incurring no cash discounts or alteration costs, maintained markup and gross margin would be the same.

The gross margin, therefore, is the most accurate determination of the difference between what merchandise is sold for and its actual cost. From the gross margin, expenses are deducted; what's left over is the profit. The next chapter discusses more about how sales, costs, gross margin, expenses, and profit interrelate. But let's first focus on the important relationships among initial markup, maintained markup, and gross margin.

How Initial Markup, Maintained Markup, and Gross Margin Are Related

As suggested above, there is a very close relationship between the initial markup and the maintained markup, and between the maintained markup and the gross margin. This relationship is reflected in retailing practice—the buying, pricing, and selling of merchandise. It can be expressed arithmetically. To better understand the arithmetic relationships, let's first consider an example that demonstrates the various interactions. Several of the concepts studied already are integrated, so the example is somewhat long. But you now have sufficient knowledge to follow each step of the example. Stay with it! You will also be reviewing your understanding of concepts introduced earlier.

Fred's Tuxedo Shop

Upon graduation from college with a degree in music, Fred Mullan joined a band. For the next few years he toured with the band playing at clubs, schools, shows, shopping malls, concerts, and just about any place the band's agent could find work. There were good times and bad; good weeks and bad. Finally tired of the traveling, concerned that the bad weeks were outnumbering the good ones, and anxious to settle down, Fred returned to his hometown. With the encouragement and financial backing of his father, a wealthy industrialist, Fred decided to open a retail store. He thought tuxedos represented a good opportunity. He had bought several as a musician; he thought that if he offered musicians a special discount, they would patronize his store. While most tuxedo shops not only sold but also rented tuxedos, Fred decided not to offer rentals. "I want a clean business," he said, "I don't want to mess with all those dirty rental garments that people bring back."

Opportunistically, Fred heard of a major manufacturer anxious to close out last year's lines. He acquired 1,000 brand new, first quality tuxedos, in a range of styles, colors, and sizes for $100 each. The regular wholesale price of these tuxedos was $200 each. He set his initial retail price at $200 and told his friends to spread the word; he was "selling tuxedos at cost." After several months, Fred began to tire of the tuxedo business and started to feel the urge "to get back on the road with a band." He began marking down tuxedos and eventually sold the remaining ones at his cost and closed the store. His sales and reductions were:

		Reductions	Sales
600 tuxedos	sold at the original retail of $200	$ 0	$120,000
200 tuxedos	marked down $25 and sold for $175	5,000	35,000
100 tuxedos	marked down $50 and sold for $150	5,000	15,000
50 tuxedos	marked down $75 and sold for $125	3,750	6,250
28 tuxedos	marked down $100 and sold for $100	2,800	2,800
20 tuxedos	sold to musicians who were given a special "25% off" discount. These sold for $150.	1,000	3,000
	2 store employees were allowed to buy a tuxedo at cost. These sold for $100.	200	200
Totals		$17,750	$182,250

Thus, *total sales* of Fred Mullan's store were $182,250. *Reductions* totaled $17,750, comprising:

Markdowns	$16,550
Special customer discounts	1,000
Employee discounts	200
Total	$17,750

The *initial markup* taken by Fred in originally pricing his merchandise was 50%.

$$\frac{\text{Original retail} - \text{Billed cost}}{\text{Original retail}} = \frac{\$200 - \$100}{\$200} = 50\%$$

As all the merchandise was originally priced at the same markup, the *cumulative markup* was also 50%.

The total billed cost of the merchandise was $100,000. (This represents 1,000 tuxedos purchased for $100 each.)

Thus the store's *maintained markup was*:

Sales	$182,250
Billed cost of goods sold	100,000
Maintained markup	$ 82,250

The manufacturer of the tuxedos offered Fred a cash discount of 6% of the billed cost of the merchandise if he paid for the tuxedos within 10 days of the invoice date. Fred took advantage of this offer and before the end of the 10-day period, he sent the manufacturer a check for $94,000.

As a service to customers who purchased tuxedos, Fred offered free tailoring of the trousers. He had hired a tailor to hem the trousers, and Fred paid the tailor a fixed sum per job for this work. For other alterations, the tailor charged customers directly. Fred determined that he had incurred a total cost for alterations of $3,645.

So the actual total cost of goods sold was:

Billed cost	$100,000
Minus cash discounts	(6,000)
Plus alteration costs	3,645
Total net cost of goods sold	$ 97,645

We can now determine the *gross margin* generated by Fred in the operation of the tuxedo store:

Sales	$182,250
Net cost of goods sold	97,645
Gross margin	$ 84,605

As we have learned, retailers calculate percentages in analyzing operating results. Let's now calculate the maintained markup and the gross margin percentages:

$$\text{Maintained markup \%} = \frac{\text{Sales} - \text{Billed cost of goods sold}}{\text{Sales}} = \frac{\$82,250}{\$182,250}$$

$$= 45.13\%$$

$$\text{Gross margin \%} = \frac{\text{Sales} - \text{Net cost of goods sold}}{\text{Sales}} = \frac{\$84,605}{\$182,250} = 46.42\%$$

For Fred's operation, the gross margin was greater than the maintained markup. Why was this so? Because the cash discount exceeded the alteration costs. The cash discount of $6,000, reduced the cost of goods more than the alteration costs of $3,645 increased the cost of goods. The net effect of these two factors was a reduction in the actual cost of the goods. Consequently, the true difference between what the goods cost and what they were sold for, the gross margin, was somewhat greater than the maintained markup that was based only on the billed cost of goods.

Retailers Calculate Gross Margin Often

The example and calculations presented above were based on an historical analysis. The figures were gathered and the numbers determined after the sales had taken place. In fact, these figures were organized after the business ceased. In practice, retailers periodically calculate the gross margin. All retailers, of course, must make annual calculations for income tax purposes. But for control purposes, many will calculate the gross margin on a quarterly, monthly, and some on a weekly basis. It is a key measure, along with sales, of how well a retailer is doing.

Accurate determination of the cost of goods sold requires a physical inventory. In the case of Fred's Tuxedo Shop, the inventory on hand when the store was closed was zero. All the tuxedos had been sold. However, in the normal course of retailing there is inventory on hand to be counted to determine the cost of what was sold. But retailers do not take a physical inventory every time that the gross margin is calculated. One of the major results of the physical inventory is the determination of shortages. When retailers calculate the gross margin without taking an actual physical inventory, they estimate the shortages based upon historical experience. Inaccurate estimates are corrected when the next physical inventory is taken. In Chapter 8 we will learn how this is done.

A major purpose for determining the gross margin is to compare the result with what was planned. To plan and set objectives for such measures as gross margin, retail executives must quickly figure the interrelationship among several factors. These can be readily determined by use of relationships now to be introduced.

Using the Cost of Reductions Percentage to Calculate Maintained Markup

Recall that in our analysis of Fred's Tuxedo Shop we calculated the initial markup to be 50%. After determining the sales and allowing for the markdowns, special customer discounts, and employee discounts, we calculated the maintained markup to be 45.13%. But by simply subtracting the **cost of the reductions** percentage from the initial markup percentage, we can determine the maintained markup.

To calculate the cost of the reductions percentage, we must first determine the reductions as a percentage of sales. Let's use the figure from Fred's Tuxedo Shop:

$$\text{Markdown percentage} = \frac{\$16,550}{\$182,250} = 9.08\% \text{ sales}$$

$$\text{Special customer discounts percentage} = \frac{\$1,000}{\$182,250} = .55\% \text{ sales}$$

$$\text{Employee discounts percentage} = \frac{\$200}{\$182,250} = \underline{.11\%} \text{ sales}$$

$$\text{Total reductions percentage} = \frac{\$17,750}{\$182,250} = 9.74\% \text{ sales}$$

So, the reductions are 9.74% of sales. Now to get the cost of the reductions percentage we multiply reductions as a percentage of sales by the cost complement of the initial markup percentage. (Remember that the cost complement of the initial markup percentage is 100% minus the initial markup percentage). As the initial markup for Fred's Tuxedo Shop is 50%, the cost complement is 50%.

Therefore, the cost of the reductions would be:

$$\text{Cost of reductions \%} = \text{Reductions \%} \times \text{Cost complement \%}$$

$$\text{Cost of reductions \%} = 9.74\% \times 50\% = 4.87\%$$

Now by subtracting the cost of the reductions percentage from the initial markup percentage we get the maintained markup percentage:

$$\text{Maintained markup \%} = \text{Initial markup \%} - \text{Cost of the reductions \%}$$

$$\text{Maintained markup \%} = 50\% - 4.87\% = 45.13\%$$

This of course agrees with the result obtained by accounting for each markdown, special customer discount, and employee discount experienced by Fred in operating the store.

Applying the Cost of the Reductions Percentage

The practical application of this calculation can be readily understood by assuming that Fred was not going out of business but instead planning for his next period of operation. Suppose that were the case and Fred said, "I'm pleased with my results for last period, but I think I've really been lucky in not having any shortages. One of these days I'm afraid someone is going to walk out of the store with a tux when no one's looking. I know I've heard about it happening. Suppose my shortages were to run 1% of sales, what would that do to my maintained markup?"

If we assume that shortages would be 1% of sales, and that the other reductions would remain the same, we could recalculate the maintained markup as follows:

New total reductions = 9.74% (former total) + 1% (shortages) = 10.74%

Cost of reductions % = Reductions % $\times$ Cost complement %

Cost of reductions = 10.74% $\times$ 50% = 5.37%

$$\text{Maintain markup} = \text{Initial markup \%} - \text{Cost of reductions \%}$$
$$= 50\% - 5.37\% = 44.63\%$$

Recalculating the Initial Markup

But suppose Fred then said, "I'd like to shoot for the same maintained markup I generated last period, but allow in my initial markup for shortages. What if shortages were 1% of sales and the other reductions percentages were the same as last period. What would my initial markup have to be?"

Because we are recalculating the initial markup, we cannot simply use the cost of reductions calculated above and add it to the maintained markup. That cost of reductions of 5.37% was calculated based upon an initial markup of 50%. We are now changing the initial markup. So we must recalculate the initial markup as follows:

$$\text{Initial markup} = \frac{\text{Maintained markup \% + Reductions \%}}{100\% + \text{Reductions \%}}$$

$$= \frac{45.13\% + 10.74\%}{100\% + 10.74\%}$$

$$= \frac{55.87\%}{110.74\%}$$

$$= 50.45\%$$

Now let's check our answer. Does an initial markup of 50.45% with total reductions of 10.74%, result in a maintained markup of 45.13%, Fred's objective?

$$\text{Maintained markup \%} = \text{Initial markup \%} - \text{Cost of reductions \%}$$

$$= 50.45\% - (10.74\% \times 49.55\%)$$

$$= 50.45\% - 5.32\%$$

$$= 45.13\%$$

It checks!!!

Problems

6–1. A hobby shop had sales and reductions for the last quarter as follows: total sales $34,000; markdowns $2,500; senior citizen discounts $200; shortages $135; and employee discounts $18. The billed cost of goods sold was

$17,680. There were no alteration costs; and cash discounts totaled $300. What was the maintained markup? What was the gross margin?

6–2. A dress shop had total sales of $25,000 for the last month. The billed cost of goods sold was $12,000. Cash discounts totaled $1,500 and alteration costs were $100. Calculate the maintained markup and the gross margin.

6–3. A shoe department with an initial markup of 49.5% had total reductions of 12%. What maintained markup was generated in the department?

6–4. A fabric department had the following figures: markdowns 9%; employee discounts 2%; and shortages 1%. The initial markup in the department was 52%. What was the maintained markup?

6–5.   A toy store generated a maintained markup of 44.5%. If markdowns totaled
       10%, employee discounts were 2%, and shortages were 2.5%, what was the
       initial markup?

Relationship between Maintained Markup and Gross Margin

When we calculated the gross margin for Fred's Tuxedo Shop in dollars, we subtracted the cash discounts from the billed cost of goods sold, and added the alteration costs to the billed cost of goods sold. Our calculation was as follows:

Billed cost	$100,000
Minus cash discounts	(6,000)
Plus alteration costs	3,645
Total net cost of goods sold	$ 97,645

$$\text{Gross margin} = \text{Sales} - \text{Net cost of goods sold}$$
$$= \$182,250 - \$97,645$$
$$= \$84,605$$

Instead of subtracting the cash discounts from the billed cost of goods sold, and adding the alteration costs, we could add the cash discounts to the maintained markup and subtract the alteration costs. Still using Fred's figures:

Maintained markup ($82,250) + Cash discounts ($6,000)

$$- \text{Alteration costs (\$3,645)} = \text{Gross margin (\$84,605)}$$

It should be evident that the net effect of subtracting a given amount from the cost of goods has the same impact as adding it to the maintained markup. Similarly, adding a given amount to the cost of goods sold has the same effect as subtracting it from the maintained markup. We may now express these relationships as follows:

Gross margin = Maintained markup + Cash discounts − Alteration costs

and correspondingly,

Maintained markup = Gross margin − Cash discounts + Alteration costs

Once again, we can use percentages and apply the relationships to Fred's Tuxedo Shop:

Cash discounts $6,000 ÷ Sales ($182,250) = 3.29% sales

Alteration costs $3,645 ÷ Sales ($182,250) = 2% sales

So:

Gross margin = Maintained markup + Cash discounts − Alteration costs

$$= 45.13\% + 3.29\% - 2\%$$

$$= 46.42\%$$

This checks with the gross margin percentage calculated earlier by using dollar figures.

Similarly, we can convert from gross margin to maintained markup:

$$\text{Maintained markup} = \text{Gross margin} - \text{Cash discounts} + \text{Alteration Costs}$$
$$= 46.42\% - 3.29\% + 2\%$$
$$= 45.13\%$$

This answer agrees with the results obtained by using dollar figures and also by applying the cost of the reductions shortcut.

Applying the Maintained Markup to Gross Margin Relationship

While in the above calculations we used percentages to check on the results we had figured using dollars, the major benefit of understanding these relationships is the ease with which one can move between the two measures. Suppose Fred had asked us, "What will happen to my gross margin, if I provide free alterations of all types to my customers? I know from what the tailor charged them that my alteration costs would just about double to 4%."

The impact of a doubling of alteration costs would be:

$$\text{Gross margin} = \text{Maintained markup} + \text{Cash discounts} - \text{Alteration costs}$$
$$= 45.13\% + 3.29 - 4\%$$
$$= 44.42\%$$

"Now suppose that, in addition, I didn't take the cash discounts. What would my gross margin be then?" Fred inquired.

$$\text{Gross margin} = \text{Maintained markup} + \text{Cash discounts} - \text{Alteration costs}$$
$$= 45.13\% + 0\% - 4\%$$
$$= 41.13\%$$

The reduction in gross margin would be:

$$\text{Old gross margin } (46.42\%) - \text{New gross margin } (41.13\%) = 5.29\%$$

Multiplying this reduction by the sales reveals the dollars of gross margin that would be lost because of these two changes in policy:

$$\text{Sales } (\$182,250) \times \text{Gross margin lost } (5.28\%) = \$9,641$$

Some "What If" Calculations Useful in Planning

We can now quickly make calculations that incorporate these relationships among initial markup, maintained markup, and the gross margin. For example, a department selling sportswear had an initial markup of 48%. If markdowns were 12%, employee discounts 4%, shortages 1.5%, cash discounts 4%, and there were no alteration costs, what would the maintained markup and the gross margin be?

$$\text{Maintained markup \%} = \text{Initial markup \%} - \text{Cost of reductions \%}$$
$$= 48\% - [(12\% + 4\% + 1.5\%) \times 52\%]$$
$$= 48\% - (17.5\% \times 52\%)$$
$$= 48\% - 9.1\%$$
$$= 38.9\%$$

$$\text{Gross margin \%} = \text{Maintained markup \%} + \text{Cash discounts \%}$$
$$= 38.9\% + 4\%$$
$$= 42.9\%$$

Similarly, if the above department desired a gross margin of 40%, we could determine what the initial markup had to be, assuming that the other values were as originally estimated.

$$\text{Maintained markup \%} = \text{Gross margin \%} - \text{Cash discount \%}$$

$$= 40\% - 4\%$$

$$= 36\%$$

$$\text{Initial markup \%} = \frac{\text{Maintained markup \%} + \text{Reductions \%}}{100\% + \text{Reductions \%}}$$

$$= \frac{36\% + 17.5\%}{100\% + 17.5\%}$$

$$= \frac{53.5\%}{117.5\%}$$

$$= 45.53\%$$

These calculations are especially useful to managers planning store or department operations and objectives. We will apply these again in Chapter 9 when we develop a merchandise budget.

Problems

6–6. A store had a maintained markup of 35%, cash discounts of 6%, and alteration costs of 3%. What was the gross margin?

6–7. Calculate the maintained markup for a department with a gross margin of 40%, alteration costs of 2%, and cash discounts of 5%.

6–8. In a sporting goods department the initial markup was 48%. Markdowns were 11%, special customer discounts were 3%, and employee discounts were 5%. There were no alteration costs or cash discounts. What was the maintained markup? The gross margin?

6–9. A men's shop with an initial markup of 52% had markdowns of 15%, employee discounts of 2.5%, special customer discounts of 4%, shortages of 1.5%, cash discounts of 5%, and alteration costs of 7.5%. What was the gross margin? What was the maintained markup?

6–10. What would the initial markup be for a department with the following figures: gross margin 42%; cash discounts 3%; markdowns 12%; shortages 3%; employee discounts 2%; and alteration costs 3.5%? What percentage of the potential dollar gross margin is lost because of reductions?

How It All Ties Together

Recall that when we recalculated Fred's initial markup to allow for shortages, we used the following relationship:

$$\text{Initial markup \%} = \frac{\text{Maintained markup \% + Reductions \%}}{100\% + \text{Reductions \%}}$$

We also know that:

$$\text{Maintained markup \%} = \text{Gross margin \%} - \text{Cash discounts \%} + \text{Alteration costs \%}.$$

Furthermore, we know that:

$$\text{Gross margin \%} = \text{Expenses \%} + \text{Profits \%}.$$

Now by substituting (Gross margin % − Cash discount % + Alteration costs %) for Maintained Markup %; and then substituting (Expenses % + Profits %) for Gross margin %, we can state:

$$\text{Initial markup \%} = \frac{\text{Expenses \% + Profit \% − Cash discounts \%}}{100\% + \text{Reductions \%}} \frac{+ \text{ Alteration costs \% + Reductions \%}}{}$$

This, of course, is the relationship that we learned in Chapter 3 to determine the initial markup percentage. We have now "come full circle" and should be able to confidently perform and understand relationships among: profits, expenses, reductions, initial markups, maintained markups, and gross margins. Let's try an integrated example.

The following data were available for a clothing store:

Profit	5%
Expenses	36
Markdowns	14
Employee discounts	3
Senior citizen discounts	2
Cash discounts	5
Alteration costs	3
Shortages	2

What are the initial markup percentage, the maintained markup percentage, and the gross margin percentage?

To determine the initial markup percentage:

$$\text{Initial markup \%} = \frac{\text{Expenses \% + Profit \% + Reductions \%}}{100\% + \text{Reductions \%}} \frac{- \text{ Cash discounts \% + Alteration costs\%}}{}$$

$$= \frac{36\% + 5\% + (14\% + 3\% + 2\% + 2\%) - 5\% + 3\%}{100\% + 21\%}$$

$$= \frac{60\%}{121\%}$$

$$= 49.59\%$$

The maintained markup would be the initial markup percentage minus the cost of the reductions percentage:

$$\text{Maintained markup \%} = 49.59\% - (21\% \times 50.41\%)$$

$$= 49.59\% - 10.59\%$$

$$= 39\%$$

The gross margin percentage would be the maintained markup percentage plus the cash discounts percentage minus the alteration costs percentage:

$$\text{Gross margin \%} = 39\% + 5\% - 3\% = 41\%$$

This, of course, checks with the determination of the gross margin percentage obtained by adding the expenses percentage and the profit percentage:

$$\text{Gross margin \%} = \text{Expense \% + Profit \%}$$

$$= 36\% + 5\%$$

$$= 41\%$$

To check even further, let's work back from the gross margin to the maintained markup by subtracting the cash discounts and adding the alteration costs:

$$\text{Maintained markup} = 41\% - 5\% + 3\% = 39\%$$

Now let's recalculate the initial markup:

$$\text{Initial markup \%} = \frac{\text{Maintained markup \% + Reductions \%}}{100\% + \text{Reductions}}$$

$$= \frac{39\% + 21\%}{121\%}$$

$$= \frac{60\%}{121\%}$$

$$= 49.59\%$$

It all ties together!

Problems

6–11. Calculate the initial markup percentage, the maintained markup percentage and the gross margin percentage from the following data: markdowns 16%; cash discounts 3%; alteration costs 3.4%; employee discounts 2%; expenses 32%; profit 3%; and shortages 3%.

6–12.   A video shop had the following operating figures: expenses 30%; mark-downs 12%; employee discounts 3%; profits 7% and shortages 3%. There were no cash discounts or alteration costs. Calculate the initial markup per-centage, the maintained markup percentage, and the gross margin percentage.

6–13.   A bicycle shop had expenses of 29%. Markdowns were 12%; alteration costs for assembling bicycles were 6%; shortages were 1.5%; and there were no cash discounts or employee discounts. The initial markup was 39%. What were the maintained markup percentage, and the gross margin per-centage? What was the profit percentage?

6–14. If a department has an initial markup of 50%; cash discounts of 5%; alteration costs of 2%; shortages of 1%; no employee or special customer discounts; and a gross margin of 45%; what is the markdown percentage?

6–15. A new fishing tackle and supplies shop had markdowns of 15%; employee discounts of 2%; senior citizen discounts of 2%; shortages of 1%; expenses of 30%; and an operating loss of 5%. There were no cash discounts or alteration costs. What was the initial markup of the shop?

Mellow Music Store Applications

John and Julie Martin were anxious to know how well they were doing operating their new store. They decided to examine results for the first four weeks. Sales had been $10,400. For each customer transaction, a written sales slip was prepared. This provided a record of every item sold. On the price tickets that were attached to each item of merchandise, along with the retail price, the cost had been indicated in code. Prepriced merchandise also had a coded sticker.

The code presented the cost with the numbers reversed, preceded by 10. Thus an item that cost $195 was coded 10591. An item that cost $2.50 was coded 1005.2. Because the code was entered on the sales slips, by summing the sales slips, John and Julie were able to determine the cost of goods sold. It was $6,221. They then calculated the maintained markup:

Sales	$10,400	
Cost of goods sold	6,221	
Maintained markup	$ 4,179,	(40.18%)

John and Julie had also maintained careful records of all markdowns. These totaled $1,842. There had been no employee discounts, but John had given special discounts amounting to a total of $200 to professional musicians. With these figures, they calculated the maintained markup using the cost of the reductions method as follows:

$$\text{Reductions \%} = \frac{\text{Markdown + Special customer discounts}}{\text{Sales}}$$

(Note: No employee discounts or shortages)

$$\text{Reductions \%} = \frac{\$1,842 + \$200}{\$10,400}$$

$$= \frac{\$2,042}{\$10,400}$$

$$= 19.63\%$$

$$\text{Maintained markup \%} = \text{Initial markup \%} - \text{Cost of reductions \%}$$

$$= 50\% - (19.63\% \times 50\%)$$

$$= 50\% - 9.82\%$$

$$= 40.18\%$$

John was pleased that the maintained markup he had calculated both ways agreed. There had been no cash discounts offered by suppliers. John had hired a piano tuner to tune three of the pianos in the store. For one that was later sold, he provided a free in-home tuning after the piano had been delivered to the customer's home. John thought that the cost of the tunings ($60) should be applied to the piano that had been sold. He then determined the gross margin earned during the first four weeks of operation.

$$\text{Gross margin \%} = \text{Maintained markup} - \text{Alteration costs}$$

(Note: No cash discounts)

$$\text{Gross margin} = \$4,179 - \$60$$

$$= \$4,119$$

$$\text{Gross margin \%} = \frac{\$ \text{ gross margin}}{\$ \text{ sales}}$$

$$= \frac{\$4,119}{\$10,400}$$

$$= 39.61\%$$

He compared the result to the gross margin projected from the figures estimated for the store's first year of operation:

$$\text{Gross margin} = \text{Expenses} + \text{Profit}$$

$$= \$50,000 + \$15,000$$

$$= \$65,000$$

$$\text{Gross margin \%} = \frac{\$ \text{ gross margin}}{\$ \text{ sales}}$$

$$= \frac{\$65,000}{\$165,000}$$

$$= 41.67\%$$

John was very concerned that the gross margin was less than targeted. He decided to compare the reductions for the first four weeks with those projected:

	First Year Estimates	Results First Four Weeks
Sales	$156,000	$10,400
Reductions	13,000	2,042
Reductions percentage	8.33%	19.63%

As most of the reductions were markdowns, John concluded, "I guess we are selling too much merchandise at sale prices. We've got to sell a higher proportion of the regularly priced goods."

On the next visit to the store of Mr. James Flynn, John and Julie showed him the figures. He shared their disappointment, but reminded them that it often took a while to get a new store established. "You have to run these specials to get people to try your store. Initially, markdown sales represent a higher proportion of total sales, but it should taper off."

Mr. Flynn asked if John and Julie had taken inventory in order to determine the cost of goods sold. John explained his use of the cost codes and sales slips to determine the cost of goods sold. Mr. Flynn pointed out, "I hope you realize your system does not allow for shortages. You may not have had any, but the only way to really tell is by taking a careful inventory."

John agreed and said that at the end of the first quarter (13 weeks) an inventory would be taken. "But I wonder if we should increase advertising to try to increase sales?"

Original plans called for $10,000 in advertising for the year (6.41% of sales). John decided to recalculate the initial markup incorporating an increase in advertising to 8.41% and an increase in reductions to 10%. Profits, alteration costs, and other expenses would be kept at planned levels.

John figured as follows:

Expenses at former level	32.05%	($50,000 ÷ $156,000)
Increase	2.0	
Total expenses	34.05%	

$$\text{Profit } \% = \frac{\$15,000}{\$156,000} = 9.61\%$$

$$\text{Alteration costs } \% = \frac{\$3,000}{\$156,000} = 1.92\%$$

$$\text{Gross margin } \% = \text{Expenses } \% + \text{Profit } \%$$

$$\text{Gross margin } = 34.05\% + 9.61\%$$

$$= 43.66\%$$

$$\text{Maintained markup } \% = \text{Gross margin } \% + \text{Alteration costs } \% \\ - \text{Cash discounts } \%$$

$$\text{Maintained markup } = 43.66\% + 1.92\% - 0\%$$

$$= 45.58\%$$

$$\text{Initial markup } \% = \frac{\text{Maintained markup } \% + \text{Reductions } \%}{100\% + \text{Reductions } \%}$$

$$\text{Initial markup } = \frac{45.58\% + 10\%}{110\%}$$

$$= \frac{55.58\%}{110\%}$$

$$= 50.53\%$$

"Wow," John said, "That's just what our cumulative markup was. I think we'll be OK, if we can increase our sales at regular prices. I hope a little extra advertising helps."

Review Problems

6–1R. What were the maintained markup and the gross margin in dollars and percentages of a department with these results: sales $125,000; billed cost of goods sold $65,000; alteration costs $2,000; and cash discounts $7,000?

6–2R. A jewelry store had an initial markup of 52.5%. Reductions totaled 18.5%. There were no cash discounts or alteration costs. What were the maintained markup percentage and the gross margin percentage?

6–3R. The small appliance department had markdowns of 18%. Shortages were 2% and employee discounts 5%. If the maintained markup was 40%, what was the initial markup percentage?

6–4R. Calculate the maintained markup percentage for a store with these results: initial markup 46%; markdowns 16%; employee discounts 6%; senior citizen discounts 4%; shortages 2%; alteration costs 3%; and cash discounts 5%.

6–5R. A millinery department had markdowns of 20%; shortages of 1%; cash discounts of 5%; and an initial markup of 54%. What was the gross margin percentage?

6–6R. The Young Men's Shop had markdowns of 17.5%; shortages of 2.5%; alteration costs of 4%; cash discounts of 6%; and employee discounts of 5%. If the initial markup was 50%, what were the maintained markup percentage and the gross margin percentage?

6–7R. Calculate the profit percentage of a garden shop with the following figures: initial markup 48%; markdowns 16%; discounts to special classes of customers 2.5%; shortages 2%; employee discounts 3%; and expenses 32%. There were no cash discounts or alteration expenses.

6–8R. A young women's boutique had markdowns of 17%; employee discounts of 3%; expenses of 30%; shortages of 3%; cash discounts of 6%; alteration costs of 2%; and profits of 6%. What were the initial markup percentage, the maintained markup percentage, and the gross margin percentage?

6–9R. What are the markdowns in a T-shirt shop with the following figures: initial markup 44%; cash discounts 4%; employee discounts 5%; gross margin 40%; and shortages 2%?

6–10R. A store with total sales of $250,000 experienced an operating loss of $10,000. Cash discounts were 4% of sales and alteration costs 2.5% of sales. Operating expenses were $75,000. What was the gross margin percentage? The maintained markup percentage?

CHAPTER 7

Operating Profit, Expenses and Contribution

Earlier chapters have occasionally referred, in simplified form, to the components of a retail operating statement, or income statement. Traditionally also called a *profit and loss* statement, this report is the most important summary presentation of the achievements of a retail unit. It reveals whether all the activity involved in operating a company, a store, or a department, during a particular period of time has been profitable. We will start with the simplest form of operating statement and then gradually increase the amount of detail.

Basic Components of a Retail Operating Statement

Table 7–1 presents what we might call a "skeleton statement." It is just bare bones! But it provides the framework for our understanding of a fully developed statement.

Table 7–1 Skeleton Operating Statement

Sales	$100,000
Cost of goods sold	60,000
Gross margin	40,000
Expenses	35,000
Profit	$ 5,000

Table 7–1 presents a simple, logical story. The store sold $100,000 worth of goods. Those goods cost the store $60,000. The difference between what the store paid for the goods and what it sold them for, the gross margin, was $40,000. Expenses of $35,000 were incurred in operating the store. Remaining was a profit of $5,000.

As a way of helping yourself remember the relationships, imagine the $100,000 coming into a big cash register in the store. Then picture $60,000 being sent to the suppliers of the goods sold; $35,000 being given to those who provided the expenses; and the remaining $5,000 being deposited in the owner's bank account. Keep this model in mind as we examine each component in more detail.

How Net Sales Differ from Gross Sales

The sales entered on Table 7–1 are more accurately labeled *net sales*. They are net of customer *returns* and the *allowances* to customers. A return would represent a refund of the retail purchase price granted to a customer who decided for some reason to bring back merchandise previously purchased. For example, a customer purchases a dress for $100. Two days later the customer returns the dress to the store and is given a refund of $100. The refund is recorded as a *return*.

An allowance would represent a partial refund granted after purchase to a customer dissatisfied with a product. For example, a customer buys a chair for $300 and has it delivered home. Upon inspection of the chair after delivery, the customer discovers a slight scratch that occurred during the delivery. The customer complains to the store, which offers a $25 refund if the customer will keep the chair. The customer accepts the $25 refund. It is recorded as an *allowance*.[1]

The return of $100 and the allowance of $25 were originally reported as part of sales. Accordingly, retailers have two classifications of sales as indicated in Table 7–2.

Table 7–2 Sales Part of Operating Statement

Gross sales	$112,500
Returns and allowances	12,500
Net sales	$100,000

The *gross sales* would include all sales transactions for a given period of time. Every sale punched into a cash register, entered into a point-of-sale terminal, written up on a sales slip, or processed as a charge slip, would be included in gross sales. *Net sales* would, therefore, be net of any returns and allowances.

At this point, we should become aware of one exception to the general rule that retailers use net sales as the base for percentage calculations. *The returns and allowances percentage is based on gross sales.* So, for the data presented in Table 7–2, the returns and allowances percentage would be:

$$\text{Returns and allowances percentage} = \frac{\text{Returns and allowances}}{\text{Gross sales}} = \frac{\$12,500}{\$112,500}$$
$$= 11.1\%$$

The Net Cost of Goods Sold

The cost of goods sold figure entered in Table 7–1 is also more precisely labeled as *net cost of goods sold.*

In the summary to Chapter 6, we saw that John and Julie Martin kept track of each item they sold. From codes placed on the merchandise, they determined the cost of each item sold and, thereby, figured the total cost of goods sold. This procedure is possible in a small volume store. In the typical retailing operation, however, the cost of goods sold is determined by a process of deduction based on inventories.

Retailers have inventory on hand at the beginning of a period of business; they purchase merchandise during the period; and they usually have inventory on hand at the end of the period. There may also be cash discounts available from vendors and alteration costs, as we learned in Chapter 6. Furthermore, just as a customer may return merchandise to a store, a store may return merchandise to its suppliers. Also, a supplier may grant a store an allowance for merchandise not fully satisfactory. Table 7–3 indicates how these elements are related.

At the beginning of the period reported in Table 7–3, there was an inventory on hand of $32,000. Merchandise that cost $56,000 was purchased from suppliers, but returns to suppliers and allowances granted by suppliers totaled $1,000. Thus, the net cost of the purchases was $55,000. Transportation costs of $3,000 were incurred in having the purchases shipped to the store, so the total cost of the purchases was $58,000.

During the period, a total of $90,000 worth of merchandise was available for sale, consisting of the opening inventory and the purchases. We have labeled this amount "total merchandise handled," but as indicated in parenthesis it is sometimes labeled "goods available for sale." At the end of the period, merchandise that cost

---

[1]This transaction would also be recorded as a markdown of $25.

Table 7–3 Cost of Goods Sold Part of Operating Statement

Opening inventory		$32,000
Gross purchases	$56,000	
Less: Returns and allowances	1,000	
Net purchases		55,000
Plus: Transportation costs		3,000
Total purchases		58,000
Total merchandise handled (or goods available for sale)		90,000
Ending inventory		29,000
Gross cost of goods sold		61,000
Less: Cash discounts on purchases		4,000
Plus: Net alteration costs		3,000
Net cost of goods sold		$60,000

$29,000 was still in inventory. By subtracting this from the $90,000 available, we determine that the cost of goods sold was $61,000. This amount has been labeled "gross cost of goods sold" because there were cash discounts and alteration costs. Had there been no cash discounts or alteration costs, the $61,000 figure would represent the net cost of goods sold. However, the retail operation presented in Table 7–3 took cash discounts of $4,000 on purchases and incurred net alteration costs of $3,000. Thus, the actual, or final, or *net cost of goods sold* was $60,000.

Note the internal logic of determining the cost of goods sold in Table 7–3. If you started with a certain amount of merchandise on hand, added more via purchases, then subtracted what was left, the difference is what was sold. Of course this assumes that none "walked out the door," or was shoplifted or damaged. There is a method for determining accurately these *shortage* amounts. The arithmetical procedure is presented in Chapter 8. The effect of any shortage is to increase the cost of goods sold. The retailer had to pay for the goods involved, but received no revenue from them.

Problems

7–1. A store with expenses of $57,000 had a loss of $2,000. What was the store's gross margin?

7–2. The returns and allowances were $15,000 in a store with net sales of $150,000. What were the gross sales?

7–3. A department had an opening inventory of $88,000; a closing inventory of $82,000; and total purchases of $102,000. What was the cost of goods sold?

7–4. From the following data, develop a retail operating statement: profit $2,000; purchases $36,000; gross sales $52,000; closing inventory $34,000; customer returns and allowances $2,000; and beginning inventory $28,000.

7–5. From the following data, determine the net cost of goods sold: cash discounts on purchases $1,200; transportation costs $900; ending inventory $8,700; returns to suppliers $250; alteration costs $900; allowances from suppliers $50; opening inventory $9,600; and gross purchases $16,800.

Expenses for a Single Store

The "skeleton statement" in Table 7–1 reported expenses of $35,000. This part of the operating statement is where the widest variation in reporting format is encountered. Prior to this point in the statement, there is little room for differences. Sales are basically sales, and costs of goods are costs of goods. But there are all kinds of expenses and different ways of classifying and accounting for them. We will now discuss these differences. The magnitude of expenses has direct impact on the amount of profit. Most retail managers are at some point evaluated on the basis of the profit that is generated. Thus, it is very important to understand how the classification and determination of expenses influence that profit.

Let's start with the simplest situation to understand and assume that the figures in Table 7–1 represent a small retail store owned and operated by an individual who has no other stores. For this store, expenses might be classified as presented in Table 7–4.

Table 7–4 Operating Expenses of Single Store

Rent	$ 8,500
Utilities	2,500
Advertising	3,500
Owner's salary	10,500
Other payroll	5,000
Insurance	1,500
Supplies	1,000
Depreciation	1,800
Bad debts	200
All other	500
Total	$35,000

The expenses reported in Table 7–4 are readily identifiable. They represent costs clearly associated with operating the store. When we subtract these expenses from the gross margin generated by the store, there is no doubt that the balance, the $5,000 shown in Table 7–1, represents the profits made by the store (of course before income taxes) during the period under consideration.

When There Is More Than One Store

But let's suppose that the owner of this single store decides to open two additional stores. He now appoints managers for each of his three stores and becomes the president-general manager of the company. He does all the supervision of the three stores, all the buying, all the advertising, and uses a company station wagon to drive from store to store, occasionally bringing needed merchandise or supplies.

Should we assign his salary to the expenses of the individual stores? Surely if we did not, the profit of each store would be overstated. If we decide to charge each store for a portion of the owner's salary, how do we determine how much to charge? Should we keep track of each minute of the owner's time and divide the owner's salary on the basis of amount of time spent at each store? What about occasions when the owner is working at home, after closing time, on matters that affect one store? Should we include that? And what should be done when the owner is in one store, but making decisions that involve all three?

Perhaps the solution would be to have the owner record, for each minute, the particular store he was working on, indicating when two or three were involved for later resolution. How long do you think the owner would keep such a record?

If the owner was working on the advertising for the stores, should that portion of his salary be included in the advertising expense? When an advertisement in the newspaper is for all three stores, how should the cost be assigned? Divided in thirds? What if, because of location differences, the circulation of the paper is more favorable to one of the stores?

How should the cost associated with owning and operating the company station wagon be assigned to the stores?

We have raised enough questions to this point to focus on the problems involved in accurately determining the expenses of a retailing unit. Our example included only three stores with one major common expense, the president-general manager. Consider the problem from the point of view of a retail chain organization with hundreds of stores and a major headquarters facility and staff.

Expenses for Departments in a Large Store

This difficult problem is not only present when there is more than one store. It also exists in a large department store that may be organized into a hundred or more departments. How should the rent for the store be assigned to individual departments, each of whose manager or buyer will need to be evaluated? Is it accurate to assign the total rent for the store to each department on the basis of the department's space as a percentage of total space? Doesn't that penalize the department on the 10th floor and favor the one on the first floor? Clearly as retail space, the first floor would command a higher rent per unit of space than the 10th floor.

While additional examples could be considered, those presented indicate the difficulty involved in trying to determine accurately the *profit* generated by an individual retail subunit, be it a department or a store that is part of a larger retailing organization. Different companies take different approaches to the resolution of the problem. Some evaluate only on the basis of gross margin generated. Others relate expenses to subunits. It is important, when being evaluated on the basis of systems of allocation that attempt to assign common expenses to subunits, to understand precisely how these common expenses are being assigned. Because of the judgment or even arbitrariness that may be involved, a different method of expense assignment could result in a different level of profit. Managers being evaluated should understand the system well enough to be able to challenge methods that seem unreasonable.

A complete discussion of the different methods of expense assignment that might be employed is beyond the scope of this book. Major techniques and concepts will be introduced to provide a fundamental understanding.

Direct and Indirect Expenses

There are different ways of classifying expenses. Some analysts refer to *direct* and *indirect* expenses. Direct expenses would be those that unquestionably relate to the operation of a particular store or department. For example, the store or department manager's salary would be a direct expense. Indirect expenses would be those incurred by the company that could not be definitively related to a particular store or department, for example, the top management salaries of a large, multistore, retail company. Indirect expenses, if assigned to subunits, would be assigned on some basis of allocation, such as, a percentage of sales.

Controllable and Noncontrollable Expenses

A further complication is the element of control over expenses, and their classification as *controllable* or *noncontrollable* by the manager of the store or department being evaluated. Controllable expenses would be those that the responsible manager could be held accountable for. Wages of selling personnel and supplies might be included. Many direct expenses are also controllable expenses, but some are not. For example, rent which could be directly related to a particular store, might have been negotiated by the real estate department many months earlier, and not be under the control of the present store manager.

Utilities present another perplexing example. Clearly the cost of oil to heat the store and the cost of electricity to light it are direct expenses. Are they controllable? The rapid increase in the cost of oil during the mid to late 1970s and early 1980s was not controllable by retail store managers. And likewise, the decline in oil prices experienced during 1986 was beyond managers' control. Similarly, the corresponding impact on electric rates. On the other hand, store managers do have control on utility waste, for example, heating buildings hotter than needed, or using lights when not needed. But some analysts would argue that utility expenses should be considered noncontrollable because if store managers were held directly accountable, they would tend to minimize these expenses, limiting heat and light in the stores and making them less attractive to customers!

Some Retailers Use Contribution to Evaluate Performance

So, even though we can make some distinctions about expenses, obtaining agreement about how they should be handled is very difficult. Judgment is involved. As a consequence, different retail companies have approached the problem in different ways. Some do not attempt to use net operating profit (so-called bottom line) as the overall index of a subunit's performance and, correspondingly, of the subunit manager's performance. Instead, a measure called *contribution* is used. Contribution would be the difference between the gross margin and the limited expenses judged to be within the responsibility of the store or department manager. In some companies these might be the direct expenses, in other situations controllable expenses. It is likely that you will confront situations where the expenses used in calculating contribution seem to be a combination of what we have called direct and controllable, recognizing, of course, that some expenses like selling payroll are clearly both direct and controllable.

You may also see the term *controllable margin* used as a synonym for contribution. Given the difficulty in ascertaining just what is definitely controllable, we shall use the term *contribution*. It has the advantage of clearly suggesting what it is, the residual revenue that contributes to the balance of expenses and to profit. We must not forget that all expenses, no matter how categorized, must be met before a profit can be declared.

Some Simplifying Assumptions

In the examples that follow and for the problems to be done, we will make the following simplifying assumptions to resolve the dilemma of classifying expenses: (1) when calculating the contribution of a department in a multi-department store, we shall consider only the controllable expenses, those that the responsible manager can control; and (2) when calculating the contribution of a store that is a branch store, or unit in a chain, we shall consider only the direct expenses, those that can be attributed to the unit without any allocation. For the department we will calculate a *department contribution*, and for the store a *location contribution*.

A Departmental Contribution Statement

The following data are for the spring season, February 1 through July 31, for the silverware department of a large department store:

Sales	$100,000
Cost of goods sold	60,000
Buyer's salary	15,000
Clerical's salary	6,000
Buyer's travel	500
Sales personnel	7,000
Supplies	1,000
Departmental advertising	800

An operating statement focusing on departmental contribution is presented in Table 7–5 following our working assumption:

Table 7–5 Contribution Statement for Silverware Department

Sales	$100,000
Cost of goods sold	60,000
Gross margin	40,000

(continued)

Table 7–5 (continued)

Controllable expenses:		
Payroll		
Buyer	$15,000	
Clerical	6,000	
Sales	7,000	
		28,000
Buyer travel		500
Advertising		800
Supplies		1,000
Total		$ 30,300
Contribution		$ 9,700

As Table 7–5 indicates, the buyer is considered to have responsibility for expenses totaling $30,300. Subtracting these controllable expenses from the gross margin leaves a contribution of $9,700 to other expenses and to profit.

Allocating the Noncontrollable Expenses

As suggested earlier, in order to estimate the department's net profit the noncontrollable expenses would have to be allocated to the department. For illustrative purposes, we shall assume that these noncontrollable costs include rent, utilities, delivery, corporate management, and a catchall, "all other." We will assume that under the system used by the company, rent and utilities expenses are allocated to individual departments on the basis of amount of space occupied. Delivery is allocated on the basis of number packages delivered. Corporate management and all other are allocated on the basis of sales. Relevant figures are listed below:

	Company Expense	Basis of Allocation	Silverware Department Proportion
Rent	$400,000	Space occupied	.5% total space
Utilities	100,000	Space occupied	.5% total space
Delivery	100,000	Packages delivered	.3% of packages delivered
Corporate management	300,000	Sales	1% of total sales
All other	350,000	Sales	1% of total sales

Based on these figures, the amounts allocated to the silverware department would be as follows:

Rent allocation	.5% × $400,000 =	$2,000
Utilities allocation	.5% × 100,000 =	500
Delivery allocation	.3% × 100,000 =	300
Corporate management allocation	1% × 300,000 =	3,000
All other allocation	1% × 350,000 =	3,500
Total allocated expenses		$9,300

Under this system, the operating statement for the silverware department would be as presented in Table 7–6.

Table 7–6 Operating Statement for Silverware Department

Sales		$100,000
Cost of goods sold		60,000
Gross margin		40,000
Expenses:		
Controllable		
Payroll		
Buyer	$15,000	
Clerical	6,000	
Sales	7,000	
	28,000	
Buyer travel	500	
Advertising	800	
Supplies	1,000	
Total controllable expenses	30,300	
Allocated		
Rent	2,000	
Utilities	500	
Delivery	300	
Management	3,000	
All other	3,500	
Total allocated expenses	9,300	
Total expenses		$39,600
Operating profit		$ 400

A Location Contribution Statement

The following data are for the first quarter, February 1 through April 30, for a store located in Lakewood, operated by a large supermarket chain. The store advertises in the local newspaper and is the only store owned by the chain that is located within the circulation area of the newspaper.

Sales	$600,000	Rent	$10,000
Cost of goods sold	460,000	Snow removal	3,000
Store manager salary	10,000	Window washing	500
Department managers' salaries	8,000	Floor cleaning	500
Payroll	40,000	Repairs	1,000
Advertising	7,500	Music	100
Promotion	3,000	Supplies	7,000
Depreciation	4,000	All other	4,400
Utilities	3,000		

An operating statement focusing on the contribution of the Lakewood store is presented in Table 7–7.

As Table 7–7 indicates, the store at the Lakewood location generated a contribution of $38,000 to other company expenses and profit. Here we see that many more types of expenses can be clearly attributed to the particular location. In contrast, the silverware department in a larger, multidepartment store would have many more common expenses that would be shared with other departments. For example, the snow removal expenses at the location in Lakewood would be for that particular store. Snow removal for the department store that houses the silverware department would be a common expense for the entire store.

Table 7–7 Location Contribution Statement

Sales		$600,000
Cost of goods sold		460,000
Gross margin		140,000
Direct expenses:		
Managers	$18,000	
Other payroll	40,000	
Total salaries	58,000	
Rent	10,000	
Advertising and promotion	10,500	
Depreciation	4,000	
Utilities	3,000	
Supplies	7,000	
Snow removal	3,000	
Repairs	1,000	
Maintenance	1,000	
Music	100	
All other	4,400	
Total direct expenses		102,000
Location contribution		$ 38,000

Allocating Chainwide Expenses

Many companies would apply an allocated charge to the Lakewood store for common indirect and overhead expenses, including: warehousing, delivery, and central office (corporate management, buyers, personnel, advertising, promotion, public relations, and accounting departments). Such expenses are usually allocated on a percentage of total sales basis. Let's assume that the Lakewood store represented 2% of total company sales. If total indirect (overhead) expenses for the company were $1,500,000, then Lakewood would be allocated 2% or $30,000. The condensed operating statement for Lakewood is shown in Table 7–8.

Table 7–8 Condensed Operating Statement Lakewood Store

Sales		$600,000
Cost of goods sold		460,000
Gross margin		140,000
Expenses		
Direct location	$102,000	
Indirect allocated	30,000	
Total		132,000
Operating profit		$ 8,000

Evaluating Marginal Operations

We have recognized that judgment is needed in deciding which expenses are controllable and in developing the basis for allocating noncontrollable and indirect expenses. Likewise, judgment must be utilized in interpreting the operating profit that results. Sometimes after indirect expenses have been allocated, a department or store may appear to be just barely profitable or even unprofitable.

For example, Table 7–9 represents a condensed quarterly operating statement for store No. 19 in a chain of paint stores.

Table 7–9 indicates that store No. 19 had a quarterly loss of $10,000. But if we examine the contribution, we find that store No. 19 met all its direct location expenses and made a contribution of $10,000 to overhead and profit:

Gross margin		$100,000
Direct location expenses		90,000
Contribution		$ 10,000

Table 7–9 Condensed Operating Statement Store No. 19

Sales		$400,000
Cost of goods sold		300,000
Gross margin		100,000
Expenses		
Direct location	$90,000	
Indirect allocated	20,000	
Total		110,000
Operating profit (Loss)		($ 10,000)

When consideration is being given to closing a store or eliminating a department that is making a contribution to overhead and profit, but not covering all allocated expenses, a very careful analysis must be conducted. Would closing the department or store eliminate anything other than direct expenses? Usually one unit in a large organization has little or no impact on overhead and general office type expenses typically allocated. These activities must continue to be carried out for the remaining departments or stores. If the unit is making a contribution, it may be preferable to continue to operate it, while seeking ways to increase contribution. A marginal department in a department store may be desirable because it complements other departments, and customers expect it to be part of the overall assortment. A marginal store in a large chain may have an outstanding long-term lease liability.

One Further Complication

Remember that in the following problems the contribution calculated for a department, that is part of a larger departmentalized store, will be based on controllable expenses; the contribution calculated for a store that is part of a multistore chain will be based upon direct location expenses. These problems will not include an additional complication which you have probably thought of and of which you should be aware.

Refer back to the silverware department whose contribution we figured by including the buyer's salary and travel expenses as a controllable departmental expense. If the buyer was also responsible for silverware departments in other branch stores of the company, these expenses could not be applied only to one store. They would have to be allocated among the stores for which the buyer had responsibility along with other expenses common to all branch stores.

Problems

7–6. The following data were provided by the owner-manager of a small convenience store. It is the only store the proprietor operates. Prepare an operating statement.

Sales	$260,000
Cost of goods sold	161,200
Rent	22,100
Advertising and promotion	8,800
Manager's salary	27,000
Clerks' salaries	13,000
Supplies	2,500
Depreciation	4,000

(continued)

Accountant	$	500
Insurance		2,000
Utilities		9,100
All other		1,600

7–7. Prepare a departmental contribution statement for the notions department of a department store that had the following results:

Net sales	$80,000
Gross margin	40%
Markdowns	10,000
Buyer's salary	12,500
Buyer's travel	800
Customer returns and allowances	2,500
Departmental advertising	3,000
Salaries of salespeople	6,000
Supplies	800

7–8. Prepare a departmental operating statement for the toy department of a department store that allocated noncontrollable expenses to departments on a percentage of sales basis. Relevant figures for the department and the company were:

	Toys	*Company*
Net sales	$120,000	$18,000,000
Gross margin	33%	46%
Buyer salaries	25,000	1,500,000
Buyer travel	500	30,000
Customer returns and allowances	5,000	180,000
Advertising	7,000	720,000
Salespeople salaries	8,400	1,250,000
Depreciation		500,000
Management salaries		850,000
Warehouse		280,000
Interest		600,000
Occupancy		800,000
All other		1,000,000

7–9. Prepare a location contribution statement for store No. 231 that is part of a large discount department store chain. Store No. 231 had the following results:

Cost of goods sold	$3,500,000		
Departmental managers	50,000	Supplies	$48,000
Gross sales	5,008,500	Customer returns and	
Markdowns	450,000	allowances	8,500
Utilities	75,000	Maintenance	3,000
Store manager	45,000	Depreciation of	
Advertising	150,000	equipment	4,000
Clerk wages	350,000	Music	125
Rent	125,000	All other	18,000

7–10. Prepare an operating statement for store No. 451, a unit in a large chain of audio video electronics stores. Corporate headquarters allocated all nonlocation expenses on a percentage of sales basis. Relevant figures for the store and the company are as follows:

	Store No. 451	Company
Net sales	$900,000	$60,000,000
Gross margin	265,000	
Total store payroll	108,000	
Rent	35,000	
Supplies	7,200	
Utilities	15,000	
All other	18,000	

(continued)

	Store No. 451	*Company*
Advertising		3,000,000
Warehousing and logistics		750,000
General office		1,750,000

Natural and Functional Expenses

There is another facet of expense control in retailing with which students should be familiar. It applies elements of so-called expense center accounting. To this point the only bases for categorizing or classifying expenses that we have utilized have been direct versus indirect, and controllable versus noncontrollable.[2] We have used these classifications to illustrate calculations of the contributions of retail selling subunits, either departments or individual stores. It is obviously very important to determine whether a unit is contributing to common and/or overhead expenses and to company profits. The expenses we have been considering, such as payroll, rent, supplies, advertising, travel, and insurance, are labeled *natural* expenses. They refer to a particular kind or type of expenditure.

Retail companies engage in various support functions or specific duties, such as credit and accounts receivable management, personnel management, building operation and management, warehousing, and delivery. along with the fundamental tasks of buying and selling merchandise, and performing advertising and sales promotion activities. In a very large retail organization, these major functions, duties, tasks, and activities would be subdivided into a limited number of responsibilities and assigned to a manager. For example, within the category of advertising and sales promotion, there could be individual responsibility for media advertising,

---

[2]Fixed expense and variable expense classification and analysis are discussed in Chapter 11.

direct mail advertising, window display, in-store display, special events, and public relations. A large store such as Macy's that uses a big parade as a major promotional device, might even have a separate category for parades and give an executive that responsibility.

Each responsibility center is called a *function*. Then in order to effectively analyze and control expenses, the natural expenses would be classified by function. This would permit careful assessment of the cost of performing each function. A simplified hypothetical example is presented in Table 7–10.

Table 7–10 Hypothetical Example of Functional Expense Analysis

	Functional Expense Centers				
Natural Expense	*Advertising and Promotion*	*Building Operations*	*Warehousing and Transportation*	*Personnel*	*Credit*
Payroll					
Manager	$ 60,000	$ 48,000	$ 55,000	$ 40,000	$ 45,000
Other	100,000	120,000	200,000	110,000	115,000
Telephone	800	500	900	1,000	1,200
Office supplies	300	200	800	900	1,000
Vehicle supplies			2,000		
Rent		500,000			
Maintenance		50,000	20,000		
Bad debts					6,000

As Table 7–10 illustrates, the assignment of natural expenses to expense centers permits careful analysis of the cost of performing different functions. It permits comparisons with industry figures developed by trade associations and provides the basis for establishing objectives and budgets. Such an analysis would also enable management to consider, for example, the alternative of utilizing a major credit service, such as Visa or American Express, rather than operating the company's own credit program.

Table 7–11 lists natural expenses and expense centers usually associated with retail businesses.

Table 7–11 Typical Natural Expenses and Expense Centers for Retailers

Natural Expenses	*Expense Centers*
Payroll	Corporate management
Advertising	Real estate and equipment
Taxes	Accounting and control
Supplies	Credit
Services purchased	Sales promotion
Travel	Building operations
Communications	Personnel
Pensions	Warehousing and delivery
Insurance	Selling
Depreciation	Buying and merchandising
Maintenance	
Property rental	
Equipment rental	
Bad debts	
Professional services	

Each retail organization must develop a system tailored to be most useful for its purposes. A company, for example, that provided no home delivery and acquired all merchandise from wholesalers who delivered directly to the stores, would not need a warehouse and delivery expense center.

Mellow Music Store Applications

John and Julie Martin noticed a gradual increase in sales during the second month of operation of their store. "I think that extra advertising is having some effect," Julie said. "More people know about us now. And there have been some repeat customers," she added, "but I wonder if we are making any money?"

In an effort to determine whether the store was profitable, John and Julie began to prepare an operating statement for the first eight weeks of business. From their records they determined the sales and estimated cost of goods using their cost codes. These results were:

Gross sales	$22,734	
Returns and allowances	128	
Net sales		$22,606
Cost of goods sold from codes	13,275	
Tunings	150	
Total cost of goods sold		13,421
Gross margin		$ 9,185

They calculated the gross margin percentage ($\frac{\$9,185}{\$22,606} = 40.63\%$) and were relieved that it had increased over the figure for the first four weeks (39.61%—Chapter 6).

They then accumulated canceled checks and receipts to determine expenses to date. Results were:

Salaries	$4,308
Rent	1,800
Utilities	277
Advertising	3,200
Bad check	95
Donations	55
Other	239
Total	$9,974

The summary estimated operating statement revealed:

Sales	$22,606
Cost of goods sold	13,421
Gross margin	9,185
Expenses	9,974
Estimated loss	($ 789)

"I guess this retailing isn't as easy as I thought," John concluded, "We're losing money."

"Well, John, I'm not sure your figures are that accurate," Julie replied. "After all we've only been open two months, but we rented the store for a month before opening to get it ready. And don't you think some of the advertising we've done will have an effect in the future? Besides we may still collect on that bad check."

John quickly reworked his figures, reducing the rent by $600, scratching out the bad check, and reducing advertising by $200. His revised figures showed an estimated profit of $106. "That's more like it, we're doing OK," he shouted.

"That's great, John, but you forgot the insurance bill we haven't paid yet, and what about taking some depreciation on our fixtures?" Julie asked.

This chapter also discussed the direct versus indirect, controllable versus noncontrollable, and natural versus functional methods of classifying expenses. The concept of contribution was introduced and illustrated for a department of a department store and a single store of a retail chain. Application of expense center analysis in retailing was also considered.

Because the Mellow Music Store is a single outlet and not departmentalized, calculations employing the concepts of controllable versus noncontrollable expenses, direct versus indirect expenses, and illustrating contribution have not been presented. Likewise, in such a small operation there is no opportunity to realistically apply expense center analysis.

One can envision, however, a larger retailer selling musical instruments, sheet music, and supplies in a departmentalized store, also engaged in instrument repair and offering music lessons. For such an operation these concepts would have direct applicability.

Review Problems

7–1R. The gross sales of a department were $88,000. Customer returns totaled $4,000. Four customers were granted allowances of $25 each. What were net sales?

7–2R. What was the gross margin of a store with expenses of $48,000 and a profit of zero?

7–3R. Calculate the cost of goods sold from the following data: gross purchases $44,000; ending inventory $27,000; returns to vendors $5,600; freight on purchases $850; and beginning inventory $31,000.

7–4R. Prepare a retail operating statement from the following data: expenses $142,000; closing inventory $190,000; gross sales $482,000; purchases $260,000; opening inventory $220,000; and customer returns and allowances $8,000.

7–5R. Prepare a retail operating statement from the following data: payroll $42,000; cash discounts $12,000; customer returns and allowances $26,000; ending inventory $98,000; freight on purchases $10,000; advertising $22,000; rent $12,000; net sales $348,000; opening inventory $102,000; net purchases $248,000; utilities $10,000; and other expenses $14,000.

7–6R. Prepare a retail operating statement from the following data: expenses $103,000; closing inventory $139,000; customer returns $10,000; transportation on purchases $12,000; gross sales $417,000; markdowns $29,000; beginning inventory $121,000; allowances to customers $2,000; gross margin $133,000; and cash discounts $20,000.

7–7R. Prepare a retail operating statement from the following data: customer returns and allowances $25,000; freight on purchases $26,000; closing inventory $111,000; rent $20,000; net sales $639,000; net purchases $502,000; salaries $60,000; cash discounts $38,000; total merchandise handled $666,000; utilities $12,000; and other expenses $38,000.

7–8R. Prepare a departmental contribution statement for the infant's department of a department store with the following results: gross sales $137,000; net sales $125,000; gross margin 36%; buyer's salary $23,000; departmental advertising $3,000; sales personnel $12,000; supplies $500; and buyer's travel $500.

7–9R. Prepare a location contribution statement for store No. 77 of a supermarket chain with the following results: gross sales $2,010,000; gross margin 24%; customer returns and allowances $10,000; salary of store manager $36,000; department managers' salaries $60,000; rent $50,000; other store expenses $30,000; utilities $40,000; supplies $20,000; divisional advertising $2,000,000; general office 4.5%; and other store payroll $100,000.

7–10R. Prepare an operating statement for store No. 678, a unit in a convenience store chain where corporate headquarters allocates nonlocation expenses on a percentage of sales basis. Relevant figures are:

	Store No. 678	*Company*
Net sales	$1,800,000%	$717,000,000
Gross margin	32.7%	33.1%
Manager's salary	32,000	
Other store payroll	108,000	
Rent	60,000	
Supplies	12,000	
Utilities	70,000	
Advertising	18,000	14,000,000
All other expenses	20,000	
Warehousing and logistics		20,000,000
General office		35,000,000

CHAPTER 8

Stockturn and Inventory Management

At the heart of merchandising is merchandise, that which is bought and sold. For many retailers, it represents the major investment. Stores are often rented and many major items of equipment—computers, point-of-sale terminals, vehicles—may be leased. But merchandise, once acquired, is owned. It becomes inventory. Retailers strive to manage well their investment in inventory utilizing concepts and techniques that will be discussed in this chapter.

Retailers Can't Stock Everything

Solely as customers, unconcerned with the problems associated with the management of a retail business, we would like retailers to provide us with every possible variation of all types of merchandise that we might want, always in stock—a customer's Utopia. But for retailers this would provide an impossible situation. Consider the financial investment that would be required to acquire this unlimited choice, and then the physical facility that would be needed to house and display it.

There is an axiom in retailing, "You can't be all things to all people!" Most retailers generally specialize in a limited line of goods, which they can profitably acquire and sell to their customers. A supermarket that may sell 10,000 food items is stocking only a small percentage of all the brands, styles, and varieties of food stuffs available. Even retailers who present a very narrow line of goods, with a great range of choice provided, such as a specialty hardware store, or a button shop, cannot stock every possible item available.

So retailers try to balance their inventory of goods with the needs and wants of customers and financial considerations in mind. In the short run, space considerations are also a factor. Merchandise must be stored. Over the longer run, space can be expanded to accommodate increases in inventory if the decision is judged to be financially beneficial.

Inventories Tend to Depreciate

Unlike other kinds of investments that may be generating income or appreciating in value, retailers' investments in inventory that are not being converted into sales tend to depreciate (with perhaps the exception of antique shops). Dresses go out of fashion as styles change; new seasons bring new colors; new appliance models have innovating features; this year's model of automobiles obsoletes last year's model. Staple merchandise sitting in inventory can become shopworn, and perishables can become unsalable. Moreover there are expenses of storage, insurance, and refrigeration associated with inventories.

As a result, retailers analyze carefully and regularly the rate at which inventories are converted into sales. The process is an ongoing one for the prospering retailer. Cash is converted into inventory, which is converted into sales, which provides the cash to acquire more inventory to be converted into sales, and so on. To measure the relationship between inventories and sales, retailers employ a concept called **stockturn.**

Stockturn Calculations

Stockturn can be defined as the relationship between the sales of goods measured in units, retail dollars, or cost dollars, and the average inventory of goods measured in units, retail dollars, or cost dollars. When sales are measured in units, the average inventory must be measured in units. Likewise, if sales are measured in retail dollars, the average inventory must be valued in retail dollars. If sales are measured at cost (that is, cost of goods sold), average inventory must be valued at cost.

Stockturn is measured in *turns* or *times*. For example, during the past year a shoe retailer sold 4,000 pairs of shoes. During this period the retailer had an average inventory of 1750 pairs of shoes. The retailer's stockturn in units was:

$$\text{Stockturn} = \frac{\text{Sales in units}}{\text{Average inventory in units}} = \frac{4{,}000}{1{,}750}$$

$$\text{Stockturn} = 2.3$$

The shoe retailer had 2.3 turns during the past year, or turned the inventory 2.3 times.

A junior dress department in a department store had sales the past year of $246,000. The average inventory of dresses in this department valued at retail prices was $84,238. The stockturn was:

$$\text{Stockturn} = \frac{\text{Sales at retail}}{\text{Average inventory at retail}} = \frac{\$246{,}000}{\$84{,}238}$$

$$\text{Stockturn} = 2.9$$

The junior dress department had a stockturn of 2.9.

An appliance store had an average inventory measured in cost dollars of $96,400. For the past year the store's cost of goods sold was $461,320. The stockturn for the store was:

$$\text{Stockturn} = \frac{\text{Cost of goods sold}}{\text{Average inventory at cost}} = \frac{\$461{,}320}{\$96{,}400}$$

$$\text{Stockturn} = 4.8$$

The appliance store had 4.8 turns.

Whether stockturns are measured in units, at retail, or at cost depends on the particular retailer being analyzed. Generally dollar figures are used. Stores that maintain inventories at cost values, usually smaller stores, will correspondingly use cost figures. Stores on the retail method of inventory, most large stores, will use retail figures. Unit calculations are usually done only by stores selling very homogeneous merchandise, such as automobiles or shoes. Because the merchandise is very similar, a stockturn measure based on units, easily determined, can have value. For a large retailer selling a heterogeneous mix of different goods, a unit based calculation would not only have little meaning, but would be time consuming to calculate. Because inventories represent cash investments, stockturn measures based on dollar figures are generally more useful. It is important to make certain that the figures used in the numerator and denominator are on the same basis, that is, either cost or retail.

Stockturns Vary for Different Goods

Retailers like to keep stocks turning, that is, to be selling existing stocks and bringing in new ones. The turnover of stocks keeps merchandise fresh and epitomizes the essence of retailing, that is, the buying and selling of goods. Rates of stockturn vary widely among merchandise categories. For example, perishable food items such as milk and bread are often restocked daily, have limited variety, are purchased frequently, and sell in large volumes with a much higher stockturn than staple hardware items that are occasionally ordered, have wide variety, and sell infrequently in small quantities. Measures of stockturn are most meaningfully used when compared with industry figures or figures for other similar stores.

Stockturn Must Be Carefully Managed

In general, retailers try to increase stockturn. A higher stockturn is associated with: having up-to-date merchandise in the stores to stimulate sales; lower storage and inventory maintenance costs; a greater return on investment; and overall better management of financial assets. However, an increased stockturn can also result in higher merchandise procurement costs and greater stockouts. While retailers regularly set stockturn goals and periodically calculate stockturn rates, efforts to make major changes in merchandising tactics to improve stockturn must be very carefully assessed. Obviously, if sales could be increased while stocks were kept constant, stockturn would increase. But efforts to further increase sales via additional markdowns for sale specials or increased advertising and promotion, have costs in terms of lost markup and added expenses that might reduce profits. Likewise, reducing stocks while maintaining sales volume would increase stockturn, but if reduced stocks resulted in less assortment and out of stocks, sales might decline.

So stockturn must be very carefully managed. The best opportunities for improvement usually occur when there is evidence from better performing departments or stores that higher stockturn is associated with a higher contribution or profit. Generally, in such a situation the poorer performing unit will have excess duplicate stocks, out-of-fashion and/or shopworn stocks, and possibly heavy inventories of very slow moving substitute brands.

The Inventory Figure in Stockturn Calculations

Stockturn is a very simple calculation as was indicated above, a measure of sales being divided by a measure of average inventory. While the sales figure can be readily and accurately obtained, the average inventory figure is less reliable. An absolutely accurate average inventory figure would require frequent physical countings to obtain a sufficient number of measures to average. It is probably reasonable to conclude, given what we know about retailing and the seasonal variations in sales, that to get an accurate average inventory a retailer would need to count the stock weekly and then average the 53 inventories taken to determine the average for a year.[1]

But there aren't very many retailers taking weekly inventories. Consider the thousands of items that would have to be counted in a large department store. It would be very costly. As a result, many retailers take inventory just twice a year, and some do only what is necessary for income tax and annual financial reports. They take inventory once a year. With inventory taken just once a year, the average inventory would reflect two measures, the beginning of the year and the ending of the year inventories added together and divided by 2. If you observe that such a measure cannot be very accurate, you are correct, especially given the degree to which retailers use preinventory sales as a promotional stimulus and, also, to reduce the amount of stock to be counted and reported on balance sheets.

---

[1]53 not 52, because there would be beginning of the year and end of the year figures (i.e., January 1st and December 31st).

The Book Inventory

But many large retailers do maintain a book inventory or perpetual inventory system that keeps track of inventories by adding purchases, subtracting sales, and correcting for markdowns and other reductions and price changes. Such a system will provide figures on a monthly basis that are more representative than those based solely on an annual physical inventory. Other companies also may take quarterly physical inventories. When calculating stockturn, one has to use the best figures available.

Annual, Seasonal, Quarterly, Monthly, and Weekly Stockturns

When stockturn figures are reported, they are usually annual figures, based upon annual sales and an average inventory for a year. However, stockturn may be calculated for shorter time periods. It is common in the department store industry to calculate a seasonal stockturn, a season being a six month period; the spring season, February 1, to July 31; the fall season, August 1 to January 31. Stockturn can also be calculated on a quarterly, monthly, or weekly basis. For an ongoing retail business, the variation over time in sales will far exceed the variation in average inventory. For example, for a reasonably staple retail operation, the sales for the year will approximate something like 12 times the sales for a month. But the average inventory for each month is likely to be roughly similar. The sales are a cumulative figure, the inventory is a more static, average figure. Keep this in mind to help you remember the following conversion relationships:

Seasonal stockturn × 2 = Annual stockturn
Quarterly stockturn × 4 = Annual stockturn
Monthly stockturn × 12 = Annual stockturn
Weekly stockturn × 52 = Annual stockturn

Many large chain organizations divide the year into 13 four week periods. An estimated annual stockturn rate would be the stockturn for a period multiplied by 13.

Calculating Seasonal Stockturn

Let's calculate a seasonal stockturn for the men's clothing department in a department store that takes physical inventory twice per year. The relevant figures are:

Inventory at Retail First of Month			*Retail Sales for Month*
February	Physical	$49,375	$11,236
March	Book	51,332	14,374
April	Book	53,118	16,661
May	Book	54,636	17,777
June	Book	52,347	16,539
July	Book	50,131	10,322
August	Physical	48,359	

The total sales for the six-month spring season were: $86,909.

Notice that we have seven inventory figures. But recognize that the beginning inventory for the first of August would be the same as the ending inventory for the 31st of July. So we will use the best data available to calculate the average inventory, that is, the physical inventories for the start and end of the spring season and the book inventories for the intervening months.

Thus the average inventory would be the sum of the seven inventories, $359,298, divided by 7, equaling $51,328.

The stockturn would then be:

$$\text{Stockturn} = \frac{\text{Sales at retail}}{\text{Average inventory at retail}}$$

$$= \frac{\$86,909}{\$51,328}$$

$$= 1.69$$

The seasonal stockturn is 1.69. To get an estimated annual stockturn rate, we would multiply the seasonal rate by 2:

$$\text{Estimated annual stockturn} = 1.69 \times 2 = 3.38$$

Problems

8–1. Calculate the stockturn for a hardware store with the following annual figures: sales $188,000; cost of goods sold $98,000; beginning inventory at cost $62,500; and ending inventory at cost $59,250.

8–2. The home furnishings department in a department store had the following figures for the fall season: physical retail inventories, August 1 $77,456, February 1 $66,898; book retail inventories, September 1 $78,996, October 1 $81,456, November 1 $82,567, December 1 $78,555, January 1 $71,442; and sales $101,324. Calculate the seasonal stockturn and the estimated annual stockturn.

8–3. A unit in a drug chain had sales of $653,785 for the past calendar year. Inventories were as follows:

January 1	Cost book	$125,576
February 1	Cost physical	120,878
March 1	Cost book	129,898
April 1	Cost book	131,422
May 1	Cost book	134,422
June 1	Cost book	135,543
July 1	Cost book	130,093

(continued)

August 1	Cost physical	$124,036
September 1	Cost book	129,665
October 1	Cost book	131,757
November 1	Cost book	132,734
December 1	Cost book	135,548
January 1	Cost book	129,823

The gross margin for the year was 39.4%. Calculate the annual stockturn.

8–4. A shoe department classified merchandise as follows: dress, casual, sneakers, and stormwear. Inventories, sales, and gross margins for the last quarter are presented below. Calculate the stockturn for each classification and for the entire department for the last quarter.

	Sales	Beginning Inventory Cost	Ending Inventory Cost	Gross Margin
Dress shoes	$12,578	$10,858	$9,246	45.5%
Casuals	14,643	8,990	8,144	42.5
Sneakers	9,432	4,475	5,127	39.5
Stormwear	434	1,240	1,014	48.0

Estimate the annual stockturn for the department.

8–5. A department had sales during the past year of $184,000 and a stockturn of four. Management of the store believed that the department was carrying an inventory of outdated merchandise that was not selling. The buyer was instructed to improve the stockturn by liquidating the old merchandise and replacing it with fresh stocks. Management set as an objective a stockturn of eight. The gross margin in the department was 42%. If the buyer was able to maintain the sales volume, what average inventory at cost should be planned?

The Stock-Sales Ratio

Stockturn provides a general measure of the relationship between sales and stocks. It is a rough guide. For planning purposes, that is deciding how much stock should be on hand at a particular time, retailers also use other relationships. One common, easy-to-understand-measure is the *stock-sales ratio*. It literally relates the stock on hand at either the beginning or end of a month to the projected sales for that month. In practice, it is usually the beginning of the month ratio that is used because of the desire to relate the onhand stock level at the start of the month to the anticipated sales volume for that month. For example, in a department that uses the stock-sales ratio to set inventory levels, the beginning of the month ratio, known as BOM, for June is 2.2. Sales for June have been forecasted to be $23,000. What amount of stock (at retail values) should be on hand on June 1st?

The stock-sales ratio of 2.2 for the beginning of the month indicates that the stock should be 2.2 times the expected sales. Therefore, $23,000 × 2.2 = $50,600, and is the amount of inventory to have on hand June 1st. (Note that this is a retail value. To determine the cost value of the inventory we would multiply $50,600 by the cost complement of the initial markup.)

Calculating Stock-Sales Ratios

Stock-sales ratios are usually determined for a store or department based upon its historical figures. Below are last year's figures, rounded for illustration, for the sleepwear department of a department store:

	Sales	*BOM Retail Stock*
August	$ 9,000	$27,000
September	10,000	31,000
October	12,000	33,000
November	15,000	36,000
December	18,000	33,000
January	8,000	24,000
February		$33,000

To calculate the monthly BOM stock-sales ratios we would divide each BOM stock figure by the corresponding month's sales:

August	$27,000/$ 9,000 = 3.0 stock-sales ratio
September	$31,000/$10,000 = 3.1 stock-sales ratio
October	$33,000/$12,000 = 2.8 stock-sales ratio
November	$36,000/$15,000 = 2.4 stock-sales ratio
December	$33,000/$18,000 = 1.8 stock-sales ratio
January	$24,000/$ 8,000 = 3.0 stock-sales ratio

Note how readily we can also use these figures to check on the overall stockturn. The total sales for the season (the sum of August through January sales) were $72,000. The average inventory (the sum of the BOM stocks divided by 7)[2] was $31,000. So the seasonal stockturn was $\frac{\$72,000}{\$31,000} = 2.3$.

If this stockturn were disappointing to management, adjustments in the monthly stock-sales ratios might be made. Let's assume, however, that a stockturn of 2.3 is satisfactory. To get the planned stocks for the upcoming fall season we apply the stock-sales ratios to planned sales:

	Planned Sales	×	BOM Stock-Sales Ratio	=	Planned Retail BOM Stocks
August	$ 9,500	×	3.0	=	$28,500
September	11,000	×	3.1	=	34,100
October	12,500	×	2.8	=	35,000
November	16,000	×	2.4	=	38,400
December	18,500	×	1.8	=	33,300
January	8,500	×	3.0	=	25,500

Stock-sales ratios are also developed and published for retailers by trade associations.

The Weeks' Supply Method

Another simple technique of relating inventories to anticipated sales is known as the *weeks' supply* method. It has applicability to staple merchandise that does not fluctuate much in sales from week to week. For example, the housewares department forecasts sales of $65,000 for the fall season. The annual stockturn objective for this department is 6. How much stock should be on hand on average at any given time?

If the annual stockturn is 6, the seasonal stockturn would be $\frac{6}{2} = 3$. There are 26 weeks in a season. With a stockturn of 3 for the season, the average inventory would be $\frac{26}{3} = 8.7$ weeks' supply. Average sales per week would be $\frac{\$65,000}{26 \text{ weeks}} = \$2,500$. So to have in stock 8.7 weeks' supply, the stock would have to be $2,500 \times 8.7 = \$21,750$ at retail value. (To determine the stock at cost, we would multiply by the cost complement of the initial markup.) Would an average inventory of $21,750 provide a stockturn of 3?

$$\text{Stockturn} = \frac{\$65,000}{\$21,750} = 2.99 \quad \text{(Rounding discrepancy)}$$

Problems

8–6. In a department that uses the stock-sales ratio to determine monthly stocks, sales for March are planned to be $15,400. If the beginning of the month stock-sales ratio is 3.1, how much inventory should be on hand on March 1? Is this result in retail or cost dollars?

8–7. In a small women's shop the proprietor uses the stock-sales ratio to plan stocks. The initial markup in the shop is 48%. Sales for September are planned to be $12,500. The BOM stock-sales ratio for September is 2.2.

(continued)

---

[2]The February BOM figure is also the ending inventory for January.

How much money should the store owner plan to have invested in merchandise on September 1?

8–8. A leather goods department in a department store uses the stock-sales ratio calculated from historical figures to determine beginning of the month inventories. Inventory and sales data for last season, and planned sales for the upcoming season are presented below. Determine planned BOM stocks.

	Last Season Sales	*Last Season BOM Retail Stocks*	*Planned Sales*
February	$11,686	$18,979	$12,500
March	12,535	18,755	13,000
April	14,889	22,678	15,500
May	15,756	22,545	16,000
June	14,342	20,698	15,000
July	12,676	16,834	13,000

8–9. For a store using the weeks' supply method to determine inventories, what is the average number of weeks' inventory on hand if the annual stockturn is eight?

8–10. A department using the weeks' supply method to determine stock on hand anticipates sales of $72,000 for the fall season. The seasonal stockturn objective is three. How much stock should be on hand on average at any given time?

The Basic Stock Method

The techniques introduced above for planning stocks can be simply calculated and understood. They illustrate well the difficult task of systematically trying to determine how much inventory should be on hand to support anticipated sales. Much more complex techniques using computer based mathematical models have been developed and applied by some retailers. They are beyond the scope of this volume. However, we will introduce two classic techniques widely applied by retailers. Though more complicated than the stock-sales or weeks' supply techniques, they can be calculated with pencil and paper (or calculator). They will illustrate two approaches to balancing stocks.

The so-called *basic stock* method presumes that there should always be on hand a base assortment of goods (the basic stock) that remains constant no matter what rate of sales is being achieved. This basic stock is defined as the average inventory, determined by the stockturn, minus the average monthly sales. For example, consider that planned sales in the men's furnishings department are as presented below. The seasonal stockturn objective is 2.

	Planned Sales
August	$11,000
September	15,000
October	16,000
November	18,000
December	21,000
January	15,000
Total for season	$96,000

The average monthly sales would be $\frac{\$96,000}{6} = \$16,000$.

With a seasonal stockturn of 2, the average inventory at retail would be:

$$\text{Average inventory} = \frac{\text{Sales}}{\text{Stockturn}} = \frac{\$96,000}{2} = \$48,000$$

The basic stock would be calculated as follows:

$$\text{Basic stock at retail} = \text{Average inventory} - \text{Average monthly sales}$$

$$= \$48,000 - \$16,000$$

$$= \$32,000$$

Then to determine the beginning of the month stocks, we would add the basic stock to the planned sales for the month.

So, the beginning of the month stock for August would be:

$$\text{BOM} = \text{Planned sales } (\$11,000) + \text{Basic stock } (\$32,000) = \$43,000$$

Likewise the beginning of the month retail stocks for the other months would be:

Month	*Planned Sales*	+	*Basic Stock*	=	*BOM Stock*
September	$15,000	+	$32,000	=	$47,000
October	16,000	+	32,000	=	48,000
November	18,000	+	32,000	=	50,000
December	21,000	+	32,000	=	53,000
January	15,000	+	32,000	=	47,000

Limitations of the Basic Stock Method

The basic stock method, therefore, assumes that it is necessary or desirable to maintain this fixed quantity of merchandise throughout the season. It is generally applied when the annual stockturn rate is 6 or less, because at higher stockturns it produces an unrealistic basic stock. For example, let's apply a seasonal stockturn of 6 to the example above (equivalent to an annual rate of 12).

Now the average inventory would be:

$$\text{Average inventory} = \frac{\text{Sales (\$96,000)}}{\text{Stockturn (6)}} = \$16,000$$

With an average inventory of $16,000, the basic stock would be:

$$\text{Basic stock} = \text{Average inventory} - \text{Average sales}$$

$$= \$16,000 - \$16,000$$

$$= \$0$$

Consequently, at an annual stockturn rate of 12 there would be no basic stock, and at higher stockturns a negative basic stock, if such can be imagined!

The Percentage Variation Method

To overcome these limitations of the basic stock method, a technique known as the *percentage variation* method has evolved. It modifies stocks in some proportion to the change in sales volume. Using this method requires solution of a simple algebraic formula. As presented below, the formula varies stocks by half the variation in sales. Other fluctuations could be developed algebraically, but this one based on the one half, or 50%, variation has usually been applied.

$$\text{BOM stock (at retail)} = \text{Average inventory} \times \frac{1}{2}\left(1 + \frac{\text{Sales for month}}{\text{Average monthly sales}}\right)$$

To illustrate the application of the percentage variation method we will use the same planned sales figures presented earlier for the men's furnishings department, but assume a seasonal stockturn objective of 4.

	Planned Sales
August	$11,000
September	15,000
October	16,000
November	18,000
December	21,000
January	15,000
Total for season	$96,000

The average monthly sales would be $\frac{\$96,000}{6} = \$16,000$.

With a seasonal stockturn of 4, the average inventory at retail would be:

$$\text{Average inventory} = \frac{\text{Sales}}{\text{Stockturn}} = \frac{\$96,000}{4} = \$24,000$$

Now, to determine the beginning of the month stocks we insert the relevant values into the formula. The mathematical steps are not as difficult as they might appear at first glance. Notice also the shortcut presented in the footnote for those using calculators.

$$\text{BOM stock August} = \text{Average inventory} \times \frac{1}{2}\left(1 + \frac{\text{Sales for month}}{\text{Average monthly sales}}\right)$$

$$\text{BOM stock August} = \$24,000 \times \frac{1}{2}\left(1 + \frac{\$11,000}{\$16,000}\right)$$

(Steps in calculation)

$$= \$24,000 \times \frac{1}{2}\left(\frac{16}{16} + \frac{11}{16}\right)$$ (Substituting $\frac{16}{16}$ for 1, dividing by 1,000)

(continued)

$$= \$24{,}000 \times \frac{1}{2}\left(\frac{27}{16}\right) \qquad \text{(Adding } \tfrac{16}{16} \text{ and } \tfrac{11}{16}\text{)}$$

$$= \$24{,}000 \times \left(\frac{27}{32}\right) \qquad \text{(Multiplying by 1/2)}$$

$$= \$20{,}250 \qquad \text{(Multiplying by 27 and dividing by 32)}^3$$

$$\text{BOM stock for September} = \$24{,}000 \times \frac{1}{2}\left(1 + \frac{\$15{,}000}{\$16{,}000}\right)$$

$$= \$24{,}000 \times \frac{1}{2}\left(\frac{16}{16} + \frac{15}{16}\right)$$

$$= \$24{,}000 \times \frac{1}{2}\left(\frac{31}{16}\right)$$

$$= \$24{,}000 \times \left(\frac{31}{32}\right)$$

$$= \$23{,}250$$

$$\text{BOM stock for October} = \$24{,}000 \times \frac{1}{2}\left(1 + \frac{\$16{,}000}{\$16{,}000}\right)$$

$$= \$24{,}000 \times \frac{1}{2}(1 + 1)$$

$$= \$24{,}000 \times \frac{1}{2}(2)$$

$$= \$24{,}000$$

$$\text{BOM stock for November} = \$24{,}000 \times \frac{1}{2}\left(1 + \frac{\$18{,}000}{\$16{,}000}\right)$$

$$= \$24{,}000 \times \frac{1}{2}\left(\frac{16}{16} + \frac{18}{16}\right)$$

$$= \$24{,}000 \times \frac{1}{2}\left(\frac{34}{16}\right)$$

$$= \$24{,}000 \times \left(\frac{34}{32}\right)$$

$$= \$25{,}500$$

$$\text{BOM stock for December} = \$24{,}000 \times \frac{1}{2}\left(1 + \frac{\$21{,}000}{\$16{,}000}\right)$$

$$= \$24{,}000 \times \frac{1}{2}\left(\frac{16}{16} + \frac{21}{16}\right)$$

$$= \$24{,}000 \times \frac{1}{2}\left(\frac{37}{16}\right)$$

$$= \$24{,}000 \times \left(\frac{37}{32}\right)$$

$$= \$27{,}750$$

---

[3]Students using a calculator can make one calculation as follows: starting at the right of the formula and working back to the left: divide $11,000 by $16,000, result .6875; add 1, result 1.6875; divide by 2, result .84375; multiply by $24,000, result $20,250.

$$\text{BOM stock for January} = \$24,000 \times \frac{1}{2}\left(1 + \frac{\$15,000}{\$16,000}\right)$$

$$= \$24,000 \times \frac{1}{2}\left(\frac{16}{16} + \frac{15}{16}\right)$$

$$= \$24,000 \times \frac{1}{2}\left(\frac{31}{16}\right)$$

$$= \$24,000 \times \left(\frac{31}{32}\right)$$

$$= \$23,250$$

Choosing between Basic Stock and Percentage Variation Methods

Remember, in applying these two approaches to use the percentage variation method when the annual stockturn is greater than 6 and the basic stock method when the annual stockturn is less than 6. At an annual stockturn rate of 6, both methods will give the same result. Because the basic stock method is easier to calculate, we will use that approach when the stockturn is 6. But to review and to check our understanding of the calculations used for each method, we will now assume an annual stockturn of 6 and the same planned sales for the men's furnishing department that we used in the above examples.

	Planned Sales
August	$11,000
September	15,000
October	16,000
November	18,000
December	21,000
January	15,000
Total for season	$96,000

The average monthly sales are $\frac{\$96,000}{6} = \$16,000$.

With an annual stockturn of 6, the seasonal stockturn would be 3, and the average inventory would be:

$$\text{Average inventory} = \frac{\text{Sales}}{\text{Stockturn}} = \frac{\$96,000}{3} = \$32,000$$

Using the basic stock method, basic stock would be:

$$\text{Basic stock} = \text{Average inventory} - \text{Average sales}$$

$$= \$32,000 - \$16,000$$

$$= \$16,000$$

The beginning of the month retail stocks using the basic stock method would be:

Month	*Planned Sales*	+	*Basic Stock*	=	*BOM Stock*
August	$11,000	+	$16,000	=	$27,000
September	15,000	+	16,000	=	31,000
October	16,000	+	16,000	=	32,000
November	18,000	+	16,000	=	34,000
December	21,000	+	16,000	=	37,000
January	15,000	+	16,000	=	31,000

Using the percentage variation method, the average monthly sales are the same, $\frac{\$96,000}{6} = \$16,000$.

With the seasonal stockturn of 3, the average inventory would be $\frac{\$96,000}{3} =$ $32,000. Using the formula for the percentage variation method,

$$\text{BOM stock} = \text{Average inventory} \times \frac{1}{2}\left(1 + \frac{\text{Sales for month}}{\text{Average monthly sales}}\right)$$

gives the following results for each month:

$$\text{BOM for August} = \$32,000 \times \frac{1}{2}\left(1 + \frac{\$11,000}{\$16,000}\right)$$

$$= \$32,000 \times \frac{1}{2}\left(\frac{16}{16} + \frac{11}{16}\right) \qquad \text{(Substituting } \tfrac{16}{16} \text{ for 1, dividing by 1,000)}$$

$$= \$32,000 \times \frac{1}{2}\left(\frac{27}{16}\right) \qquad \text{(Adding } \tfrac{16}{16} \text{ and } \tfrac{11}{16}\text{)}$$

$$= \$32,000 \times \left(\frac{27}{32}\right) \qquad \text{(Multiplying by 1/2)}$$

$$= \$27,000 \qquad \text{(Dividing by 32)}$$

$$\text{BOM for September} = \$32,000 \times \frac{1}{2}\left(1 + \frac{\$15,000}{\$16,000}\right)$$

$$= \$32,000 \times \frac{1}{2}\left(\frac{16}{16} + \frac{15}{16}\right)$$

$$= \$32,000 \times \frac{1}{2}\left(\frac{31}{16}\right)$$

$$= \$32,000 \times \left(\frac{31}{32}\right)$$

$$= \$31,000$$

$$\text{BOM for October} = \$32,000 \times \frac{1}{2}\left(1 + \frac{\$16,000}{\$16,000}\right)$$

$$= \$32,000 \times \frac{1}{2}(1 + 1)$$

$$= \$32,000 \times \frac{1}{2}(2)$$

$$= \$32,000 \times (1)$$

$$= \$32,000$$

$$\text{BOM for November} = \$32,000 \times \frac{1}{2}\left(1 + \frac{\$18,000}{\$16,000}\right)$$

$$= \$32,000 \times \frac{1}{2}\left(1 + \frac{18}{16}\right)$$

$$= \$32,000 \times \frac{1}{2}\left(\frac{34}{16}\right)$$

$$= \$32,000 \times \left(\frac{34}{32}\right)$$

$$= \$34,000$$

$$\text{BOM for December} = \$32,000 \times \frac{1}{2}\left(1 + \frac{\$21,000}{\$16,000}\right)$$

$$= \$32,000 \times \frac{1}{2}\left(\frac{16}{16} + \frac{21}{16}\right)$$

$$= \$32,000 \times \frac{1}{2}\left(\frac{37}{16}\right)$$

$$= \$32,000 \times \left(\frac{37}{32}\right)$$

$$= \$37,000$$

$$\text{BOM for January} = \$32,000 \times \frac{1}{2}\left(1 + \frac{\$15,000}{\$16,000}\right)$$

$$= \$32,000 \times \frac{1}{2}\left(\frac{16}{16} + \frac{15}{16}\right)$$

$$= \$32,000 \times 1/2\left(\frac{31}{16}\right)$$

$$= \$32,000 \times \left(\frac{31}{32}\right)$$

$$= \$31,000$$

It does check out! With an annual stockturn rate of 6, we get the same results with both methods.

Problems

8–11. For a department with the following planned sales and an annual stockturn objective of 4, calculate the average monthly sales and the average inventory.

February	$12,600	May	$16,100
March	14,200	June	15,500
April	15,800	July	12,200

8–12. A specialty shop has an annual stockturn objective of 3. Calculate BOM stocks if planned sales are:

August	$10,700	November	$16,900
September	13,500	December	18,200
October	15,100	January	10,700

8–13. For a department with an annual stockturn objective of 8, and the following planned spring sales, calculate the BOM stocks:

February	$22,000	May	$15,000
March	24,000	June	27,000
April	22,000	July	21,000

8–14. A department has an annual stockturn objective of 6. Planned sales for the
fall season are presented below. Calculate BOM stocks using the basic stock
method. Use the percentage variation method to check your results.

August	$ 8,000	November	$16,000
September	10,000	December	20,000
October	12,000	January	6,000

Calculating Inventory Shortages with Retail Book Inventories

From time to time we have referred to the retail method of inventory. It is a widely used system, particularly, in the department store part of the retailing industry. It is rather complicated and the specific details are beyond our concern in this chapter. As part of the retail method, a book or perpetual inventory is maintained. Even stores that do not use the so-called retail system may keep a book inventory, usually at cost values. As suggested in the discussion of operating statements, by maintaining a book inventory, it is possible to prepare periodic financial statements of high accuracy without having to take a physical inventory.

At this point in our consideration of inventory management, we will consider the techniques that enable store management to detect inventory shortages. The term shortage is used by retailers to include: shoplifting or other theft (by customers, professional thieves, employees, or suppliers); damaged or broken merchandise that is disposed of or sold at reduced price without recording the loss or markdown; errors by store personnel that result in customers being given more merchandise than was paid for; and clerical errors that occur in the maintenance of stock records.

In a store that keeps track of all inventory at retail values, determining the amount of shortage is a simple task. A major assumption, however, is that the physical inventory counting is very accurately done. A haphazardly conducted physical inventory is of no value. But presuming counting accuracy, the process is very reliable. At the start of a period, the store has an inventory of merchandise measured at retail value. During the period, merchandise is sold: markdowns are recorded; damages are recorded; employee and special customer discounts are recorded; purchases are recorded at retail value; and other changes in stock position such as returns of merchandise to suppliers, and transfers from or to other stores are recorded. Then the opening inventory at retail is added to all increases in the value of stock at retail, and all decreases in value of stock at retail are subtracted. The balance is the value of the inventory at retail in the store.

For example, on February 1st a women's specialty store had an opening inventory, valued at retail, of $225,655. During February, March, and April net purchases at retail totaled $310,909. Total net markdowns were $24,878. Employee and special customer discounts were $2,196. There were no transfers or damages to stock. Net sales for the three month period were $272,678. What should be the value of the inventory at retail on April 30th?

Opening inventory at retail		$225,655
Increases in value of inventory:		
Purchases at retail		310,909
Total merchandise handled		536,564
Decreases in value of inventory:		
Sales	$272,678	
Markdowns	24,878	
Employee and customer discounts	2,196	299,752
Closing inventory at retail		$236,812

By adding the increases in stock value and subtracting the decreases in stock value, we have determined what the closing inventory **should be**. What the closing inventory should be is the **book** inventory. It is what the books say the inventory is. But the only way to determine what the inventory **really is**, is to count it. Let's say that we have a completely accurate physical counting of the stock after the close of business on April 30th. The count reveals an inventory in the store of $231,113. The inventory is short by $236,812 − $231,113, or $5,699.

To calculate a shortage percentage, the dollar inventory shortage would be related to the dollar net sales during the period. Here, the shortage percentage would be $\frac{\$5,699}{\$272,678} = 2.1\%$. In recent years, shortages of 2% of sales and higher are not unusual in retailing. Our analysis cannot detect the specific causes of the shortage. Because of the major impact of shortages on profits, retailers are striving to improve systems for reducing shortages of all types.

Using Book Inventories at Cost

The use of a retail book inventory system is relatively straightforward because reductions in stock value (sales, markdowns) are recorded at retail values. While a book inventory can be maintained at cost, its application is made somewhat more difficult by the need to keep track of decreases in stock at cost values. The system used by John and Julie Martin at the Mellow Music Store (chapter applications) of recording on sales slips in code the cost of each item sold, provides an example of how a book inventory at cost could be used in a small volume store, where each customer transaction consists of the purchase of only one or a few items. Such a system would be unworkable in a high volume store, where customers may purchase many items at a time. But the use of a computerized checkout system would enable such a store to quickly and accurately record the cost of each product sold.

The example provided below is for a cost based book inventory system. Markdowns and employee and special customer discounts would not be included, because they are reductions in retail value. The cost value would not be reduced because of these reductions. This would provide the control desired to determine the amount of stock shortage. (However, it would not be accurate for determining the precise cost value of the inventory, because of the need to depreciate the inventory for any markdowns that would reflect reductions in the market value of the goods. Remember the accounting principle that inventories should be valued at the lower of cost or market!)

A small appliance store selling major appliances had an opening inventory at cost of $32,354 at the start of the third quarter. During the quarter, purchases at cost totaled $71,175. Sales during the third quarter valued at cost from codes entered on sales slips were $69,533. What should be the value of the inventory at cost at the end of the third quarter?

Opening inventory at cost	$ 32,354
Increases in value of inventory:	
Purchases at cost	71,175
Total merchandise handled	103,529
Decreases in value of inventory:	
Sales at cost (from codes on sales slips)	69,533
Closing book inventory at cost	$ 33,996

Let's now suppose that the owner-manager of the store takes a physical inventory. The value at cost of the inventory is determined to be $33,996. There is no shortage! (Well, we wouldn't expect a major appliance to be shoplifted, would we?)

When the Physical Inventory Exceeds the Book Inventory

Is it possible, you may be asking, for the physical inventory to be higher than the book inventory? Yes. Such a condition is known as an *overage*. Because merchandise is not likely to be added to stocks, free of all charges and billings, overages are usually the result of clerical errors.

For example, let's suppose that in counting the inventory, the owner of the appliance store came up with a total of $34,496. There would then be an overage of $500. Subsequent rechecking of inventory sheets might reveal that an entry of $300 for an item was misadded as $800 in compiling the total physical inventory. Correcting the physical inventory total for the extra $500 would result in the correct figure, $33,996.

Estimating Shortages

On the basis of historical experience, retailers will usually include an estimated shortage in the calculation of book inventories. For example, let's suppose that in the illustration presented above of the women's specialty store using the retail book system, experience had indicated that stock shortages were usually about 2% of sales. Then from the book inventory at retail of $236,812 (summarized below) an estimate for shortages would be subtracted, as illustrated below:

Opening inventory at retail	$224,655
Purchases at retail	310,909
Total merchandise handled	536,564
Decreases in value (sales, markdowns, discounts)	299,752
Book inventory at retail	$236,812
Estimated shortages (2% × Sales − $272,678)	5,454
Estimated physical inventory at retail	$231,358

After the physical inventory revealed a value of $231,113, the shortage would be increased by $231,358 − $231,113, or $245, making the true shortage, $5,454 + $245, or $5,699, the same result obtained earlier.

Problems

8–15.   If the book inventory at retail is $47,546, and the physical inventory is $45,457, is there a shortage or an overage? Of what amount?

8–16. A small store maintaining a book inventory at cost based upon sales slips, had the following figures: cost of goods sold from sales slips $67,775; purchases at cost $65,433; and opening inventory (physical) at cost $32,787. Calculate the closing book inventory.

8–17. The women's coat department in a department store on the retail inventory method had the following figures for the first three months of the spring season: sales $88,874; opening inventory at retail $54,234; markdowns $10,230; employee discounts $1,089; and purchases at retail value $76,242. Calculate the closing book inventory. If a physical count revealed an inventory of $29,136 at retail, what was the shortage percentage?

8–18.   A department using a retail book inventory system had the following figures: sales $162,236; book inventory at retail $68,986; and estimated shortages 1.7% sales. Calculate the estimated physical inventory. If a physical inventory indicated a stock valued at retail of $65,338, what was the shortage percentage?

Mellow Music Store Applications

William Flynn's comments (summary Chapter 6) had made John and Julie Martin sensitive to inventory shortages.

"We are trusting people," said Julie, "and I don't like the atmosphere you find in some stores where they make you feel that you are under surveillance. But I guess Dad is right when he talks about the need to be alert. You shouldn't create an environment that encourages those who might attempt to shoplift. It would be impossible to steal a piano, but I suppose someone could walk out with a portable keyboard or an amplifier. I don't think we've had any theft, but we'll find out after we take inventory."

At the end of the first quarter of operation (13 weeks) of the Mellow Music Store, John and Julie, with the help of Mr. Flynn took a physical inventory of the contents of the store. The initial inventory had totaled $62,044 at cost. Purchases at cost had totaled $7,340. John and Julie had continued the practice of recording on sales slips the cost codes of the items sold. Periodically they tallied the cost of goods sold, and at the end of the first quarter it totaled $21,388.

John estimated what the physical inventory at cost should be as follows:

Initial inventory at cost	$62,044
Purchases at cost	7,340
Total merchandise handled	$69,384
Cost of goods sold (tallied from cost codes on sales slips)	21,388
Estimated closing inventory	$47,996

A careful counting of the stock in the store, utilizing the cost codes, resulted in a total value at cost of $47,838. This indicated a shortage of $47,996 − $47,838, or $158.

While John and Julie were disappointed that there had been any shortage at all, Mr. Flynn observed that the figure was very low and that it might not reflect customer shoplifting. He remarked that attention should also be focused on the stockturn. He calculated the stockturn for the quarter and estimated an annual stockturn as follows:

Beginning inventory	$ 62,044
Ending inventory	47,838
	$109,882

$$\text{Average inventory (cost)} = \frac{\$109,882}{2} = \$54,941$$

$$\text{Stockturn} = \frac{\text{Cost of goods sold}}{\text{Average inventory (cost)}}$$

$$= \frac{\$21,388}{\$54,941}$$

$$= .39 \text{ for quarter}$$

Estimated stockturn for year $= .39 \times 4 = 1.56$

"I guess that's not too good," said John. "At this rate we're not even turning over our inventory twice a year."

"But don't forget," Mr. Flynn said, "You're just getting started. You had to stock the store from scratch so that you could provide your customers with a good selection and also to create the impression that you're a legitimate music store. Most of the merchandise you sell is expensive and people don't buy it every day. It's not fast turning stuff. But you'll notice that some items are moving well and others are catching dust. You're starting to get a good reading on what your customers want. Once you weed out the poor selling merchandise, your stockturn will go up. But in a music store it will never be very high."

The other concepts discussed in this chapter, stock-sales ratios, the weeks' supply, the basic stock, and the percentage variation methods for determining inventory levels are typically not applied in a small retail operation selling expensive, slow turnover merchandise, as exemplified by the Mellow Music Store.

Review Problems

8–1R. In a department with a seasonal stockturn of 4, management wishes to increase the stockturn to 5. If sales were constant, what percentage decrease in average inventory would be required?

8–2R. Determine the seasonal stockturn by classification and overall for a unit in a menswear chain with the following figures for the spring season:

	Beginning Inventory Retail	*Ending Inventory Retail*	*Sales*
Suits	$32,599	$21,565	$23,545
Jackets and slacks	29,454	20,888	38,457
Shirts	6,654	5,045	9,343
Accessories	5,325	2,459	4,588

8–3R. A retailer began the year with an opening inventory at cost of $69,757. The end of the year inventory at cost was $97,435. During the year purchases totaled $269,443 at cost. What was the stockturn?

8–4R. Determine BOM stock for the fall season in a department that uses stock-sales ratios to plan stocks when the following data are available:

(continued)

| | Sales | | BOM Retail Stocks |
	Last Year	Planned	Last Year
August	$22,456	$23,000	$36,769
September	25,098	26,500	39,566
October	27,890	29,500	41,456
November	29,866	31,000	43,544
December	31,654	33,000	41,322
January	19,756	21,000	29,888

8–5R. What would be the investment in merchandise on March 1 for the proprietor of a specialty shop that uses the stock-sales ratio method of planning stocks if planned sales for March are $32,500, the BOM stock-sales ratio for March is 2.8, and the initial markup is 52%?

8–6R. A department with an annual stockturn objective of 4.2 has planned sales of $340,000 for the upcoming six month season. If the weeks' supply method is used to determine stocks, what would be the average inventory value at retail?

8–7R. Calculate BOM stocks for a department with a seasonal stockturn objective of 3.5, and the following planned sales:

August	$33,400	November	$38,800
September	39,600	December	40,600
October	36,400	January	31,000

8–8R. Calculate BOM stocks for a department with an annual stockturn objective of 4.5 and the following planned sales for the next season:

February	$52,500	May	$50,000
March	48,000	June	55,000
April	48,500	July	46,000

8–9R. What is the closing book inventory for a department with the following figures for the past month:

Gross sales	$55,580
Customer returns	4,437
Net purchases at retail	53,595
Markdowns	8,778
Employee discounts	2,865
Opening inventory retail	65,560

8–10R. What was the dollar shortage and the shortage percentage for a department using a retail book inventory that had the following figures:

Gross sales	$332,238
Gross purchases	348,565
Customer returns	10,434
Customer allowances	2,456
Purchase returns to vendors	6,650
Markdowns taken	40,545
Markdown cancellations	10,980
Employee discounts	4,555
Opening inventory	131,780
Estimated shortages	1.5% sales
Closing physical inventory	121,954

CHAPTER 9

The Seasonal Merchandise Plan and Open-to-Buy

Planning is an essential management function. Most large retailers, and many smaller ones, engage in comprehensive planning activities. A plan not only provides direction, but also is the basis for control—for a carefully developed plan that establishes realistic objectives becomes the measuring stick against which results are assessed. The best aspects of *management by objectives* can be realized through effective planning.

In earlier chapters we have become familiar with several of the specific objectives that retailers plan, such as initial markup, maintained markup, gross margin, and stockturn. In learning how to calculate initial markup, we saw that essential elements were estimates of sales, expenses, reductions, and profits. These variables become parts of the overall plan for a retailing unit.

Need for Planning

The need for careful planning can perhaps be best appreciated by considering the situation in a large department store. There may be more than 100 individual departments, each the responsibility of a buyer. Sales are many millions of dollars. Thousands of items are stocked. Each buyer can commit the store to purchases of hundreds of thousands of dollars worth of inventory. This inventory represents a major investment of funds. It may be the store's largest asset. A carefully designed system for planning and controlling this investment is essential.

Environmental Factors Influencing Sales Planning

Planning begins with an estimate of sales. Retailers carefully maintain historical sales data. A starting point for forecasting future sales is an analysis of historical sales, seeking trends or patterns and questioning their applicability to the future. Factors that may have had a major influence on sales for the past few years must be assessed. A strike, or adverse business conditions at a major employer in the area could have had a strong negative impact on sales. Future expectations for the economic climate in the retailer's area must be weighed. Similarly, customer access to the store could be: (*a*) limited by traffic dislocations caused by construction projects or the ending of public transportation to the area; or (*b*) improved by the opening of a new access road or new public transportation service to the area.

Changing demographics of the customers that normally patronize the store are another important consideration. Changes in the number of people, their age characteristics, and their socioeconomic levels can have effects on the sales of specific stores.

An important input to the sales planning activity is an assessment of competition. Changes in the amount and nature of competition will influence future sales. The likely effect of a major new competitor coming into a store's area, or of a long-standing competitor leaving, are key considerations to be weighed in predicting future sales.

Management Actions Influencing Sales Planning

The factors discussed above are environmental, and very important, but not within the control of the retailer. Also of major significance are actions that have been or are planned to be taken by the store that could influence future sales. A major store remodeling, a planned increase in promotional activities, a new pricing policy, addition or elimination of certain merchandise categories or customer services, and other actions could have an appreciable impact on sales.

Forecasting Sales Requires Judgment

There is a certain amount of crystalballing involved in forecasting sales. Some retailers use consultants or rely on the input of commercial forecasting services. Processes within individual companies will vary. In the end it becomes an informed judgment. This does not diminish its importance. All subsequent decisions, ranging, for example, from a decision about the number of stores to operate to a decision about the number of sewing needles to stock, must ultimately stem from the forecast of sales. Because informed judgments are developed from many interacting factors and incorporate planning in great detail, providing a realistic practice problem in retail sales planning is beyond the modest purposes of this book.

Hopefully the reader appreciates the importance of careful sales planning and some of the related issues. We will proceed by assuming the sales forecasts needed to understand the merchandise planning or budgeting process are in hand. The sales plan, when finally developed, will range from an overall plan for the total company, to a plan for each store in the company, for each major subdivision, for each department, and, in some instances, for major classifications of merchandise within a department. The sales plan will also be broken down by month within a department and may be further subdivided by weeks. We will consider the plan most beginning retailers will have as their initial experience—the seasonal merchandise plan (or budget) developed on a monthly basis.

Developing a Seasonal Merchandise Plan for Junior Sportswear

Laura Winter was the buyer for junior sportswear in a large department store. In planning sales for the next spring season, she studied and analyzed results for the spring season just concluded. She also examined figures for previous seasons. Laura compared figures for her department with industry statistics published in the MOR.[1] She had several discussions with her divisional merchandise manager considering corporate and storewide plans, likely actions by competitors, environmental trends, and expected changes. She then prepared preliminary sales estimates for her department. After further deliberations and revisions, and with the final concurrence of her merchandise manager, Laura established $220,000 as the planned total sales for junior sportswear for the next spring season. The percentages of planned sales to be achieved in each month of the season were estimated to be:

February	14.0%	May	17.7%
March	15.5	June	19.8
April	17.6	July	15.4

Laura then calculated planned monthly sales for the season:

February	$220,000 × 14.0% =	$ 30,800
March	220,000 × 15.5 =	34,100
April	220,000 × 17.6 =	38,720
May	220,000 × 17.7 =	38,940
June	220,000 × 19.8 =	43,560
July	220,000 × 15.4 =	33,880
		$220,000

---

[1]Known as the MOR, the *Merchandising and Operating Results of Department and Specialty Stores* is an annual publication of the National Retail Merchants Association, New York, New York.

The total reductions for the season were planned to be 22% of sales. These consisted of markdowns and employee discounts of 21% and shortages of 1%. Reductions were estimated to be distributed by month as follows:

February	15%	May	16%
March	12	June	20
April	14	July	23

On the basis of these data, Laura calculated the reductions planned for each month.

$$\text{Total reductions} = \$220,000 \times 22\% = \$48,400$$

Monthly estimated reductions:

February	$48,400 \times 15\%$	=	$ 7,260
March	$48,400 \times 12$	=	5,808
April	$48,400 \times 14$	=	6,776
May	$48,400 \times 16$	=	7,744
June	$48,400 \times 20$	=	9,680
July	$48,400 \times 23$	=	11,132
			$48,400

The annual stockturn objective established by Laura and her merchandise manager for the junior sportswear department was 4.2. Laura then established the beginning of the month stock levels using the basic stock method as follows:

$$\text{Seasonal stockturn} = \frac{\text{Annual stockturn}}{2} = \frac{4.2}{2} = 2.1$$

$$\text{Average inventory} = \frac{\text{Sales for season}}{\text{Stockturn}} = \frac{\$220,000}{2.1} = \$104,762$$

$$\text{Average monthly sales} = \frac{\text{Sales for season}}{6} = \frac{\$220,000}{6} = \$36,667$$

$$\text{Basic stock} = \text{Average inventory} - \text{Average monthly sales}$$

$$= \$104,762 - \$36,667$$

$$= \$68,095$$

Planned Sales			**Basic Stock**		**BOM Stock**
February	$30,800	+	$68,095	=	$98,895
March	34,100	+	68,095	=	102,195
April	38,720	+	68,095	=	106,815
May	38,940	+	68,095	=	107,035
June	43,560	+	68,095	=	111,655
July	33,880	+	68,095	=	101,975

Reflecting on the sales projections, and prior merchandising results, Laura and her merchandise manager agreed upon the following additional objectives for the department:

Total expenses	38%
Total controllable expenses	21
Planned profit	8
Alteration costs	.1
Cash discounts	5.2

She then calculated the planned initial markup:

$$\text{Initial markup \%} = \frac{\begin{array}{c}\text{Expenses \%} + \text{Profits \%} + \text{Reductions \%} + \\ \text{Alteration costs \%} - \text{Cash discounts \%}\end{array}}{100\% + \text{Reductions \%}}$$

$$= \frac{38\% + 8\% + 22\% + .1\% - 5.2\%}{100\% + 22\%}$$

$$= \frac{62.9\%}{122\%}$$

$$= 51.56\%$$

Laura then calculated the maintained markup:

$$\text{Maintained markup \%} = \text{Initial markup \%} - \text{Cost of reduction \%}$$

$$= 51.56\% - (22\% \times 48.44\%)$$

$$= 51.56\% - 10.66\%$$

$$= 40.9\%$$

She then calculated the gross margin:

$$\text{Gross margin \%} = \text{Maintained markup \%} - \text{Alteration costs \%} + \text{Cash discounts \%}$$

$$= 40.9\% - .1\% + 5.2\%$$

$$= 46\%$$

Laura then checked to see whether her calculation of the gross margin percentage agreed with the result obtained by adding together the total expenses and the planned profit:

$$\text{Gross margin \%} = \text{Expenses \%} + \text{Profits \%}$$

$$= 38\% + 8\%$$

$$= 46\%$$

She was pleased that her calculations checked out. She then calculated the planned contribution:

$$\text{Contribution \%} = \text{Gross margin \%} - \text{Controllable expenses \%}$$

$$= 46\% - 21\%$$

$$= 25\%$$

Filling Out the Form

Laura then began to assemble the various parts of the spring season merchandise plan on the form her company used for that purpose. (The specific arrangement of items on the forms used by different retailers for merchandise planning vary somewhat. A composite model is presented in Figure 9–1. As indicated, these forms include space for entering the figures that represent last year's results—designated LY—along with the planned and actual figures for this year—designed TY. To enhance readability and comprehension of the form the LY figures are omitted.)

She entered the sales projections in the appropriate columns of Figure 9–1; then the corresponding reductions and BOM stocks.

She then entered end of the month (EOM) inventories on Figure 9–1 reasoning as follows:

Figure 9–1 Seasonal Merchandise Plan

Department __1910 Junior Sportswear__

Spring ~~Fall~~	Feb. ~~Aug.~~	Mar. ~~Sep.~~	April ~~Oct.~~	May ~~Nov.~~	June ~~Dec.~~	July ~~Jan.~~	Total
Sales LY							
TY plan	$30,800	$34,100	$38,720	$38,940	$43,560	$33,880	$220,000
TY actual							
Reductions LY							
TY plan	7,260	5,808	6,776	7,744	9,680	11,132	48,400
TY actual							
BOM stocks LY							
TY plan	98,895	102,195	106,815	107,035	111,655	101,975	628,570
TY actual							
EOM stocks LY							
TY plan	102,195	106,815	107,035	111,655	101,975	104,762	634,437
TY actual							
Retail planned purchases	41,360	44,528	45,716	51,304	43,560	47,799	274,267
Cost planned purchases	20,035	21,569	22,145	24,852	21,100	23,154	132,855

	LY	TY plan	TY actual
Initial markup		51.56%	
Maintained markup		40.9%	
Gross margin		46.0%	
Markdowns		21.0%	
Shortages		1.0%	
Cash discounts		5.2%	
Alteration costs		0.1%	

	LY	TY plan	TY actual
Controllable expenses		21%	
Contribution		25%	
Total expenses		38%	
Profit		8%	
Stockturn		2.1	

Signed by: BUYER: _____ DMM: _____ GMM: _____
ASST. BUYER: _____

The BOM stock for March is the same amount as the EOM stock for February. Thus, the BOM figure for March, $102,195, was entered in the EOM column for February. Likewise, she entered EOM figures for March, April, May, and June:

$$\text{EOM for March} = \text{BOM for April} = \$106,815$$
$$\text{EOM for April} = \text{BOM for May} = 107,035$$
$$\text{EOM for May} = \text{BOM for June} = 111,655$$
$$\text{EOM for June} = \text{BOM for July} = 101,975$$

Laura was not able to use this technique to establish the EOM stock for July, lacking August figures. She therefore used the average inventory for the season based upon BOM stocks for the six months to set an EOM stock level for July:

Total BOM stocks February through July = $628,570.

$$\frac{\$628,570}{6} = \$104,762$$

She noted that this figure checked with the average inventory she had calculated earlier based upon seasonal sales and stockturn figures ($\frac{\$220,000}{2.1} = \$104,762$).

The final step in completing the merchandise plan for her department was to calculate planned purchases. She did this for each month reasoning as follows, "I need enough merchandise to meet my planned sales and reductions and the planned EOM stock level. By subtracting from the sum of these three amounts the BOM stock, I determine how much I need to purchase. This of course is a retail figure. By multiplying it by the cost complement of the initial markup, I'll get the purchases at cost." The calculations for each month are:

Month	EOM		Sales		Reductions		BOM		Retail Purchases		Cost Complement		Cost Purchases
Feb.	$102,195	+	$30,800	+	$ 7,260	−	$ 98,895	=	$41,360	×	48.44%	=	$20,035
Mar.	106,815	+	34,100	+	5,808	−	102,195	=	44,528	×	48.44	=	21,569
Apr.	107,035	+	38,720	+	6,776	−	106,815	=	45,716	×	48.44	=	22,145
May	111,655	+	38,940	+	7,744	−	107,035	=	51,304	×	48.44	=	24,852
Jun.	101,975	+	43,560	+	9,680	−	111,655	=	43,560	×	48.44	=	21,100
Jul.	104,762	+	33,880	+	11,132	−	101,975	=	47,799	×	48.44	=	23,154

She entered these purchase figures at retail and cost into the plan (Figure 9–1) and completed it by entering the other merchandising and operating figures that now were objectives for the next season. Her next task was to sign the form and schedule a meeting with her divisional merchandise manager. The divisional merchandise manager would have to also sign the form before it could be submitted to the general merchandise manager.

The Seasonal Merchandise Plan as a Control Tool

As you have worked through the preparation of the merchandise plan with Laura Winter, you have also reviewed many of the concepts and calculations discussed earlier in this book. The merchandise plan ties together many of these concepts, and it also becomes the basis for monitoring and appraising Laura's performance in managing the junior sportswear department. On a monthly basis, a comparison can be made between the planned figures and the actual results achieved. One, of course, would not expect dollar for dollar accuracy. Usually the planned numbers in Figure 9–1 would be rounded to hundreds of dollars. They are best estimates, not precise facts. But, we have kept the figures unrounded so that students can follow the exact calculations.

It should be apparent that if actual sales, reductions, or stock levels differ markedly from the forecasts, the purchases will be directly influenced. For example, if sales are much higher than forecast for February, acquiring only the amount of merchandise calculated in Figure 9–1 will leave the department short of inventory going into March, unless purchases are increased. Similarly, if sales are much lower than forecast, purchasing the amount previously calculated will leave the department overstocked going into the following month. We will see how retailers control the amount of purchasing authorized for buyers in the section that follows the problems.

One can also see how the seasonal plan provides the basis for monitoring and controlling the other operating and merchandising activities. For example, by comparing the cumulative markup with the planned initial markup, a check can be made of pricing. Similar assessments of markdowns, maintained markup, and gross margin, planned against actual, provide a check on the amount of reductions, the taking of cash discounts, and the level of alteration costs. Expenses can be similarly monitored.

Consequently, management is able to quickly detect deviations from expected conditions and results. Reasons for these deviations can then be readily sought out and, if possible, corrective action taken. The cause may or may not be related to the buyer's performance. For example, sales may be less than predicted. The cause may be a major promotional effort by the principal competitor involving advertising expenditures higher than the competitor's usual level, and increased markdowns that are boldly advertised as lower prices in the competitor's ads. Given this assessment, management must decide whether and, if so, how to retaliate. Another scenario might have sales less than predicted, but investigation revealing that a new buyer has misjudged customer desires and fashion shifts, acquiring an inventory that is not selling. In either case because of its planning efforts, management has a system that alerts it to the situation. Corrective and/or retaliatory action can be taken. The plan will have to be revised and a new one developed. But management is able to respond in a timely manner. Consider the alternative, having no plan, having no benchmarks, not being aware of the need to react in a timely way.

Problems

9–1. The furniture department had spring season sales for last year of $124,560. For the upcoming spring season, a 12% increase in sales is forecasted. Reductions last year were 15% of sales. The forecast is that they will stay at this level. Develop the monthly forecast of sales and reductions if estimates for the monthly distribution of sales and reductions are as follows:

	Sales	*Reductions*
February	14%	18%
March	18	14
April	20	13
May	21	16
June	17	18
July	10	21

9–2. The buyer for the girls' clothing department had projected the following figures for the month of October: sales $22,900; BOM inventory $65,455; reductions $3,760; and EOM inventory $69,458. What are the planned purchases for October? Is this a retail or a cost figure?

9–3. What are the planned purchases at cost for March in a department that has the following planned figures: sales $37,870; reductions $4,565; EOM inventory $74,888; BOM inventory $72,576; and initial markup 46%?

9–4. Using the figures presented below prepare a seasonal merchandise plan for the luggage department for the fall season. Enter your final numbers on Figure 9–2.

Annual stockturn	2.4
Markdowns and employee discounts	10%
Shortages	2%
Cash discounts	4%
Total expenses	38%
Controllable expenses	22%
Planned profit	10%
Planned sales	$200,000

	Planned	
	Sales	*Reductions*
August	15%	15%
September	14	16
October	16	15
November	19	18
December	24	14
January	12	22

Figure 9–2 Seasonal Merchandise Plan

Department _____

Spring Fall	Feb. Aug.	Mar. Sept.	April Oct.	May Nov.	June Dec.	July Jan.	Total
Sales LY							
TY plan							
TY actual							
Reductions LY							
TY plan							
TY actual							
BOM stocks LY							
TY plan							
TY actual							
EOM stocks LY							
TY plan							
TY actual							
Retail planned purchases							
Cost planned purchases							

	LY	TY plan	TY actual		LY	TY plan	TY actual
Initial markup				Controllable expenses			
Maintained markup				Contribution			
Gross margin				Total expenses			
Markdowns				Profit			
Shortages				Stockturn			
Cash discounts							
Alteration costs							

Signed by: BUYER: _____   DMM: _____   GMM: _____
              ASST. BUYER: _____

The Need for Careful Control of Purchasing

Preparation of the seasonal merchandise plan resulted in the calculation of the planned purchases figures for each month of the season. If we assume for the moment the accuracy of the estimates, the planned purchase figure at cost is an authorization for the buyer to spend the store's funds to acquire merchandise. Referring back to Figure 9–1, the buyer for junior sportswear needs to acquire $20,035 worth of merchandise for the department for February. In practice, merchandise for a given month is usually not purchased all at once, and for various items it may be ordered far in advance of delivery. So a buyer may be simultaneously ordering merchandise for delivery during several different months and have outstanding several orders for delivery during a given month. Furthermore, full or partial deliveries may already have been made, sometimes in advance of the expected month of sale. Remember that in a large department store there may be over 100 buyers engaged in these activities. How does the store management control this purchasing activity so that the merchandise needed is acquired, but so that excessive investment in inventory is avoided?

Open-to-Buy Control

A control concept known as **open-to-buy** is the device used to manage the purchase activities of buyers.

Let's assume for purposes of illustration that Laura Winter, the buyer for junior sportswear whose seasonal merchandise plan is presented in Figure 9–1, had acquired no merchandise for delivery in February and had on hand on February 1 a BOM stock of $98,895 — exactly according to plan. Let's further assume that her planned sales, reductions, and EOM stocks are as indicated in Figure 9–1. Then Laura's open-to-buy for February would be the planned purchases already determined: $41,360 at retail, $20,035 at cost.

Open-to-Buy with Merchandise on Order

On the other hand, let's assume that the sales, reductions, and inventory figures are as indicated, but that Laura had on order for delivery during February merchandise with a retail value of $10,000. Then she would have already committed $10,000 for purchases and her open-to-buy for February would be $31,360 at retail ($31,360 × 48.44% = $15,191 at cost).

Open-to-Buy with Revised BOM Position

As we suggested above, it is not very likely that buyers will forecast sales, reductions, and inventories precisely. So let's complicate the situation involving Laura Winter by assuming she had $10,000 at retail on order and that while sales, reductions, and EOM inventory figures remain as listed in Figure 9–1, the BOM figure with which she started the month was actually $101,434. Then to calculate her open-to-buy balance for the month of February, we would first determine the merchandise needed to meet the month's objectives. These are:

Needed for February:

Sales	$ 30,800
Reductions	7,260
EOM stock	$102,195
Total needed	$140,255

As the above figures indicate, Laura needs enough merchandise to meet the sales and reductions projections of $30,800 and $7,260, respectively, and the desired EOM stock position of $102,195.

Next we determine the merchandise on hand and on order:

On hand for February: BOM	$101,434
On order for February	10,000
Total available	$111,434

The open-to-buy would be the difference between what was needed for February and what was available:

$$\text{Open-to-buy February} = \$140{,}255 - \$111{,}434$$
$$= \$28{,}821 \text{ (at retail value)}$$

Another way to calculate the open-to-buy for February would be to recalculate the planned purchases and then subtract the on order amount. Let's do that as a check on our answer. The revised planned purchases for February, assuming again the higher BOM inventory figure (\$101,434) and the same sales, reductions, and EOM figures for February would be:

$$\text{Planned purchases} = \text{EOM} + \text{Sales} + \text{Reductions} - \text{BOM}$$
$$= \$102{,}195 + \$30{,}800 + \$7{,}260 - \$101{,}434$$
$$= \$38{,}821$$

Then open-to-buy, February 1st, would be planned purchases minus the on order:

$$\text{Open-to-buy} = \text{Planned purchases} - \text{On order}$$
$$= \$38{,}821 - \$10{,}000$$
$$= \$28{,}821 \text{ (at retail value)}$$

This is the same amount as calculated earlier.

Open-to-Buy with Revised Sales and Reductions

When actual sales and reductions are not occurring as forecasted as the month progresses, there is a need to further revise the open-to-buy. For example, if for some reason, sales are much lower than forecasted, the need for additional merchandise will decrease. Correspondingly, if sales are surpassing the forecasted amount by a substantial margin, there will be a need for more merchandise than had been planned. Let's continue with the situation in Laura Winter's department and say that in the first 14 selling days of February sales had been \$21,000. The merchandise on order, \$10,000, had been received. An additional \$20,000 had been purchased and received. Reductions to date had totaled \$4,200. In the judgment of Laura and her merchandise manager it was expected that the sales and reductions pattern for the balance of the month would follow that of the first 14 days. There would be 28 selling days during the month.

If the sales and reductions for the balance of the month equaled those for the first half, then total sales and reductions would be much higher than forecast:

$$\text{Revised sales} = \$21{,}000 \times 2 = \$42{,}000$$
$$\text{Revised reductions} = \$4{,}200 \times 2 = \$8{,}400$$

We have made the situation easy by dividing the month into two halves. This isn't always the case, so let's illustrate how we would determine the sales and reductions by calculating the daily averages so that this method can be applied when you confront a situation involving other than exactly a half month's sales.

$$\text{Average daily sales to date} = \frac{\$21{,}000}{14 \text{ days}} = \$1{,}500 \text{ per day}$$

$$\text{Projected sales for 28 day month} = \$1{,}500 \times 28 = \$42{,}000$$

$$\text{Average daily reductions to date} = \frac{\$4{,}200}{14 \text{ days}} = \$300$$

$$\text{Projected reductions for 28 day month} = \$300 \times 28 = \$8{,}400$$

Let's first calculate the revised open-to-buy by determining the merchandise needed and the amount on hand to meet the need.

Needed for balance of February:

Sales	$ 21,000
Reductions	4,200
EOM stock	102,195
Total needed	$127,395

On hand after 14 selling days:

BOM stock	$101,434
Purchases received	30,000
	$131,434
Less: Sales	$ 21,000
Reductions	4,200
Amount on hand	$106,234

The open-to-buy would be the amount needed minus the amount on hand, or $127,395 − $106,234 = $21,161.

Now, as a check, we will determine the revised open-to-buy by recalculating the planned purchases and subtracting the purchases ordered and received.

With higher sales and reductions figures, the planned purchases should have been:

$$\text{Planned purchases} = \text{EOM} + \text{Sales} + \text{Reductions} − \text{BOM}$$

$$= \$102,195 + \$42,000 + \$8,400 − \$101,434$$

$$= \$51,161$$

$$\text{Open-to-buy} = \text{Planned purchases} − \text{Purchases ordered and received}$$

$$= \$51,161 − \$30,000$$

$$= \$21,161$$

Once again we see that it all checks out.

The Open-to-Buy Control Responds to Changes

As one final reconciliation and to help understand the purpose of the open-to-buy control, we will make one additional analysis. Recall that before we considered the increases in sales and reductions, we had calculated Laura's open-to-buy to be $28,821, assuming $10,000 on order and a revised BOM stock of $101,434. If we had not revised Laura's open-to-buy, midway through February it would have been $28,821 minus the $20,000 she had purchased and received, or $8,821. Thus, she would be authorized to acquire an additional $8,821 worth of goods (at retail). However, sales are much ahead of forecast and reductions somewhat ahead. The difference in sales and reductions would be:

$$\text{Sales difference} = \text{Revised forecast} − \text{Original forecast}$$

$$= \$42,000 − \$30,800$$

$$= \$11,200$$

$$\text{Reductions difference} = \text{Revised forecast} − \text{Original forecast}$$

$$= \$8,400 − \$7,260 = \$1,140$$

So, the total additional needs are $11,200 + $1,140 or $12,340. Adding this amount to the $8,821 results in the figure of $21,161, calculated as the revised open-to-buy. So the system responds to the expected increases in sales and reductions and provides for the purchase of additional merchandise. Similarly, if sales and/or reductions were less than forecasted, the system would signal the need to reduce purchases.

   Furthermore, had the buyer acquired too much merchandise, that is more than needed to meet sales, reductions, and EOM stock projections, the system would signal that the buyer was "overbought". This becomes a flag for the buyer and the buyer's supervisor to determine whether any additional merchandise purchases should be authorized. In the absence of such a control system, a store could have a hundred or so buyers yielding to the ever present appeals of manufacturers' sales representatives with all the items "I know will be big sellers in your store." The system also gives buyers the convenient reason, "I have no open-to-buy," to politely refuse the overly persistent sales appeal!

Problems

9–5. A clothing department had the following figures for the month of May: planned sales $27,500; planned reductions $3,000; BOM stock $63,140; and planned EOM stock $61,370. Merchandise with a retail value of $18,000 was on order for May delivery. What was the open-to-buy on May 1st?

9–6. A sportswear buyer planning a buying trip is calculating the open-to-buy for September. Sales for the month of $56,800 have been forecasted. The BOM and EOM stock objectives are $111,400 and $115,200, respectively. Merchandise for September with a retail value of $15,000 had been received and $15,000 is on order for September delivery. Reductions of $8,000 are expected and the initial markup is 48%. How many cost dollars may the buyer spend on the trip?

9–7. The seasonal merchandise plan for the men's accessories department had the following figures for October: sales $30,976; reductions $5,420; BOM stock $85,450; and EOM stock $85,620. On October 1st the BOM stock as indicated by the book inventory was $88,731. Merchandise valued at $8,000 retail had already been acquired for October and an additional $8,000 was on order. What was the buyer's open-to-buy on October 1st? If the department's initial markup was 50%, how much could the buyer actually spend to acquire merchandise for October?

9–8. After the first 10 selling days in November, sales in the glassware department were running 15% above planned sales. The buyer conferred with the merchandise manager and they concurred in the judgment that sales for the balance of the month would continue at this higher than forecasted level. They also expected reductions to remain as originally planned. There were to be 30 selling days in November. Calculate the revised open-to-buy at retail and cost if the other relevant figures were: planned sales $33,520; planned EOM stock $110,300; initial markup 52%; November purchases received $8,000; on order for November delivery $11,000; planned reductions $4,000; and inventory November 1st $122,552.

Open-to-Buy as a Dollar Control

Open-to-buy control, as introduced above, is a system for controlling dollar investments in inventory. While we have illustrated it in the context of an entire department using monthly planning, the basic concept could also be applied to categories of merchandise within a department, known as classifications, and for time periods other than a month. The dollar open-to-buy system indicates how much money the buyer is authorized to spend. It does not determine what specific items should be purchased and the timing of the purchases. The process of converting dollars of authorization into purchases of units is obviously critical, as it brings together the investment in merchandise and the demand of customers. In practice, processes for deciding "what to buy, when," range from buyer judgment and decision based upon "eyeball" inspection of the stock, experience, and familiarity with suppliers, all the way to sophisticated inventory control systems utilizing complicated mathematical models. The former approach is more likely to be confronted in smaller operations and those selling dynamic, fashion oriented goods with less predictable demand; the latter in larger operations selling staple goods with highly predictable demand.

In considering the problem of converting from dollars of open-to-buy to units of purchases, we need to recognize that whereas dollars are dollars, that is homogeneous in kind, units are heterogeneous, varying in style, color, size, fabric, brand, and price. Units also vary in rates of sale, distance of supplier to store, minimum order sizes, factory pack sizes, and so forth. Fortunately, we now have computers available as tireless slaves that can capture unit sales information at the point of sale and incorporate it into sophisticated analyses of merchandise resupply variables, producing lengthy sales and inventory reports along with suggested reorder amounts.

Buyer Judgment Always Needed

But buyers still have to exercise judgment in deciding exactly how the open-to-buy should be applied to the reorder suggestions. Remember the computer cannot tell you to order the new market style that will be the next "hot" item. Likewise, no model can forecast the degree of acceptance of a style that is new and just being introduced. Like many other facets of retailing discussed earlier, good judgment is a necessary accompaniment of success. This good judgment causes the buyer not to put any further open-to-buy into an item for which demand is about to fall, and to have open-to-buy available for the next item about to become a big seller.

Unit Open-to-Buy for Neckties

To provide familiarity with the process of converting dollar open-to-buy into orders of units, we will consider a simple example. In so doing, we will introduce a *unit* open-to-buy system.

Many retailers utilize stock plans to indicate how inventory should be distributed across the various individual items stocked. These stock plans reflect the expected sales and the factors that will influence sales such as style, color, size, price, brand, and so forth. For example, George Herman, the buyer for men's accessories in a department store, forecasted November sales of $24,500. He further estimated that 30% of these sales would be in the neckties classification. Thus, the planned November sales for neckties were $7,350. The BOM stock-sales ratio was 3.5. Thus, George determined that beginning of the month inventories should be $25,725. George further forecasted the distribution of sales among the three necktie price lines carried in his department to be:

35% at $ 7.95

45% at $ 9.95

20% at $12.95

He used these estimates to forecast sales in units:

Price line $7.95

Planned dollar sales $= 35\% \times \$7,350 = \$2,573$

Planned unit sales $= \dfrac{\$2,573}{\$7.95} = 324$

Price line $9.95

Planned dollar sales = 45% × $7,350 = $3,308

$$\text{Planned unit sales} = \frac{\$3,308}{\$9.95} = 332$$

Price line $12.95

Planned dollar sales = 20% × $7,350 = $1,470

$$\text{Planned unit sales} = \frac{\$1,470}{\$12.95} = 114$$

He then calculated the distribution of the BOM inventory:

$ 7.95 ties: 35% × $25,725 = $ 9,004

$ 9.95 ties: 45% × $25,725 = $11,576

$12.95 ties: 20% × $25,725 = $ 5,145

He further calculated the number of units of each price line to be in the BOM stock:

$$\frac{\$9,004}{\$7.95} = 1,133 \text{ units}$$

$$\frac{\$11,576}{\$9.95} = 1,163 \text{ units}$$

$$\frac{\$5,145}{\$12.95} = 397 \text{ units}$$

With a similar set of calculations, George determined that EOM stocks should be:

$ 7.95: 1,254 units

$ 9.95: 1,363 units

$12.95:   538 units

These inventory amounts would represent the ideal or model stock levels, assuming that the sales forecasts are accurate and given the stockturn objective implicit in the stock-sales ratio. Of course, it is unrealistic to expect that forecasts will be precisely met. Correspondingly, inventory levels will vary with actual sales. Based upon October's actual sales, the inventory of ties in George's department, and the amounts on order for November delivery as of November 1st are:

Price Line	On Hand	On Order
$ 7.95	1,175 ties	288 ties
$ 9.95	1,202 ties	288 ties
$12.95	365 ties	144 ties

Thus, George's unit open-to-buy for each price line on November 1st was:

For $7.95 ties:

Needs: 1,254 (EOM) + 324 (sales) = 1,578

Available: 1,175 (BOM) + 288 (on order) = 1,463

Unit open-to-buy: 1,578 − 1,463 = 115

For $9.95 ties:

Needs: 1,363 (EOM) + 332 (sales) = 1,695

Available: 1,202 (BOM) + 288 (on order) = 1,490

Unit open-to-buy: 1,695 − 1,490 = 205

For $12.95 ties:

Needs: 538 (EOM) + 114 (sales) = 652

Available: 365 (BOM) + 144 (on order) = 509

Unit open-to-buy: 652 − 509 = 143

To convert the unit open-to-buy figures (indicating how much of which items need to be acquired) into dollar open-to-buy (the controlling limit on dollar expenditures) we would take the additional step of multiplying the unit open-to-buy figures by the price lines:

$$115 \text{ units} \times \$\ 7.95 = \$\ \ 914.25$$
$$205 \text{ units} \times \$\ 9.95 = \$2,039.75$$
$$143 \text{ units} \times \$12.95 = \underline{\$1,851.85}$$

Total open-to-buy, at retail = $4,805.85

Now George knows how much he is authorized to spend, and what items he needs to buy.

Problems

9–9. Calculate the open-to-buy in units for the $40 price line in the handbag classification. The buyer had on hand 72 units and 12 were on order for delivery during the month. Planned sales for the month were 25 units and the EOM planned stock was 75 units.

9–10. One of the classifications in the lawn and garden shop was power lawn mowers. There were four categories of power mowers: gas fueled riding mowers; gas fueled self-propelled mowers; gas fueled push mowers; and electric push mowers. Inventories were planned based upon proportions of sales. Sales were distributed as follows:

Gas riding	12%
Gas self-propelled	30
Gas push	50
Electric push	8

There were three price lines in the gas self-propelled category: $349, $399, and $469, whose percentages of gas self-propelled sales were 30%, 55%, and 15%, respectively. Planned beginning of the season retail inventory for powered mowers was $31,270. How many units of the $469 self-propelled mowers should be in stock at the start of the season? If the June BOM unit stock for the $469 self-propelled mowers was four, there were no units on order, planned sales for June were six units, and the EOM planned stock was two units, how many dollars of the retail open-to-buy should the buyer apply to the $469 self-propelled mower?

Summary of Chapter Concepts

This chapter discussed the seasonal merchandise planning or budgeting system developed and utilized in department store retailing and also in departmentalized specialty stores.

Concepts introduced in earlier chapters were integrated into an illustrated overall plan for a new season. Subsequent use of the plan as a control device to detect unexpected results and to assess performance also was explained.

The relationship of the merchandise plan to the open-to-buy system used to authorize and control buyer purchasing was also discussed and illustrated. Finally, the relationship between dollar and unit control of stocks was introduced.

These concepts and systems would have limited applicability to a small retail operation, such as the Mellow Music Store which has been used to apply many of the general concepts introduced earlier. At the Mellow Music Store, the owner-operators are selling a limited line of goods, have direct daily visual contact with the merchandise, know just what is selling, and what customers are requesting. They would wish to stock a sufficient inventory to support the image of being a reliable source of supply. They would have a limited inventory of expensive items, such as pianos and other musical instruments that would be monitored on a simple units of stock basis.

Julie and John Martin would reorder such essential supplies as guitar strings and drum sticks on a judgment basis, designed never to be out of stock. They would try to keep in stock select pieces of "classical" music in limited quantities. They would inventory "pop" music sheets hoping to have the latest hit in ample supply, but to be going out of stock on last month's hit just when its popularity dies.

It is also likely that Julie and John would provide customers with a special order service using manufacturer's catalogs for expensive items not stocked. Also, by dealing with reliable wholesalers and distributors, they would most likely be able to order for delivery within a day or two, specially requested arrangements of music or particular songs not stocked. If a wholesaler or distributor were located within reasonable proximity of the Mellow Music Store, one can imagine John or Julie Martin taking time to go to the supplier to pick up the item so as to have a requested item ready for a customer in advance of the supplier's regular delivery schedule.

Review Problems

9–1R. Calculate planned purchases at retail and at cost for the children's department with the following planned figures for April: sales $34,600; initial markup 52%; BOM inventory $68,580; EOM inventory $64,320; and reductions $3,680.

9–2R. The new buyer for men's dress shirts took over on May 1st with a BOM stock of $72,155. Planned sales and reductions were $25,500 and $3,825, respectively. The planned EOM inventory was $69,336. The previous buyer had goods on order for May delivery totaling $28,778. What was the open-to-buy on May 1st?

9–3R. A buyer planning a buying trip consulted the latest reports covering the first 12 selling days of the month. Sales were $39,567 and reductions were $3,240. These figures were somewhat at variance with those planned, but after conferring with the merchandise manager, the buyer decided to base projections for the balance of the month on these actual figures. Planned sales for the month had been $88,320, and planned reductions had been $9,000. Inventory on the first of the month was $247,296. Planned EOM inventory was $253,338. Purchases for the month already received into inventory totaled $51,300, and $25,600 was on order for delivery during the month. The initial markup in the department was 48%. There were 30 selling days during the month. What was the buyer's retail open-to-buy? How much could the buyer spend during the buying trip to purchase additional merchandise for the current month?

9–4R. Use Figure 9–3 to prepare a spring seasonal merchandise plan for the junior ready-to-wear department. The numbers that you and your merchandise manager have agreed upon are:

Total expenses	35%
Controllable expenses	22%
Planned profit	8%
Planned sales	$180,000
Seasonal stockturn	2.2
Shortages	1.5%
Markdowns and employee discounts	22%
Cash discounts	4%

	Planned	
	Sales	**Reductions**
February	15%	16%
March	17	14
April	19	14
May	22	16
June	16	19
July	11	21

Figure 9–3 Seasonal Merchandise Plan

Spring / Fall		Feb. Aug.	Mar. Sep.	April Oct.	May Nov.	June Dec.	July Jan.	Total
Department _____								
Sales	LY							
	TY plan							
	TY actual							
Reductions	LY							
	TY plan							
	TY actual							
BOM stocks	LY							
	TY plan							
	TY actual							
EOM stocks	LY							
	TY plan							
	TY actual							
Retail planned purchases								
Cost planned purchases								

	LY	TY plan	TY actual
Initial markup			
Maintained markup			
Gross margin			
Markdowns			
Shortages			
Cash discounts			
Alteration costs			

	LY	TY plan	TY actual
Controllable expenses			
Contribution			
Total expenses			
Profit			
Stockturn			

Signed by: BUYER: _____ DMM: _____ GMM: _____

ASST. BUYER: _____

CHAPTER 10

Performance Measures Based on Sales

The preceding chapters of this book have focused on many of the important "numbers" of retailing. They have introduced, discussed, and illustrated operating terms and concepts from the language of retailing. Terms such as markups, markdowns, maintained markups, gross margins, contributions, stockturns and open-to-buys, represent the essence of merchandising and control. In this chapter and in Chapter 11, we will introduce some other widely applied concepts that measure productivity and financial performance. This chapter will focus on calculations that are based on sales.

Departmental Sales Percentages

Retailers use sales as a major variable or as the base for many measures of output, productivity, or performance. Retailers regularly calculate the percentage that each department's net sales are of the total store's net sales. The sleepwear department of store No. 9, a branch of a department store company, had net sales for the past season of $380,176. Total store net sales for the same period were $34,561,477. The sleepwear department's net sales were $\frac{\$380,176}{\$34,561,477} = 1.1\%$ of total store net sales.

Similarly, the sleepwear department's percentage of total net sales for all stores operated by the department store company was calculated as follows:

$$\text{Percentage of total sales in sleepware} = \frac{\text{Total net sales of sleepwear departments all stores}}{\text{Total net sales all departments all stores}}$$

$$= \frac{\$3,793,771}{\$411,610,444}$$

$$= .9\%$$

In analyzing sales performance, retailers compare the percentage of sales for individual departments of one store with those of other stores in the company. Results for the company are also compared with industry figures. For example, department and specialty store companies compare their figures with those published by the National Retail Merchants Association in the annual *Merchandising and Operating Results of Department and Specialty Stores*. Supermarket companies compare their results with figures compiled and distributed by the Food Marketing Institute.

Comparing This Year's Sales with Last Year

As we saw in Chapter 9, while retailers are planning ahead, they are also looking back. The seasonal merchandise plan not only includes this year's planned figures, but also last year's actual figures. Once this year's actual figures are available, retailers will calculate by department the percentage change in net sales over last year.

For example, last year the housewares department had net sales of $122,343. This year's net sales were $127,048. The percentage change in net sales was calculated as follows:

$$\text{Percentage change in net sales} = \frac{\text{This year's sales} - \text{Last year's sales}}{\text{Last year's sales}}$$

$$= \frac{\$127,048 - \$122,343}{\$122,343}$$

$$= \frac{\$4,705}{\$122,343}$$

$$= 3.8\%$$

Retailers will usually further compare these figures with the merchandise plan, among individual stores in the company, and against industry figures.

Analyzing Sales by Method of Payment

Many retailers also examine the distribution of sales by method of payment. At the Modern Department Store, net sales last year were $15,347,865. Of this total, $5,709,406 were cash sales; $7,766,019 were charge sales on the store's own credit card; and the balance, $1,872,440, were charge sales on third party credit cards, such as Visa, MasterCard, and American Express. The percentages of sales by method of payment were calculated as follows:

$$\text{Cash sales} = \frac{\$5,709,406}{\$15,347,865} = 37.2\% \text{ of total sales}$$

$$\text{In-house credit sales} = \frac{\$7,766,019}{\$15,347,865} = 50.6\% \text{ of total sales}$$

$$\text{Third-party credit sales} = \frac{\$1,872,440}{\$15,347,865} = 12.2\% \text{ of total sales}$$

Problems

10–1. The luggage department of a department store had net sales for the spring season of $88,319. If total spring season net sales for the department store were $1,471,991, what percentage of total net sales were in luggage?

10–2. A supermarket chain had total third quarter net sales of $221,046,377, of which $56,092,186 were in the meat department and $20,894,231 were in the produce department. What percentage of total sales were in meat? In produce?

10–3. Records of the past month's sales at a specialty store revealed that $52,363 were paid in cash, $29,241 were on the store's credit plan, and $25,394 were on third-party credit cards. Make a percentage analysis of the month's sales by method of payment.

10–4. From the following second quarter data calculate the percentage change in net sales over last year for the men's clothing department and for the entire store.

	Second Quarter Net Sales This Year	*Second Quarter Net Sales Last Year*
Men's clothing	$ 14,844	$ 13,619
Total store	$236,438	$226,980

10–5. From the following data determine the percentage of total store sales and the percentage change in sales over last year for the jewelry department. How does the percentage change in sales of the jewelry department compare with that of the entire store?

	Net Sales This Year	*Net Sales Last Year*
Jewelry department	$ 2,094,447	$ 2,100,986
Total store	$83,443,976	$78,103,561

Sales per Square Foot: A Common Measure

One of the most common measures of productivity in retailing is *sales per square foot*. It is usually calculated for a total store and for individual departments, but also may be calculated for sections of a department or for an entire shopping center. Sales per square foot relates the net sales to the amount of selling area used to generate the sales.

$$\text{Sales per square foot} = \frac{\text{Net sales}}{\text{Square feet of selling area}}$$

In the supermarket industry, measures of sales per square foot are often calculated on a weekly basis. For example, store No. 334 in a supermarket chain had sales last week of $287,363. The store has 31,224 square feet of selling area. The store's sales per square foot last week were:

$$\text{Sales per square foot} = \frac{\$287,363}{31,224} = \$9.20$$

The produce department of store No. 334 had sales last week of $21,755. It has 2,800 square feet of selling area. The sales per square foot in the produce department last week were:

$$\text{Sales per square foot} = \frac{\$21,755}{2,800} = \$7.77$$

In the department store field, measures of sales per square foot are usually calculated on an annual basis. The downtown store of a department store company had sales last year of $35,389,576. It has 215,778 square feet of selling space. The store's sales per square foot for last year were:

$$\text{Sales per square foot} = \frac{\$35,389,576}{215,778} = \$164.01$$

The domestics department of this store had sales last year of $1,694,342. It occupied 15,220 square feet of selling space. The domestics department's sales per square foot were:

$$\text{Sales per square foot} = \frac{\$1,694,342}{15,220} = \$111.32$$

Defining Selling Area

There is no doubt about what the net sales in the above relationship are. These are the total or gross sales, net of any returns and allowances. However, selling area cannot be so clearly defined. As customers, we recognize that the checkout lanes in a supermarket, or discount department store, are usually the location of racks designed to sell us candy, gum, magazines, razor blades, cigarettes, and other merchandise. Should they be considered selling space, or excluded from selling space because the major purpose of this section of the store is the checking out and bagging of our purchases? It is a rather moot point. Industry calculations in the supermarket field do not include checkout area as part of selling area. In the department store field the definition of selling area is:

The total departmental area used in selling including clerk and customer aisles, fitting rooms, and forward stock areas contained within or contiguous to the areas used by merchandise departments for selling purposes; customer aisles that run between different selling departments are divided in calculating the selling areas of each such department.[1]

To be useful for comparative and analytical purposes, sales per square foot data must be comparable. In order to make comparisons among individual departments and stores, the same definition of selling space must be used by all. Likewise, to make comparisons with industry figures, a given company must use the same definitions as those used by the industry group.

Sales per Square Foot as a Productivity Measure

There are two major uses of sales per square foot data. One use is to monitor the productivity of a department or store. For example, if a unit is operating below company or industry standards, efforts may be taken to try to increase the sales volume, or to consider reducing the amount of space. In this regard, sales per square foot is a very useful measure. In a sense it is a rough measure of return on investment. Consider that the amount of profit earned in a retailing operation is ultimately a function of the sales volume. Likewise, the investment in a retailing unit is a function of the amount of space. For example, construction costs are usually measured as so many dollars per square foot. The amount of equipment needed is related to the amount of space. The amount of inventory is a function of the amount of space available to display and store it. While one cannot say that a given sales per square foot can be directly translated into a certain return on investment, it can be said that a very healthy sales per square foot is generally associated with a healthy return on investment. Because it is so easily calculated as a by-product of sales data that is readily captured by the cash registers or point-of-sale devices, sales per square foot is a key measure of retailing performance.

Sales per Square Foot as a Planning Measure

A second use of the sales per square foot data is in planning sales and determining space requirements. For example, a "ballpark" estimate can be made of the amount of space needed to support a given sales volume by using available sales per square foot data. If the average sales per square foot in the bakery department of a supermarket chain are $12.50 per week, then an analyst might tentatively project a weekly

---

[1]*The Buyer's Manual*, R. Patrick Cash, editor, National Retail Merchants Association, New York, 1979, p. 568.

sales volume of $15,000, if 1,200 square feet in a new store were allocated to bakery products:

$$\text{Estimated sales} = \text{Space (1,200 square feet)} \times \text{Sales per square foot (\$12.50)}$$
$$= \$15,000$$

Or, if company researchers had estimated weekly bakery department volume for a new store to be $15,000, then the amount of space needed could be estimated as 1,200 square feet:

$$\text{Amount of space} = \frac{\text{Sales volume (\$15,000)}}{\text{Sales per square foot (\$12.50)}}$$
$$= 1,200 \text{ square feet}$$

It is necessary to stress that such estimates are clearly only rough approximations that encompass a number of assumptions about the similarity between the new store and existing company stores regarding such factors as demographics, locations, and competition. While not providing a definitive answer, estimates based on sales per square foot data often provide useful starting points for further analysis.

We should not forget that sales per square foot and many other measures of performance are usually reported as averages, usually the median, the middle figure in an array of the data for contributing stores. Some companies will use as goals the so-called upper quartile result. This is the figure in the array that is better than the performance of 75% of the stores contributing data.

Sales per Linear Foot of Shelf Space

There are other measures similar to sales per square foot that you may occasionally confront. *Sales per linear foot* of shelving would literally relate sales to the number of linear feet of shelf space used by a particular department, category, or brand of merchandise. For example, in the paper towels aisle of a supermarket there are 60 linear feet of shelving. Sales per week in paper towels are $1,866. Therefore, sales per linear foot of shelving are:

$$\text{Sales per linear foot} = \frac{\text{Sales}}{\text{Linear feet of shelving}}$$
$$= \frac{\$1,866}{60}$$
$$= \$31.10$$

If an analysis were made of two brands, and the results indicated that Brand A had a much higher sales per linear foot than B, increasing the shelf space of Brand A at the expense of Brand B might be considered.

Problems

10–6. A branch department store has a total of 180,000 square feet of space. Twelve percent of the total space is considered nonselling. If the store's total sales last year were $22,965,754, what were the store's sales per square foot for last year?

10–7. A discount department store had total sales during the past week of $748,432. Eight hundred square feet of the store's total area of 56,000 square feet are used for nonselling purposes. What were the store's sales per square foot last week?

10–8. The florist department in a large supermarket had sales last week of $3,900. The department occupies 200 square feet of space. What were the department's sales per square foot?

10–9. The bridal shop of a department store had sales last year of $285,870. What were the department's sales per square foot if the amount of selling space occupied by the department was an area 30 feet wide and 40 feet deep?

Sales per Transaction

We will now introduce several other productivity measures that involve sales. *Sales per transaction* relates the total sales in a store or department to the number of transactions that were processed in the store or department. A transaction is the processing of one sale. For example, in a department store a customer buys a chair for $299. The sales clerk writes up a charge slip for $299 which is processed through a point-of-sale terminal. This is one transaction. In a discount department store, a customer walks up to a checkout counter carrying 5 quarts of oil and an oil filter. The cashier rings the six items up on the cash register and the customer pays the total amount in cash. This is one transaction. In a supermarket, a customer wheels a shopping cart laden with foodstuffs into the checkout lane. The cashier puts each item through an electronic scanner that produces a total of $76.82, which the customer pays in cash. This is one transaction.

Sales per transaction would relate total gross sales to the number of transactions processed. If total gross sales were $246,780 during a period in which 20,100 customers were processed, the sales per transaction would be:

$$\text{Sales per transaction} = \frac{\text{Gross sales}}{\text{Number of transactions}}$$

$$= \frac{\$246,780}{20,100}$$

$$= \$12.28$$

This result, $12.28, is also referred to as the average transaction, or the average sale.

Sales per Employee Hour

Some retailers, particularly in food retailing, relate sales for a period to the number of hours of labor worked during that period. The result is a measure of productivity, *sales per employee hour*. For example, during the past week sales at store No. 88 of a supermarket chain were $247,365. During the week 3,055 hours of labor were worked. Sales per employee hour were:

$$\text{Sales per employee hour} = \frac{\text{Net sales}}{\text{Number of employee hours}}$$

$$= \frac{\$247,365}{3,055}$$

$$= \$80.97$$

During the same week, sales in the produce department were $17,315. The number of employee hours worked in the produce department was 255. Sales per employee hour for the produce department were:

$$\text{Sales per employee hour} = \frac{\text{Net sales}}{\text{Number of employee hours}}$$

$$= \frac{\$17,315}{255}$$

$$= \$67.90$$

Sales per Full-Time Equivalent

A similar measure used by retailers is *sales per full-time employee*. Because of the large number of part-time employees used in many phases of retailing, this measure is actually computed on the basis of number of full-time equivalent employees. Part-time hours worked are converted into the number of equivalent full-time employees. For example, during the week in which store No. 88, cited above, had sales of $247,365, 30 full-time employees worked and, in addition, part-timers worked a total of 2,005 hours. A full-time week at this company is 35 hours. By dividing the number of hours worked by part-timers, 2,005, by 35 we determine the number of full-time equivalents, 57.3. Combining this amount with the 30 full-timers, we have a total of 87.3 full-time equivalents. To determine the sales per full-time equivalent:

$$\text{Sales per full-time employee} = \frac{\text{Net sales}}{\text{Number of full-time equivalent employees}}$$

$$= \frac{\$247,365}{87.3}$$

$$= \$2,834$$

Sales Analysis by Vendors

Retailers will also relate sales to specific vendors who supply merchandise. For example, during the past spring season, the men's clothing department had total sales of $124,860. The buyer had made relatively equal purchases of merchandise from six sources. In analyzing the results of the past season, the buyer obtained data on sales broken down by supplier. The results were:

	Sales
Vendor A	$ 40,704
Vendor B	14,109
Vendor C	10,988
Vendor D	25,472
Vendor E	6,118
Vendor F	27,469
Total	$124,860

Dividing each vendor's sales by the total sales results in the percentage of sales contributed by each vendor:

	Percentage of Total Sales
Vendor A	32.6%
Vendor B	11.3
Vendor C	8.8
Vendor D	20.4
Vendor E	4.9
Vendor F	22.0

The results indicate three relatively strong and three relatively weak vendors. The buyer would now seek explanations of the differences and try to decide what possible action might increase the volume of the weaker vendors' lines. The buyer would also consider whether lines of one or more of the weaker suppliers might be eliminated, and that space made available to the merchandise of one of the stronger vendors, or to a supplier not presently represented in the department's assortment.

As we saw in Chapter 8, the buyer might also relate each vendor's sales to that supplier's inventory to analyze vendor stockturn.

Problems

10–10. A supermarket had total gross sales last week of $345,006. 28,749 customer transactions were processed. What was the average sale per transaction?

10–11. The average sale in a discount department store was $11.43 during a week when the store processed a total of 28,433 customers. What were the store's total sales for the week?

10–12. Payroll records for a supermarket indicated that during the past week a total of 65 employees had worked. Of this total, 20 were full-timers who each worked a regular 40 hour week; 45 were part-timers who each averaged 25 hours of work. If sales for the week were $157,836, what were the sales per employee hour?

10–13. In the meat department of a supermarket, 12 employees were employed during the past week. Six each worked a full-time, 40 hour week; six were part-timers who averaged 22 hours each. If sales for the week were $23,324, what were the sales per full-time employee equivalent?

10–14. A buyer analyzing sales for the past season decided to determine the proportion of sales contributed by each vendor. Determine this result from the following data:

Vendor	Sales
1	$22,350
2	21,605
3	4,842
4	8,940
5	15,455
6	10,439
7	18,917
8	6,678
9	20,989

Analytical Ratios Based on Sales

In evaluating a department or store's performance, retailers use a number of analytical ratios based on sales. For example, in earlier chapters we have occasionally used a percentage figure, such as "the expense percentage was 35.6%" or "the profit percentage was 5.5%." In each case the base for the percentage was net sales. Individual expenses, for example, the payroll expense, the advertising expense, or the rent expense, will be analyzed by retailers. In every example, the dollar expense figure will be related to total net sales to calculate the percentage.

Table 10–1 presents sales and selected expense data for the twelve stores that comprise the Alpha district of a large regional drug and general merchandise chain.

Table 10–1

Operating Results for Alpha District Stores
First Quarter

Store	Sales	Payroll Expense	Advertising Expense	Utilities Expense	Supplies Expense
A1	$ 639,124	$ 49,149	$ 8,565	$ 9,523	$ 6,351
A2	437,325	35,460	7,085	7,129	4,242
A3	943,111	73,091	13,487	12,827	9,714
A4	889,637	72,061	12,010	13,067	10,676
A5	917,963	76,283	10,465	15,239	9,914
A6	1,206,129	92,631	17,368	19,298	10,855
A7	797,138	66,641	12,993	12,834	9,566
A8	1,006,927	79,245	13,694	12,285	9,062
A9	564,187	44,571	9,535	8,124	5,980
A10	812,346	70,106	14,134	11,779	10,561
A11	1,222,132	90,804	16,865	15,643	12,832
A12	707,135	61,803	11,526	10,961	7,778
Totals	$10,143,154	$811,845	$147,727	$149,609	$107,531

To analyze the performance of the various stores, management calculated the percentages presented in Table 10–2.

These simple calculations permit quick appraisal of the performance of the several units (and their managers). For example, payroll expense appears to be high at stores A10 and A12. Advertising expense appears to be high at stores A9 and A10. Utilities expense appears to be high at stores A2, A5, A6, and A7. Supplies expense appears high at stores A4, A7, and A10.

Like many other analytical figures, these observations are signals for further analysis and investigation. There may be acceptable explanations for them, but they may also reveal inefficiencies that need to be corrected.

The Returns and Allowances Percentage

At this point, while considering percentages based on sales we should review the exception to the general rule that analytical ratios are always based upon net sales. The percentages in Table 10–2 were all based on net sales. However, as was indicated in Chapter 7, the *returns and allowances percentage* is calculated on the basis of gross sales. For example, a department store had gross sales during the fall season of $28,976,343. Returns totaled $2,103,682 and allowances totaled $728,633. The returns and allowances percentages, individually and combined, would be calculated as follows:

Gross sales	$28,976,343
Returns	2,103,682
Allowances	728,633
Net sales	$26,144,028

Table 10–2

Percentage Analysis Alpha District Stores
First Quarter

Store	Sales Percentage[1]	Payroll[2] Percentage	Advertising[2] Percentage	Utilities[2] Percentage	Supplies[2] Percentage
A1	6.30%	7.69%	1.34%	1.49%	.99%
A2	4.31	8.11	1.62	1.63	.97
A3	9.30	7.75	1.43	1.36	1.03
A4	8.77	8.10	1.35	1.57	1.20
A5	9.05	8.31	1.14	1.66	1.08
A6	11.89	7.68	1.44	1.60	.90
A7	7.86	8.36	1.63	1.61	1.20
A8	9.93	7.87	1.36	1.22	.90
A9	5.56	7.90	1.69	1.44	1.06
A10	8.01	8.63	1.74	1.45	1.30
A11	12.05	7.43	1.38	1.28	1.05
A12	6.97	8.74	1.63	1.55	1.10
Totals	100.00%	8.00%	1.46%	1.47%	1.06%

[1]Store's percentage of total district sales.
[2]Store's expense as a percentage of store's sales.

$$\text{Returns \%} = \frac{\$2,103,682}{\$28,976,343} = 7.26\%$$

$$\text{Allowance \%} = \frac{\$728,633}{\$28,976,343} = 2.51\%$$

$$\text{Returns and allowances \%} = \frac{\$2,103,682 + \$728,633}{\$28,976,343}$$

$$= \frac{\$2,832,315}{\$28,976,343}$$

$$= 9.77\%$$

Problems

10–15. The Bedford store, in a chain of record stores, had the following results: net sales $471,134; gross margin $148,878; customer returns $15,130; markdowns $53,138; manager's salary $28,000; bad debts $335; other payroll $32,094; and customer allowances $92. Calculate the bad debts percentage, the returns and allowances percentage, and the total payroll percentage.

10–16. The following data present the spring season results for a district comprising eight stores in a large chain of women's specialty stores. Calculate the percentage of rent, payroll, sales promotion, and utilities expenses. Which stores are below the district averages? Which are above?

Store	Sales	Rent Expense	Payroll Expense	Sales Promotion Expense	Utilities Expense
201	$363,041	$29,104	$37,141	$7,131	$4,005
202	187,562	18,302	20,342	4,334	3,116
203	194,431	20,000	18,433	5,356	1,810
204	271,227	30,000	28,566	5,434	3,222
205	303,812	28,756	28,234	6,115	3,386
206	256,846	25,685	24,744	5,550	2,666
207	211,135	20,340	22,808	5,210	1,984
208	325,669	32,567	30,129	6,418	3,018

Mellow Music Store Applications

As they were reviewing the performance of their store after the first year of operation, John and Julie Martin decided to calculate some basic measures of performance. Gross sales during the first year had totaled $151,432. Returns and allowances were $4,452, or $\frac{\$4,452}{\$151,432} = 2.9\%$ of gross sales. Net sales were $146,980.

The store had a total of 1,200 square feet of selling space. Thus, sales per square foot were:

$$\frac{\$146,980}{1,200} = \$122$$

During the year the store had totaled 7,250 customer transactions. The average sale was:

$$\frac{\$146,980}{7,250} = \$20.27$$

John wondered how useful the average sale measure was for his particular store. "We sell such a wide range of merchandise, it's not a very useful average for us. One customer comes in and buys an $800 instrument; the next buys a $2.95 sheet of music."

John and Julie kept a tally of sales by method of payment. The breakdown was as follows:

Cash	$48,567 = 33% of net sales
Personal check	$77,765 = 53% of net sales
Credit cards	$20,648 = 14% of net sales

"Originally", Julie recalled, "we were only planning to accept cash, but then we realized it was unrealistic to expect people to pay for expensive items like pianos and amplifiers with cash."

Calculating sales per employee hour was also difficult. The store was open 60 hours per week. John and Julie officially were scheduled to work 40 hours each per week. Two part-time workers each worked 10 hours per week. Thus, the total employee hours per week were 100 hours.

"But," John said, "I often come in on days I'm not officially scheduled to work. And many a night I've done paperwork at home. That's what happens when you own your own business. For my store, sales per employee hour is not the useful indicator it may be for a large chain of stores. But we had 100 employee hours per week, so it's easy to figure, just not really precise:"

$$\text{Average sales per week} = \frac{\$146,980}{52} = \$2,827$$

$$\text{Average sales per employee hour per week} = \frac{\$12,827}{100} = \$28.27$$

Mellow Music Store sold the musical instruments of four manufacturers. The sales and average inventories of these suppliers were as follows:

	Net Sales	Average Inventory at Cost
Alpha Instruments	$29,346	$10,440
Beta Instruments	31,362	12,825
Gamma Instruments	21,515	14,335
Delta Instruments	28,777	8,880

From these figures John calculated the percentage of total sales contributed by each supplier and the percentage of the average inventory represented by each supplier. The results were:

	Percentage Sales	*Percentage Inventory*
Alpha	26.4%	22.4%
Beta	28.3	27.6
Gamma	19.4	30.8
Delta	25.9	19.1

John mused, "I think we ought to reexamine the proportion of our inventory that each of these different manufacturers represents. Gamma, with about 19% of sales, has almost 31% of our instrument inventory. But Delta, with almost 26% of sales, has only 19% of inventory. We'll have to look at this carefully!"

The Martins also calculated the percentage ratios for certain operating expenses. Their results were:

Payroll	17.2% of sales
Rent	7.3% of sales
Advertising	8.5% of sales
Utilities	1.4% of sales
Supplies	.6% of sales
Insurance	1.3% of sales
Bad debts	.2% of sales

"How do we compare with other small music stores?" Julie asked.

"I haven't seen any comparative figures," John replied.

"Well, I'll ask Dad, maybe he has some," Julie said.

"I hope so, I'd like to see how we did. But we also have some benchmarks to use in planning and controlling for next year," John concluded.

Review Problems

10–1R. A superstore reported the following data. Calculate for each department its percentage of total sales for both years. Which departments have increased their percentage of total sales? Did these same departments have the largest percentage increases in sales over last year?

	Net Sales This Year	*Net Sales Last Year*
Dry groceries	$10,060,131	$ 9,801,931
Frozen foods	1,885,273	1,700,322
Dairy	1,998,676	1,936,328
Meat	5,576,345	5,030,901
Produce	2,274,738	2,100,322
Delicatessen	1,354,964	1,070,193
Bakery	1,321,878	1,108,138
Flowers	898,101	732,122
Pharmacy	3,017,897	2,980,515
Health and beauty aids	1,563,756	1,440,257
Books	320,865	310,064
Cosmetics	121,545	141,343
General merchandise	8,060,708	7,654,003
Total	$38,454,877	$36,006,439

10–2R. From the data presented below for a specialty store, calculate net sales by method of payment and the returns and allowances percentage.

	Cash	Store Credit	Third-Party Credit
Gross sales	$271,877	$212,698	$175,781
Customer returns	18,666	24,917	17,432
Customer allowances	1,888	2,023	1,134

10–3R. Calculate sales per square foot by department for a specialty clothing store whose sales and departmental space allocation are as follows:

	Net Sales	Space Occupied
Women's	$1,993,345	60 feet by 200 feet
Men's	1,222,896	60 feet by 140 feet
Girl's	689,454	50 feet by 120 feet
Boy's	476,578	60 feet by 60 feet

10–4R. A supermarket chain was planning a new store. The research department estimated that given the present level of competition, a new store could achieve annual sales of $17,000,000. If the chain was averaging weekly sales per square foot of $9.76 in its newer stores, approximately how much selling space should be planned for the new store?

10–5R. The new manager of the shoe department in a large department store was concerned that the department's sales per square foot, $169, was below the average for all stores in the company which was $201. The department had 2,400 square feet of space. What percentage increase in sales would be needed to bring that department's shoe sales up to the company average?

10–6R. The women's hosiery department in a department store occupied 3,600 square feet and had sales of $702,345 last year. Management is reexamining space allocations and has asked, "If sales stayed the same, what reduction in space would bring the store's sales per square foot in line with industry average sales of $259 per square foot?"

10–7R. If a department store had gross sales last week of $1,056,877 and handled 37,774 transactions, what was the average sale?

10–8R. During the past week a discount drugstore had sales of $86,592. Twelve full-time employees worked 40 hours. Eighteen part-timers averaged 28 hours each. What were average sales per employee hour?

10–9R. A department manager organized seasonal sales and inventory data by vendor. Determine from the following data how the relative sales by vendor compare with the relative stockturn by vendor.

	Sales	Beginning Inventory	Ending Inventory
Vendor A	$67,567	$52,896	$48,454
Vendor B	29,453	43,756	36,843
Vendor C	44,324	26,346	25,758
Vendor D	18,861	28,568	26,687

10–10R. For the first quarter, a supermarket chain had the following expense ratios: occupancy 1.36%; payroll 11.6%; supplies 1.2%; and advertising 1.5%.

(continued)

How do the performances of the following stores compare with the company averages?

Store	Sales	Occupancy	Payroll	Supplies	Advertising
38	$2,656,876	$32,500	$243,188	$29,569	$35,560
82	2,246,454	35,000	244,667	31,332	36,775
146	1,964,348	30,000	220,098	28,817	32,982
157	2,257,784	36,200	254,798	25,787	29,565
181	2,011,862	28,000	233,434	22,241	32,851

CHAPTER 11

Break-Even, DPP, and Other Measures of Performance

In Chapter 10, we considered several performance measures directly related to sales that retailers regularly use. Retailers also calculate a number of other measures in planning, analyzing, and controlling departments, stores, and entire companies. These will be considered in this chapter.

The Break-Even Point

When managements plan new stores, decide whether to expand or remodel existing stores, and evaluate the performance of existing stores, they calculate and assess break-even points. The *break-even point* for a retail store is the sales volume at which all expenses are covered, but there is no profit.

Understanding the break-even point for a store operating at that level is easy. For example, the following figures represent the performance of the Village Supermarket for the past year:

Sales	$485,376
Cost of goods sold	387,043
Gross margin	98,333
Total expenses	98,333
Operating profit	0

The Village Supermarket generated sufficient revenue during the past year to cover all its expenses; it broke even!

Projecting a break-even point for a proposed store is a more complex calculation. But before we learn how to do it, we should address questions that you are probably asking at this point: Why are we concerned about the break-even point? Are we going to open a store just to break even? Shouldn't we be asking, "what volume do we need to make a profit?"

These are three good questions.

Why Retailers Calculate Break-Even Points

Retail managers usually consider break-even points as part of the overall analysis of prospects for a store that includes profit objectives. The break-even point is often a measure of the minimum achievement that may be acceptable for a new store being introduced into a new market area. While not preferable, the break-even sales volume is a level of sales at which the company is not losing money. It provides a way of assessing the risk in a proposal.

For example, if in judging a proposal for a new store, the management of Company A concludes that the break-even point is a volume of sales that seems unachievable given the population, per capita income, and competition of the area, management might decide that it would be unwise to open the store.

On the other hand, Company B's experience might be that it often enters a new market with an initial volume of sales below the break-even point. But as customers become attracted to the store, sales gradually increase to a point above break even where profits are very satisfactory.

In both cases, calculation of the break-even point is very useful. To Company A, it indicates that a new store would be very risky because the sales volume needed to cover all expenses exceeds what the company can realistically expect to achieve. For Company B, calculation of the break-even point helps management determine how much of a loss the company has to absorb until sales reach the break-even level.

Once a break-even point has been calculated it is a relatively easy task to determine what additional volume of sales would be needed to achieve a profit objective.

Fixed and Variable Expenses

The calculation of break-even points in retailing is complicated by the difficulty in precisely determining the division between fixed and variable expenses. Fixed expenses would be *fixed,* that is, they would not change with changes in sales volume. For example, the expense of heating a store would not vary with changes in store sales. Variable expenses on the other hand, would increase with increases in sales volume. For example, if sales personnel were paid a sales commission, the more merchandise they sold, the more their commissions would be. Similarly affected would be the supplies expense. The more merchandise the store sold, the greater would be the expenses of paper bags, gift boxes, and sales receipts.

Semifixed Expenses

But some expenses in retailing are semifixed (or semivariable.) When space is rented for a store, we normally consider the rent to be a fixed amount, that is, so many dollars per year, or so many dollars for each square foot of space rented.

For example, when Paul Corcoran sought space in which to open a small gift shop, he found two promising locations. The owner of one site quoted a rental of $12,000 per year. The owner of the second site quoted a price of $12 per square foot per year.

Both rentals represented fixed costs, that is, they would not vary with the volume of sales realized. At the first site the annual rental would be $12,000. At the second site, which had a total of 900 square feet of space, the annual rent expense would be $900 \times \$12 = \$10,800$.

But Paul Corcoran was not pleased with some of the features of either site. He then considered a location in a shopping center. Space was available in a mall for a rental of $10,000 plus 10% of all sales above $125,000. In this situation the rental is fixed if the sales are below $125,000. Then the rent becomes variable for all sales above $125,000, that is, the additional rent varies with the sales volume. So the total rent would be semifixed if sales exceeded $125,000.

Another example of semifixed expenses in retailing is the expense of store personnel. A store manager's salary in a supermarket is usually a fixed expense; it doesn't vary with the volume of sales the store achieves. Similarly, the expenses of department managers are usually fixed. However, the expenses for checkout personnel are not fixed. The greater the sales volume of the store, the more checkout personnel needed. But this expense doesn't vary directly with sales. That is, small increments of checkout labor are not added with each dollar increase in sales. When another checkout person is added, that person can process a considerable amount of sales. This expense, therefore, is a semifixed (or semivariable) expense.

Calculating the Break-Even Point

To calculate a break-even point in a retail store, the expected level of expenses must be divided into fixed and variable components. On the basis of experience and analysis, established retailers can make very accurate estimates.

Management of the Great Northern supermarket chain was appraising a location for a new store. It was estimated that total annual sales would be $12,000,000, and that total annual expenses of the proposed store would be $2,420,000. The division of the expenses between fixed and variable was estimated based upon experience in other stores to be:

Fixed: 45% of total expense.
Variable: 55% of total expense.

Management further estimated that the store's gross margin would be 23.5% of sales. At what sales volume would the store break even?

Recall that at the break-even point, the store generates enough gross margin to just cover all expenses.

If the variable expenses were 55% of total expenses, they would be:

$$55\% \times \$2,420,000 = \$1,331,000$$

At a sales volume of $12,000,000 the variable expenses would be:

$$\frac{\$1,331,000}{\$12,000,000} = 11.1\% \text{ of sales}$$

So, with a gross margin of 23.5% and variable expenses of 11.1%, the contribution to fixed expenses (or contribution margin) would be:

$$23.5\% - 11.1\% = 12.4\%$$

The total fixed expenses would be:

Total expenses	$2,420,000
Less: Variable expenses	1,331,000
Fixed expenses	$1,089,000

The break-even point would then be calculated by dividing the total fixed expenses by the contribution (margin) percentage:

$$\text{Break-even point} = \frac{\text{Fixed expenses}}{\text{Contribution \%}} = \frac{\$1,089,000}{12.4\%} = \$8,782,258$$

Checking the Answer

To check our result, let's see what happens at a sales volume of $8,782,258:

Sales		$8,782,258
Gross Margin ($8,782,258 × 23.5%)		2,063,831
Variable Expenses ($8,782,258 × 11.1%)	974,831	
Fixed expenses	1,089,000	
Total expenses		2,063,831
Net profit		0

As these figures demonstrate, the store breaks even at a volume of $8,782,258, covering all variable and fixed expenses.

Problems

11–1. Calculate the break-even point of a store based on the following estimates: gross margin 38%; variable expenses 17%; and fixed expenses $440,000.

11–2. The following estimates were prepared for a proposed supermarket: sales $15,000,000; gross margin $3,600,000; variable expenses $1,800,000; and fixed expenses $1,500,000. At what sales volume would the store break even?

11–3. Management of a discount department store company was appraising a location for a new store. The real estate department forecast sales of $22,500,000. Based on the experience in other stores, management made the following estimates: total expenses 25%; gross margin 30.5%; and 52% of total expenses fixed, the remainder variable. At what sales volume would the store break even?

11–4. In planning for the opening of a new superstore, management made the following estimates:

$$\text{Gross margin} = 7,644,000$$

$$\text{Sales} = 31,200,000$$

Expenses	Fixed Amount	Variable Amount
Rent	$ 374,400	
Payroll and fringes	600,000	$ 2,457,600
Advertising and promotion	280,800	187,200
Utilities	686,400	
Supplies		343,200
Maintenance	85,000	8,600
Depreciation	187,200	
Other	1,000,000	341,600

At what sales volume would the superstore break even?

Adding a Profit Objective

Now let's say that the Great Northern supermarket chain's profit objective is 3.5% of sales (before taxes). The desired profit can then be considered analogous to another variable charge. Whereas we previously considered the contribution of 12.4% to be contribution to fixed expenses only when calculating the break-even point, it now becomes a contribution to fixed expenses and profit. If the profit portion is 3.5%, then the fixed expense portion becomes:

$$12.4\% - 3.5\% = 8.9\%$$

So, to calculate the sales volume that will result in a profit of 3.5% of sales, we now divide the fixed expenses by the revised contribution to fixed expenses:

$$\frac{\$1,089,000}{8.9\%} = \$12,235,955$$

Let's check our answer by determining what happens at a sales volume of $12,235,955:

Sales		$12,235,955
Gross margin ($12,235,955 × 23.5%)		2,875,449
Variable expenses ($12,235,955 × 11.1%)	1,358,191	
Fixed expenses	1,089,000	
Total expenses		2,447,191
Net profit		$ 428,258

Is a profit of $428,258 equal to 3.5% of sales?
Let's check again:

$$\frac{\$428,258}{\$12,235,955} = 3.5\%$$

Interpreting the Results

Recall that the management of the Great Northern supermarket chain forecasted sales of $12,000,000. The calculations above indicate that the volume of sales needed to break even is

$$\frac{\$12,000,000 - \$8,782,258}{\$12,000,000} = \frac{\$3,217,742}{\$12,000,000} = 26.8\%$$

below the forecasted sales volume.
    The volume of sales needed for a profit of 3.5% of sales is

$$\frac{\$12,235,955 - \$12,000,000}{\$12,000,000} = \frac{\$235,955}{\$12,000,000} = 2\%$$

above the forecasted sales volume.
    What profit would be earned at a sales volume equal to that forecasted?

Sales		$12,000,000
Gross margin ($12,000,000 × 23.5%)		2,820,000
Variable expenses ($12,000,000 × 11.1%)	1,332,000	
Fixed expenses	1,089,000	
Total expenses		2,421,000
Net profit		$ 399,000

$$\text{Net profit percentage: } \frac{\$399,000}{\$12,000,000} = 3.3\%$$

With these results, management has sharpened its analysis of the proposed site. If based upon its experience, management has high confidence in its forecasts and is willing to accept a profit slightly below objective, or normally anticipates a gradual increase in sales and profits over time, it would probably look very favorably on the proposed location.
    Note once again that our arithmetical calculations can take us only so far in resolving the situation. Ultimately, the decision rests upon management's judgment.

Problems

11–5. An entrepreneur planning a new store made the following estimates: sales $1,000,000; variable expenses 55% of total expenses; total expenses 35% of sales; gross margin 42%; and fixed expenses $157,500. What sales volume would provide a profit of 4.5%?

11–6. A supermarket operated at a break-even level last year. Its sales were $6,916,000. Management projects that for this year the store's gross margin will be 23.4%; fixed expenses will total $830,000; and variable expenses will be 11.4% of sales. What percentage increase in sales volume will be needed to produce a pre-tax profit of 3%? A pre-tax profit of $300,000?

Revising the Break-Even Point for Changes in Expenses

In Chapter 6, we saw that retailers often consider the impact of changing one or more of the variables as they analyze a situation. There we considered what impact changes in expenses and reductions would have on the gross margin. Similarly, retailers analyze the impact on the break-even point of changing some of the variables.

For example, in the situation described above at the Great Northern supermarket chain, management wondered what would happen to the break-even point if the gross margin were kept at 23.5% while expenses were increased to support higher advertising and more in-store service. The increase in expenses was projected to be $100,000, making total expenses $2,520,000. It was further estimated by management that the division of fixed and variable expenses would now become 54.8% variable and 45.2% fixed. What would the new break-even point be?

Under these conditions, the estimated fixed and variable costs would be:

$$\text{Variable expenses} = \$2,520,000 \times 54.8\% = \$1,380,960$$

$$\text{Fixed expenses} = \$2,520,000 \times 45.2\% = \$1,139,040$$

Variable expenses are now estimated to be:

$$\frac{\$1,380,960}{\$12,000,000} = 11.5\% \text{ of sales}$$

With a gross margin of 23.5% and variable expenses of 11.5%, the contribution would be:

$$23.5\% - 11.5\% = 12\%$$

The revised break-even point would be:

$$\frac{\text{Fixed expenses}}{\text{Contribution }\%} = \frac{\$1,139,040}{12\%} = \$9,492,000$$

Thus, the break-even point has increased from $8,782,258 to $9,492,000, an increase of $709,742, or 8.1%

$$\frac{\$709,742}{\$8,782,258} = 8.1\%$$

To check our answer, let's see what happens at the revised break-even sales volume:

Sales		$9,492,000
Gross margin (23.5% sales)		2,230,620
Variable expenses (11.5% sales)	1,091,580	
Fixed expenses	1,139,040	
Total expenses		2,230,620
Net profit		0

Changing the Gross Margin and Adding a Profit

Let's take one further illustration. Great Northern management now asks, "What would the break-even point be if we raised the gross margin to 24%? And what sales volume would we need to generate a pretax profit of $100,000?"

Raising the gross margin to 24% would increase the contribution to 12.5%:

$$\text{Contribution} = \text{Gross margin }\% - \text{Variable expense }\%$$

$$\text{Contribution} = 24\% - 11.5\% = 12.5\%$$

The break-even point would now be:

$$\text{Break-even Point} = \frac{\text{Fixed expenses}}{\text{Contribution }\%} = \frac{\$1,139,040}{12.5\%} = \$9,112,320$$

To add to the conditions a pre-tax profit of $100,000, we would first add that amount to the fixed expenses. The sales volume needed would then be calculated as follows:

$$\text{Sales volume for \$100,000 profit} = \frac{\text{Fixed expenses} + \text{Profit}}{\text{Contribution }\%}$$

$$= \frac{\$1,139,040 + \$100,000}{12.5\%}$$

$$= \frac{\$1,239,040}{12.5\%}$$

$$= \$9,912,320$$

Now as a final check, let's see what happens at a sales volume of $9,912,320:

Sales		$9,912,320
Gross margin (24% sales)		2,378,957
Variable expenses (11.5% sales)	1,139,917	
Fixed expenses	1,139,040	
Total expenses		2,278,957
Net profit		$ 100,000

It checks!!!

Problems

11–7. If the planned gross margin of a store is increased from 28% to 30%, what is the change in the store's break-even point when fixed expenses are $1,000,000 and variable expenses are 15% of sales?

11–8. The planned gross margin of a store is reduced from 26% to 24%. What is the percentage change in the store's break-even point if fixed expenses are $1,200,000 and variable expenses are 14% of sales?

11–9. The following projections were made for a planned new store: sales $5,000,000; gross margin 21%; variable expenses $400,000; and fixed expenses $500,000. Management was considering the option of installing more elaborate shelving and fixturing which would increase fixed costs by $100,000, and raising the gross margin to 22%. What impact would these changes have on the break-even point of the new store?

11–10. If management changes its profit objective from 15% to 20% of the $900,000 capital investment for a new store, what percentage increase in sales is required when the projected operating figures are: gross margin 23.5%; fixed expenses $750,000; and variable expenses 13.5% of sales?

The Capital Turnover

There are other measures that retailers use to appraise the financial performance of a retail operation. In Chapter 8 we learned about stockturn. Recall that we calculated the stockturn by dividing the movement of goods by the average inventory of goods. We learned that in calculating stockturn, it was important to be sure that both measures, the movement of goods and the average inventory of goods, were valued in the same way. So if the movement of goods was measured at retail, that is as sales, the average inventory of goods had to be measured at retail. If movement of goods was measured at cost, that is, as cost of goods sold, the average inventory had to be measured at cost. We could measure stockturn either way.

However, if we divide *sales* by the average inventory at *cost,* the result is know as the *capital turnover.* It basically measures the number of times that the average dollar investment in merchandise is converted into sales. Thus, if a department in a department store had the following results:

Sales	$330,596
Average inventory at retail	100,152
Average inventory at cost	60,092

We could calculate the following measures:

$$\text{Stockturn} = \frac{\$330,596}{\$100,152} = 3.3$$

$$\text{Capital turn} = \frac{\$330,596}{\$60,092} = 5.5$$

Converting from Capital Turn to Stockturn

Now let's calculate the cumulative markup on the inventory:

Inventory at retail	$100,152
Inventory at cost	60,092
Cumulative markup on Inventory	$ 40,060

$$\text{Cumulative markup } \% = \frac{\$40,060}{\$100,152} = 40\%$$

Knowing the cumulative markup on the inventory allows us to calculate the capital turn, given the stockturn; or to determine the stockturn, given the capital turn. To do so, we must first calculate the cost complement of the cumulative markup.

Recall that in Chapter 2, we learned that the *cost complement* of a markup was defined as 100% minus the markup. So with a cumulative markup of 40%, the cost complement would be 60%. If we then divide the stockturn by the cost complement, the result is the capital turn.

In the department cited above, we had a stockturn of 3.3. Dividing that amount by the cost complement, will give the same result as our earlier calculation of the capital turn:

$$\text{Capital turn} = \frac{\text{Stockturn}}{\text{Cost complement}} = \frac{3.3}{60\%} = 5.5$$

Furthermore, if we multiply the capital turn by the cost complement, the result is the stockturn. Let's see if it checks with our previous calculation:

$$\text{Stockturn} = \text{Capital turn} \times \text{Cost complement}$$

$$= 5.5 \times 60\%$$

$$= 3.3$$

Using the Capital Turn for Analysis

We learned in Chapter 8 that stockturn is an important measure of inventory management. Capital turn is a useful measure of financial analysis. Because it can be calculated from published financial statements (sales reported in the operating statement, inventories at cost on the balance sheet), it is reported in retailing industry analyses.

It also has another important application. Multiplying the capital turn by the net profit percentage results in the return on investment in inventory. For example, if the net operating profit for the department cited above was 4%, then the return on the investment in inventory would be:

$$\text{Return on investment in inventory} = \text{Capital turn} \times \text{Net profit percentage}$$

$$= 5.5 \times 4\%$$

$$= 22\%$$

For many retail operations, the major investment in the business is the inventory of merchandise; so, the above calculation provides an approximate measure of the return on investment that can be readily calculated.

The GMROI

In a similar way, if the capital turn is multiplied by the gross margin percentage, the result is a measure many retailers calculate called **GMROI**, which means *gross margin return on the investment in inventory measured at cost*. If the department cited above had a gross margin of 38%, its GMROI would be:

$$\text{GMROI} = \text{Gross margin } \% \times \text{Capital turn}$$

$$= 38\% \times 5.5$$

$$= 209\%$$

This measure, GMROI, may be reported as a percentage, 209%, as an index of 209, or per dollar of inventory investment (calculated by dividing by 100), $2.09.

Let's check this calculation using the dollar figures for the department cited above:

Sales	$330,596
Gross margin (38%)	125,626
Average inventory at cost	60,092

$$\text{GMROI} = \frac{\text{Gross margin}}{\text{Average inventory cost}} = \frac{\$125,626}{\$60,092} = \$2.09$$

There is a gross margin of $2.09 generated for every $1.00 invested in inventory, or a return of 209%.

$$\frac{\$2.09}{\$1.00} = 209\%$$

Many retailers in the department and specialty store fields use GMROI to measure the relative performance of departments or categories of merchandise.

Problems

11–11. Calculate the capital turn from the following data: sales $342,176; cost of goods sold $212,149; beginning inventory at cost $49,171; and closing inventory at cost $55,226.

11–12. Calculate the capital turn for the following data: cost of goods sold $461,198; gross margin 38%; average inventory at retail $131,772; and cumulative markup on inventory 40%.

11–13. What is the capital turn when the stockturn is 6 and the gross margin is 36%?

11–14. What is the stockturn when the capital turn is 8.4 and the gross margin is 38%?

11–15. Calculate GMROI from the following data: sales \$235,177; beginning inventory at cost \$44,118; closing inventory at cost \$46,176; and gross margin 42%.

11–16. Calculate GMROI from the following data: cost of goods sold \$636,242; gross margin 42%; and average inventory at cost \$137,069.

Direct Product Profit

In Chapter 7, we introduced the concept of contribution. We examined the contribution for an entire store or for a department of a store. The contribution was defined as the gross margin of the store or department minus the direct (or controllable) costs involved in operating that store or department. The contribution was the amount available to meet the overhead or indirect costs of the store or department, and for profit.

In recent years, starting in grocery retailing and then spreading into other parts of retailing, a very similar concept has been developed for *individual items* of merchandise. *Direct product profit* (DPP) is the name that has been given to this calculation. It is an effort to determine more accurately the relative productivity of each item of merchandise.

Traditionally, retailers would measure an individual product's worth by assessing its *gross margin* (actually markup)[1] with some attention paid to stockturn if such information was available for an individual item. If two products had the same turnover, the one with the higher gross margin (markup) was considered a better item profitwise.

However, while two products may have the same gross margin, they may differ in other characteristics, such as size, shape, weight, and number of units per case. The amount of space needed to stock these products in a warehouse, transport them on a truck, or stock them on a store's shelves might vary. The amount of time required to open the shipping cartons, remove and price mark the individual units, and place them on the shelves might also vary. Moreover, some items, such as dairy products, require special refrigerated shelving; and frozen foods require zero degree Fahrenheit display cases.

---

[1] While grocery retailers would typically refer to a product's *gross margin,* they were usually considering the markup, that is, the difference between selling price and billed cost, not corrected for cash discounts or other allowances.

The direct product profit concept addresses these differences. It subtracts the costs directly associated with handling, storage, and sale from the gross margin of each item. These costs reflect the tasks of warehousing, transporting, receiving, price marking, displaying, and the checking out by cashiers of each item. The respective costs are determined by careful observation, including the use of time study, and analysis.

In addition, the direct product profit concept refines gross margin, usually calculated by grocery retailers solely on the basis of billed cost, to allow for any cash discounts for prompt payment, merchandising allowances, backhaul allowances, or forward buy income.[2]

Calculating DPP

The following figures compare the traditional industry gross margin with the direct product profit per case for a grocery item:[3]

	Per Case
Retail price	$18.72
Billed cost	14.98
Gross margin	3.74
Plus: discounts and allowances	
Cash discount	.30
Merchandising allowance	.50
Minus: direct costs	
Warehouse direct labor	.41
Warehouse inventory expense	.18
Warehouse operating expense	.12
Transportation to store	.14
Store direct labor	1.78
Store inventory expense	.15
Store operating expense	.81
Direct product profit	$ .95

These results show that whereas the product's gross margin is $3.74 per case, the direct product profit (DPP) is $.95 per case. The DPP indicates that each case sold contributes $.95 to overhead and profit. So, it is a more accurate measure of the contribution of each item than is the gross margin.

Applying DPP

Application of the DPP concept has been spurred by the use of scanning registers at the checkout counters in supermarkets. This equipment provides an accurate measure of the sales of individual items. Combining the sales data with DPP data provides very useful information to a merchandiser. It permits calculation of contribution per item for a period of time and for amounts of shelf space used to display the items. For example, data presented below report DPP and sales for two types of coffee in a supermarket during a one week period.[4]

	Item A–2 lb. *Ground Coffee* *Decaffeinated*	*Item B–2 lb.* *Ground Coffee* *Regular*
Gross margin per case	$ 9.33	$ 8.02
Plus discounts and allowance	.21	2.02
Less direct costs	4.22	3.80
DPP per case	$ 5.32	$ 6.24

(continued)

[2]Merchandising allowances would include introductory stocking, special display or advertising allowances; backhaul allowances would reimburse a retailer for transporting merchandise from a manufacturer in the retailer's trucks; and forward buy income would include allowances from manufacturers for retailer acquisition and warehousing of merchandise prior to actual need.

[3]Figures from John R. Phipps, "Research Perspective," *Progressive Grocer*, May 1985, p. 233.

[4]Figures from John R. Phipps, Ibid.

	Item A–2 lb. *Ground Coffee* *Decaffeinated*	*Item B–2 lb.* *Ground Coffee* *Regular*
Cases sold per week	4.2	3.1
DPP per week	$22.34	$19.34
Square feet of shelf space	1.68	.84
DPP per square foot of space per week	$13.30	$23.03

Of these two items, Item A appears to be more attractive based on its higher gross margin per case. But Item B is more profitable based on DPP because of its higher discounts and allowances and lower handling costs. The lower handling costs result because Item B is tray-packed on the shelf whereas Item A is hand stocked. Also, because Item B occupies less shelf space, it has a much higher DPP per square foot of space.[5]

As was suggested in Chapter 10 when considering sales per square foot, DPP per square foot can also be considered a rough approximation of a return on investment. It actually is a contribution per unit of space. So, to the degree that contribution relates to profit and a unit of space relates to investment, DPP per square foot can become a rough estimate of return on investment.

Grocery retailers have been using DPP analysis to help decide how much space to allot to different products; which to give preferred (eye level) shelf position; which to feature in special displays; and whether to raise prices of low DPP products.

Another Use of DPP

Food chains are also using DPP information to compare the contribution of products delivered directly to stores and placed on shelves by the manufacturer's personnel with that of similar items delivered by the manufacturer to the chain's warehouse for subsequent delivery to stores and shelving by the chain's personnel. The item that the manufacturer delivers directly to the store incurs no warehousing and related costs. With the manufacturer performing the shelf stocking, there are no direct in-store costs other than those of checking out. On the other hand, the product delivered to the chain's warehouse by the manufacturer incurs the warehousing and transportation costs along with the in-store receiving, handling, and shelf stocking costs.

The following data compare results for two similar pairs of products with the same rate of sale:

	Brand A Cookies *Store Delivery*	*Brand B Cookies* *Warehouse Delivery*
Retail price per package	$1.89	$1.85
Cost per package	1.35	1.235
Gross margin dollars	.54	.615
Gross margin percentage	28.6%	33.2%
Direct warehouse and transportation costs	—	.035
Direct in-store costs	.01	.03
Total direct cost	.01	.065
Direct product profit	.53	.55

For this comparison, the item delivered to the warehouse and requiring warehousing and store costs was slightly more profitable. The additional gross margin more than offset the higher direct costs.

---

[5]Ibid.

	Brand A Juice Drink Store Delivery	Brand B Juice Drink Warehouse Delivery
Retail price per bottle	$.59	$.59
Cost per bottle	.50	.47
Gross margin dollars	.09	.12
Gross margin percentage	15.3%	20.3%
Direct warehouse and transportation costs	—	.0375
Direct in-store costs	.035	.065
Total direct costs	.035	.1025
Direct product profit	.055	.0175

For this comparison the store delivered item, despite a much lower gross margin, was more profitable because of the high warehouse and in-store direct costs associated with the warehouse delivered item.

Using DPP Requires Good Judgment

While DPP provides a more accurate measure of the profit impact of individual items, its use, like that of any analytical tool, must be tempered with judgment. Most merchants would find many unhappy customers if they stocked only the items with the higher direct product profits. But having accurate DPP information about products enables retailers to make better informed merchandising decisions than those based only on gross margin considerations.

Problems

11–17. What is the direct product profit per case for a product with a retail price of $16.56; markup of 20%; no cash discounts or promotional allowances; direct warehousing costs of $1.08; direct transportation costs of $.12; and direct in-store costs of $1.84?

11–18. A product has the following per unit figures: retail price $1.29; billed cost $.77; direct warehouse costs $.04; direct transportation costs $.02; direct in-store costs $.12; cash discounts $.02; and display allowance $.03. What is the per unit direct product profit?

11–19. Calculate the direct product profit per week per square foot of shelf space for a product with the following figures:

Retail price	$21.36 per case
Billed cost	16.02 per case
Promotional allowance	.60 per case
Cash discount	.80 per case
Direct warehouse costs	.82 per case
Direct transportation costs	.12 per case
Direct in-store costs	2.98 per case
Sales per week	12 cases
Shelf space	1.92 square feet

11–20. Relevant figures for two brands of cookies are presented below. Which has the higher markup? Which has the higher unit DPP? Which has the higher DPP per square foot of shelf space?

	Brand A	*Brand B*
Units per case	24	12
Retail price per unit	$ 1.49	$ 1.89
Billed cost per case	28.60	16.90
Direct warehouse costs per case	1.12	0
Direct transportation costs per case	.18	0
Direct in-store costs per case	1.82	.24
Cash discount per case	0	.30
Display allowance per case	.75	0
Case sales per week	6	3
Shelf space (in square feet)	1.78	1.24

Return on Assets

Other more traditional measures of return on investment are regularly calculated by retailers. These calculations usually employ net profit after taxes as one measure that is related to a measure of investment. Different measures of investment are used. For example, one measure of return on investment (ROI) relates net profits to the total assets employed in earning those profits. The Milton Supermarket had a net profit for last year of $69,531. Total assets employed in the business were $434,570. The return on total assets was:

$$\text{Return on total assets} = \frac{\text{Net profit}}{\text{Total assets}}$$

$$= \frac{\$69,531}{\$434,570}$$

$$= 16\%$$

Return on Net Worth

Another measure of return on investment relates net profit after taxes to the net worth of the store or company earning those profits. If for the Milton Supermarket the total net worth, defined as the owners' or stockholders' total net investment in the store, was $280,000, the return on net worth was:

$$\text{Return on net worth} = \frac{\text{Net profit}}{\text{Net worth}}$$

$$= \frac{\$69,531}{\$280,000}$$

$$= 24.8\%$$

Problems

11–21. Calculate the return on total assets for a store with the following data: sales $742,136; net profit after taxes 1.7%; and total assets $86,413.

11–22. Owners of an independent supermarket observed that their net worth in the store was $326,438. If they desired a return on their investment of 18%, what dollar net profit after tax must the supermarket generate? If their objective was also a net profit after tax of 1.5% of sales, what sales volume must the supermarket achieve?

Mellow Music Store Applications

As they began to plan for the next year, John and Julie Martin, with the help of James Flynn, were analyzing some of the financial aspects of their store's operation.

Mr. Flynn pointed out that the store's expenses were mostly fixed, "No matter what happens, you have to pay the rent, lights, telephone, heat, and your salaries. About the only variable expenses you have are the part-time help you add for the busier period of the week and the bags you use for customer purchases. And actually your part-time labor cost is not strictly variable; it doesn't increase with every dollar increase in sales."

"As a matter of fact," Mr. Flynn continued, "I would judge your variable expenses to be no more than $2,000 of your total expenses of $56,831. They would represent 1.4% ($\frac{\$2,000}{\$146,980}$) of your sales. So based on this year's experience your break-even point is, let's see — your contribution is 40.9% (gross margin) minus the 1.4% variable — that would be 39.5%; and your fixed expenses were $56,831 (total expenses) minus $2,000 — that would be $54,831; so that makes your break even $54,831 divided by 39.5% — that's $138,813. Not much below what you did for sales."

"Actually," he went on, "you have the capacity to do a lot more business without really incurring any substantial increase in expenses. Your expenses are mostly fixed and since you are above the break-even point, that additional business would be relatively more profitable. Let's see what would happen if sales increased by 20% and compare that with this year:

	This Year	This Year plus 20% Increase in Sales
Sales	$146,980	$176,376
Gross margin (40.9%[1])	60,144	72,138
Variable expenses (1.4%[1])	2,000	2,469
Contribution	58,144	69,669
Fixed expenses	54,831	54,831
Profit	3,313	14,838

"Gee, that looks good", John remarked, "let's try to get those sales up."

"Would additional advertising help?" Julie inquired.

"It might, but that will increase your expenses," responded Mr. Flynn. "But let's see what the effect would be on the break even, if we double advertising. That would make our fixed expenses $67,331 — and so — the break even would be — $67,331 divided by 39.5% — that would be $170,458 — and at a 20% increase in sales and doubling of advertising, profits would only be $2,338."

Sales	$176,376
Gross margin	72,138
Variable expenses	2,469
Contribution	69,669
Fixed expenses	67,331
Profit	2,338

"Wow!" John exclaimed, "that means we really can't depend on more advertising to improve our profits."

"Well," mused Mr. Flynn, "you have to realize that you need more than just advertising to increase your sales and profits. It might draw some extra traffic to the

---

[1]Rounded calculation of this year's results applied to projected increased sales.

store, but you and Julie have to convert that traffic into sales. Let's first think about the whole operation—what you're stocking, how you're displaying, your pricing, and your selling skills, before we decide what changes to make."

"But while we're at it," Mr. Flynn added, "let's look at your return on investment. For the year, you had an average of $56,374 invested in merchandise. That means your capital turn was 2.6 $(\frac{\$146,980}{\$56,374})$. And with your pre-tax profit of 2.25% $(\frac{\$3,313}{\$146,980})$, you earned 5.9% (2.6 × 2.25%) before taxes on your merchandise investment. The store's total assets were $81,300, so your pre-tax return on assets was 4% $(\frac{\$3,313}{\$81,300})$. Our total capital investment in the store, what you and Julie put in, plus my investment, totalled $60,000. So our return on net worth was 5.5% $(\frac{\$3,313}{\$60,000})$. None of these results were very good. You've got to do better next year."

"I think we will; we'll sure try," said John.

"And we know a lot more about retailing now than when we started," added Julie.

This chapter also discussed two other major analytical concepts in modern retailing management, GMROI (the gross margin return on the investment in inventory at cost) and DPP (the direct product profit). GMROI is regularly calculated and analyzed by large retailers, particularly department and specialty store companies. DPP has been increasingly applied by large food retailing firms and is beginning to be applied to other categories of merchandise.

These measures are typically applied in retailing operations that stock and sell thousands of items. Although applicable conceptually to a small, limited line store like the Mellow Music Store, it would be unusual to find these concepts being applied in practice by such a retailer.

Review Problems

11–1R. Calculate the break-even point for a store with the following figures: total sales $14,343,756; gross margin $4,446,572; total expenses 28% of sales; and variable expenses 46% of total expenses.

11–2R. The following estimates were prepared for a new discount department store. At what sales volume would the store break even?

Sales = $20,800,000

Gross margin = 29.5%

Expenses	Fixed	Variable
Payroll	$1,097,600	$1,398,400
Rent	280,800	
Supplies	28,800	200,000
Utilities	582,400	
Depreciation	145,600	
Maintenance	93,600	62,400
Advertising	300,000	
Other	176,800	833,600

11–3R. An analyst was appraising prospects for a new store. Initial estimates were: sales $7,436,000; gross margin 25%; variable expenses 11%; fixed expenses 11%; and fixed expenses $817,960. Under consideration was an increase in expenses to be offset by an increase in gross margin. The analyst wondered: would the break-even point change (*a*) if the gross margin was increased to 27% and the variable expenses raised to 13%? and (*b*) if the gross margin was increased to 27% and the fixed expenses were raised to 13%, or $966,680?

11–4R. What sales volume would be required in a store with fixed expenses of $1,112,344; variable expenses of 11%; and a gross margin of 24.5%

(continued)

to generate a pre-tax profit of 3% of sales? To generate a pre-tax profit of $250,000?

11–5R.   Calculate the capital turn when the gross margin is 42% and the stockturn is 3.2.

11–6R.   What is the GMROI in a department with the following results: sales $265,432; gross margin 38.5%; average inventory retail $69,852; and cumulative markup on inventory 42%?

11–7R.   What is the GMROI in a department with the following data: sales $188,396; gross margin 37.6%; and capital turn 5.8?

11–8R.   Calculate the DPP for a product with the following per unit figures: cost $1.16; retail price $1.49; introductory stocking allowance $.075; display allowance $.10; direct warehousing costs $.036; direct transportation costs $.015; direct in-store costs $.12; and cash discount $.02.

11–9R.   A product has the following per case figures: retail price $28.56; markup 18.6%; promotional allowances $1.60; cash discounts $.46; direct warehouse costs $.72; direct transportation costs $.16; and direct in-store expenses $3.20. If the product occupies 2.66 square feet of shelf space and the sales per week were 8 cases, what was the direct product profit per square foot per week?

11–10R. A retailer had total net sales for the past fiscal year of $13,444,562 and after tax profits of 3.68%. Total assets were $4,122,967. Net worth equaled 56% of total assets. Calculate the return on total assets and the return on net worth.

Appendix

A

Terms of Sale and Purchase: Discounts and Dating

There are a variety of terms and practices that retailers confront in purchasing merchandise from suppliers. These terms and practices reflect the customs of different industries and the operating policies of individual suppliers. Consequently, there are variations both among industries and among suppliers in a given industry. Sometimes these terms and practices are the subject of negotiation between retailers and suppliers. This appendix presents the more common terms and practices.

Cash Discounts

Cash discounts are reductions in the cost of merchandise offered to retailers by suppliers to encourage prompt payment of bills. The discounts are expressed as a percentage of the cost of the merchandise as stated on the invoice.

Cash Discount and Date of Invoice

The simplest form of a cash discount might be expressed as "6/10 net 30." This means that the retailer is able to reduce the amount of payment by 6% if the payment is made within 10 days of the date of the invoice. So, if the invoice is dated April 5, the retailer can take a 6% discount as long as the bill is paid by April 15. If the bill was not paid within the 10 day period, the full amount is due within 30 days of the date of the invoice, May 5. When the length of the discount period is determined from the date of the invoice, it is also called *ordinary dating,* or *regular dating,* or referred to as date of invoice (DOI) dating.

Receipt of Goods

Another way of reckoning the period during which a cash discount may be taken is *receipt of goods* (ROG) dating. When this term specifies the discount period, it is counted from the date of the receipt of the goods by the retailer. An invoice is dated April 5 with the terms "6/10 net 30 ROG." The retailer receives the goods on April 10. The retailer may take the cash discount by paying the bill by April 20.

End of Month Dating

With *end of month* (EOM) dating, the period during which a discount may be taken is counted from the end of the month of the bill. Thus, with the terms "6/10 EOM," and a bill dated April 5, the cash discount could be taken until May 10.

Typically, bills dated after the 25th of the month, that is the 26th or later, are considered to be a bill of the following month. The discount period would then begin after the end of the following month. So, for a bill dated April 28, with terms 6/10 EOM, the 6% cash discount would be allowed until June 10th.

Advance Dating

Sometime the vendor lengthens the period for taking a cash discount by establishing a future date as the date for determining the discount period. For a bill dated April 5, with the terms "6/10 net 30 as of July 1," the cash discount could be taken up to 10 days after July 1 or up to July 11. If the cash discount was not taken, the net amount would be due July 31. The terms for this bill might also be abbreviated 6/10 n/30 a/o 7/1.

Extra Dating

Extra dating is another method of lengthening the discount period. For a bill dated April 5 with the terms "6/10 net 30, 60 extra," the cash discount could be taken until June 15. Thus the terms permit an additional 60 days after the normal 10 day discount period. Without the extra dating, the cash discount would have to be taken by April 15. The 60 extra days extend the discount period until June 15. The net amount would be due July 5. These terms might also be abbreviated 6/10, 60X.

Seasonal Dating

Another form of advance dating is seasonal dating which provides a lengthened payment period to encourage early purchase of seasonal merchandise. A vendor of holiday season merchandise might take orders six to nine months in advance of the season, and ship merchandise three to six months in advance, but specify as payment terms "6/10 n/30 a/o 12/20." Thus, the retailer's discount period would begin on December 20th, and the cash discount could be taken by paying the bill by December 30.

Anticipation

Another type of cash discount, actually an additional discount, is occasionally allowed by suppliers when retailers pay a bill before the end of the discount period. It is called *anticipation,* that is, the retailer anticipates the payment and makes it early. For an invoice dated April 5th the terms are 6/10 EOM, with 6% anticipation allowed. The bill is paid April 15th. The retailer takes the 6% cash discount for paying the bill before the end of the discount period, May 10th being the ending date. The retailer also takes anticipation at an annual rate of 6% for 25 days, with a year considered to be 360 days.

The retailer has paid the bill 25 days before the end of the discount period: April 15 to April 30 (15 days) plus May 1 to May 10 (10 days). So, on an invoice of $1,200, the retailer would deduct the cash discount of 6%, or $72; and anticipation of $5 ($1,200 $\times$ 6% $\times \frac{25}{360}$). The retailer's payment would be $1,200 − ($72 + $5), that is, $1,123.

Quantity Discounts

Quantity discounts are reductions in the cost of merchandise offered by suppliers to encourage larger purchases. For example, a supplier charges $200 a dozen for an item. If the retailer buys four or more dozen, the price is $190 per dozen.

The specific applications of such discounts vary. In one case the first 3 dozen purchased may cost $200 per dozen, with the fourth and subsequent dozens purchased on the same order billed at $190 per dozen. Another vendor might charge $190 per dozen if a minimum of four dozen were purchased on one order.

For still another form of quantity discount, the vendor might provide a free dozen if a certain number of dozens were purchased. For example, the vendor referenced above might offer the 20th dozen free, if 19 dozen were purchased at full price. The net result would be the same as charging the lower price for 20 dozen. (20 dozen at $190 per dozen equals a total cost of $3,800. 19 dozen at $200 per dozen plus one dozen free equals a total cost of $3,800 for 20 dozen.)

Some suppliers may also offer a discount if the total dollar amount of an order exceeds a specified amount. For example, on purchases exceeding $10,000 for one order, a 2% discount might be allowed. Such a discount might also be cumulative, applying to all purchases during a season, a year, or other time period.

Trade Discounts

Some suppliers express prices on a retail list price basis. From this list price discounts are offered to retailers. These discounts are known as trade discounts, or functional discounts. For example, a manufacturer's price schedule for a certain item is: retail list price $20; retailer's discount 40%. The retailer's cost is determined by subtracting the discount from the list price; that is, $20 - (40\% \times \$20) = \$12$, the retailer's billed cost. This result may also be calculated by multiplying the list price by the complement of the discount. (The complement is 100% minus the discount). The result is $20 \times (100\% - 40\%) = \$12$.

When the trade discount consists of a series of discounts, or chain of discounts, such as 20%, 10%, 5%, the retailer must be careful to apply the first discount to the list price and subsequent discounts to the balance after prior discounts are subtracted. For example, if the item with a list price of $20 had discounts of 20%, 10%, 5%, the cost would be calculated as follows:

$$\$20 - (\$20 \times 20\%) = \$16$$

$$\$16 - (\$16 \times 10\%) = \$14.40$$

$$\$14.14 - (\$14.40 \times 5\%) = \$13.68$$

Note that the same amount may be obtained by multiplying the list price by the complements of the discounts. So the net cost would be $20 \times 80\% \times 90\% \times 95\% = \$13.68$.

Combination of Discounts

In some situations a retailer may have the opportunity to take a cash discount, a quantity discount, and a trade discount on the same invoice. The trade discount would be taken first (establishing unit costs), the quantity discount second (establishing the aggregate costs), and the cash discount then taken on the total billed amount of the invoice.

Loading

A special category of discount, known as a loaded discount, is an inflated discount requested by some retailers who may seek to have a standard cash discount percentage, or perhaps wish to supplement their cash discount reserve. It requires an inflated billed cost. For example, a manufacturer offering a 4% cash discount is requested by a retailer to price the merchandise so that the retailer can take an 8% cash discount, but still incur the same net cost for the goods. The retailer makes purchases totalling $4,025. With the manufacturer's terms 4%/10 net 30, the retailer could take a cash discount of $161 and pay $3,864 for the merchandise.

But in order to permit an 8% cash discount, the manufacturer must price the merchandise at $4,200. Then by taking an 8% cash discount, equalling $336, the retailer would pay $3,864 for the merchandise.

The loaded cost is calculated as follows:

$$\text{Loaded cost} = \frac{\text{Actual cost} \times (100\% - \text{Actual cash discount})}{(100\% - \text{Loaded cash discount})}$$

$$= \frac{\$4,025 \times 96\%}{92\%}$$

$$= \$4,200$$

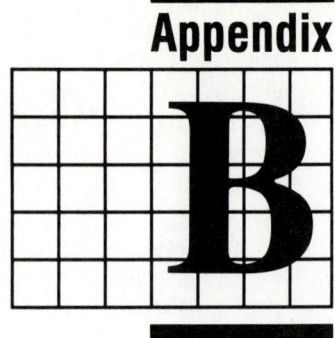

Appendix B

Answers to Odd-Numbered Problems

Chapter 2

2–1. Dollar markup $34.95
2–3. Dollar markup $119
Markup on retail 29.8%
Marketing on cost 42.5%
2–5. Cost 55%
Retail 100%
2–7. Markup on retail 35%
2–9. Markup on cost 81.8%
2–11. Markup on selling price 50%
2–13. Retail price $25.45
2–15. Cost $65
2–17. Selling price $22.50
2–19. Cost $28

Chapter 3

3–1. Initial markup 55%
3–3. Initial markup 38.8%
3–5. Initial markup 43.5%
3–7. Initial markup 47%
3–9. Initial markup 48.3%
3–11. Profit $0
3–13. Impact on prices 9.3% reduction
3–15. Cumulative markup 41%

Chapter 4

4–1. Total markup 33.5%
4–3. Markup on purchases 52.3%
4–5. Markup on balance of purchases 10.9%
4–7. Proportions: 33% of $45 tapes
67% of $42 tapes
4–9. Proportions: 67% of $2.49 melons
33% of $3.99 melons
4–11. Increase in sales 13.5%

Chapter 5

5–1. Total markdowns taken $17,360
5–3. Markdown cancellations $662 toasters, $341 can openers
Net markdowns $610 toasters, $415 can openers

5–5. Potential markup lost 18.3%
5–7. Off-retail 40%
Markdown 66.7%
Cumulative markdown 1.2%
Markdown goods 1.8%
5–9. Markdown goods 22.3%
5–11. Off-retail 45.4%
Markdown 83.3%
5–13. Reduction in price 13%
5–15. Sales target at original retail $146,250
Cumulative markdown 5.5%

Chapter 6

6–1. Maintained markup $16,320
Gross margin $16,620
6–3. Maintained markup 43.4%
6–5. Initial markup 51.5%
6–7. Maintained markup 37%
6–9. Gross margin 38.5%
Maintained markup 41%
6–11. Initial markup 46.6%
Maintained markup 35.4%
Gross margin 35%
6–13. Maintained markup 30.8%
Gross margin 24.8%
Profit −4.2%
6–15. Initial markup 37.5%

Chapter 7

7–1. Gross margin $55,000
7–3. Cost of goods sold $108,000
7–5. Net cost of goods sold $18,000
7–7. Contribution $8,900
7–9. Contribution $631,875

Chapter 8

8–1. Stockturn 1.6
8–3. Stockturn 3
8–5. Average inventory at cost $13,340
8–7. Investment in merchandise $14,300
8–9. Average inventory on hand 6.5 weeks
8–11. Average monthly sales $14,400
Average inventory $43,200
8–13. BOM stocks:

February	$32,875
March	34,375
April	32,875
May	27,625
June	36,625
July	32,125

8–15. Shortage $2,089
8–17. Closing book inventory $30,283
Shortage 1.29%

Chapter 9

9–1.

	Sales	Reductions
February	$19,531	$3,767
March	25,111	2,930
April	27,901	2,720
May	29,296	3,348
June	23,716	3,767
July	13,951	4,394

9–3. Planned purchases at cost $24,163

9–5. Open-to-buy May 1st $10,730

9–7. Open-to-buy October 1st $17,285
Amount available $8,643

9–9. Open-to-buy 16 units

Chapter 10

10–1. Luggage sales 6%

10–3. Cash sales 48.9%
Store credit plan sales 27.3%
Third party credit sales 23.7%

10–5. Jewelry sales 2.5%
Jewelry .3% decrease
Total store 6.8% increase

10–7. Sales per square foot $13.56

10–9. Sales per square foot $238

10–11. Total sales $324,989

10–13. Sales per full-time employee $2,508

10–15. Bad debts .07%
Returns and allowances 3.1%
Payroll 12.8%

Chapter 11

11–1. Break-even sales $2,095,238

11–3. Break-even sales $15,810,810

11–5. Sales $863,014

11–7. Sales to break even 13.3% decrease

11–9. Sales to break even 11.4% increase

11–11. Capital turn 6.6

11–13. Capital turn 9.4

11–15. GMROI 218%

11–17. Direct product profit $.27

11–19. Direct product profit per square foot $17.63

11–21. Return on total assets 14.6%

Index